Definitions of Sociology

Definitions of Sociology

A Historical Approach

Patricia M. Lengermann

George Washington University

Charles E. Merrill Publishing Company
A Bell & Howell Company
Columbus, Ohio 43216

Merrill Sociology Series
UNDER THE EDITORSHIP OF
Richard M. Simpson
University of North Carolina, Chapel Hill
and
Paul E. Mott

Published by
Charles E. Merrill Publishing Company
A Bell & Howell Company
Columbus, Ohio 43216

ISBN: 0-675-08896-8

Library of Congress Card Catalog Number: 73-84785

1 2 3 4 5 6 7—79 78 77 76 75 74

Printed in the United States of America

To my mother

Dorothy Edith Madoo

Acknowledgments

I wish to acknowledge the assistance given me by George Washington University, where I have taught for the whole period that this book was in preparation. Specifically I wish to thank the University Committee on Research for a Summer Research Grant which allowed me to do the preliminary research for the book; the Department of Sociology for consideration in course selection and scheduling which gave me time and opportunity to work out these ideas, and also for some assistance with typing; and most important the students, both undergraduate and graduate, who helped clarify and elaborate these ideas with their questions and discussion. I would also like to thank my husband, Joseph Lengermann, for his encouragement and support during the entire project.

Contents

1

Introduction

This book deals with the history of sociology. Instead of aiming for comprehensiveness, it is concerned with arriving at answers to a few select questions about that history. The underlying assumption is that sociology is an academic discipline characterized by a distinctive belief system. Many of these beliefs evolved out of certain concerns which affect anyone who, accepting the general need for a scientific study of social life, sets out to be more specific about the characteristics of such a field of investigation. How do sociologists conceptualize the process of "social life?" Where do they fit the human individual into this process? Of what significance is the fact that this individual can think? Questions such as these may be viewed as the basic existential problems of sociology. This book will look at the efforts made by earlier sociologists to grapple with these and other problems.

This is not to imply that there are complete continuities between past and present answers to such questions. The point has been well made that sociology tends to exaggerate its continuities with the past.[1] But the problems on which we focus in this text are constant ones for sociology, and there are sufficient links with past answers to justify an exploration of those earlier answers. Moreover, many of the earlier sociologists whose ideas will be described here rank among the most important and influential of the field's thinkers, regardless of the time factor. As such their views deserve serious consideration. This

1

group of men developed a possibly exhaustive range of answers to the problems raised by this book.

This book is a venture into the history of sociological ideas. Let us be a bit more specific about the parameters of the venture. First we need to specify a time period for the book's investigation. Our exploration starts with Auguste Comte's publications, and ends around 1920. Comte coined the name sociology, and set out to specify the details of this new subject in *The Positive Philosophy,* published in several volumes between 1830 and 1842. By 1920 almost all the important members of the earliest generations of sociologists were dead, and the first systematic exploration of the sociological belief system was over.

We must also select a bloc of writings for analysis. We will be concerned with a fairly small cluster of methodological and theoretical statements and some research reports which are regarded as major contributions to sociology's early formulation. The choice of writers, dictated partly by the traditions of the field and partly by idiosyncratic factors, is more fully described in chapter 2. At this point it is enough to say that almost all the men selected were consciously writing as sociologists. (The two exceptions are Marx and Mead, whose impact on sociology is too profound to be omitted from a text like this.)

Another cluster of decisions has to do with the selection of an approach for the analysis and presentation of this material. This text focuses on certain recurring theoretical and methodological concerns of sociology, searching through selected writings for statements relating to them. Each chapter is organized around a question about the sociological enterprise, and discusses the ideas of earlier sociologists on this question. The purpose is to make some sense of the collective ideas on each problem.

The main task of the book is to describe and analyze ideas in terms of their implications for present-day sociology. Yet it is impossible in any account of ideas not to offer some sort of explanation of why they appeared in the form that they did. This book uses a multi-causal explanation, which incorporates personality variables, social and political events, the philosophical beliefs and assumptions of the day, the arguments early sociologists had with each other, and the internal logic of each man's thoughts. On the whole though it tends to emphasize the philosophical background, and the logical development of the ideas themselves.

The text is divided into three major parts. Part one (chapters 2-4) sketches in the background to the earlier period of theoretical development, and offers a partial explanation of the ideas that will subsequently be described. Chapter 2 explores the biographies and personalities of the earlier sociologists; chapter 3 describes some of the social and political events of the day; and chapter 4 focuses on some of the intellectual characteristics of the period. Part two (chapters 5-8) contains the central discussions of this book. Chapter 5 discusses early views on sociology's subject matter; chapters 6 and 7 consider the early arguments on man and on mind, as variables which influence this subject matter; and chapter 8 reviews earlier research procedures and guidelines. Part three (chapters 9-11) looks at three general questions which seem to be at the foundations of early sociological development. Chapter 9 looks at early explorations of the dimensions of social order; chapter 10 reviews the parallel exploration of social conflict; and chapter 11 presents a series of classic statements about societal change.

One important drawback to an approach like this is that it tends to fragment the theoretical systems of each of the men being considered. The reader may well experience an unsatisfied wish to see each man's theory as a whole, interrelated complex. Broadly speaking, this problem is unavoidable, given the analytic purposes of the book. However, an effort has been made to counteract it: the summary sections and charts given at various crucial points in the text. With this aid, it is hoped that the student may be able to perceive each of the men discussed as the proponent of a distinctive and unitary sociological formulation, while understanding his place in a collective debate about the definition of a new field: sociology.

NOTES

1. Alvin Gouldner, *The Coming Crisis in Western Sociology* (New York: Basic Books, 1970).

Part One

Background to the Development of Sociology

2

The Earlier
Sociologists

Introduced here are the men whose ideas contributed in a major way to the first definitions of sociology. We will first focus on the men as a group. Each member of that group will then be individually considered, with a brief sketch of those biographical experiences and personality traits which seem relevant to the way in which he developed his views of sociology.

There is an important relationship between intellectual history and biography. Intellectual history can give the false impression that ideas directly generate ideas. Biographical accounts help dispel this impression. They make the point that one cannot causally separate ideas from the men who thought and stated them. These individuals' particular experiences and education, their communication with or isolation from each other, their personalities—these and similar individual characteristics are major intervening variables in the record of the development of ideas.

Choosing between the biographical approach and the focus on ideas is always difficult, for either choice entails a loss. Invariably one tries to minimize this loss by compromising between the two approaches. The concern here is primarily with the early ideas of sociology. This chapter's venture into biography is my own attempt at compromise.

The Early Sociologists as a Collectivity

The men on whose ideas we will focus are (listed alphabetically): Auguste Comte, Robert Cooley, Emile Durkheim, Karl Marx, George Herbert Mead, Vilfredo Pareto, Georg Simmel, Herbert Spencer, William Sumner, Ferdinand Tönnies, Lester Ward, and Max Weber. An alphabetical listing is useful only for quick reference. Our concern in viewing these men as a collectivity is to begin to understand how the sociological belief system initially developed and why it had the structure that it did. Were its original proponents really a group, communicating with each other and influencing each other? To what extent were they isolated, perhaps creating different versions of sociology? What common experiences might they have had which might produce a similar sociology, whether or not they were in communication? Were they of comparable influence in the articulation of the sociological belief system? Answering these kinds of questions necessitates rearranging the alphabetic listing in a number of ways.

The first rearrangement is presented in figure 1. The men are listed chronologically, in terms of their birth dates. The initial impression given by this chart is that sociology was unequivocally a product of the nineteenth century. Comte was born in the eighteenth century, but so late into it as to make no difference to this impression, while the "latest" members of the group, Weber and Cooley, were mature adults in their middle thirties when the century ends. If any common themes run through this period, one can expect to find them reflected in the early sociological writings. In chapters 3 and 4 we explore some of these themes.

There are limits, however, to what a chronological ordering of the life spans of early sociologists can tell us about the articulation of the sociological belief system. Obviously an individual can develop and communicate his ideas at any time in his adult life. One cannot assume that the older members of a group were necessarily the pioneers in formulating ideas, nor that the longest-lived were the final elaborators of a belief system. Figure 2 tries to compensate for this limitation by placing the major productive efforts of our sociologists on a time continuum.

This chart does not list all the written works of the group. It is limited to major works of direct sociological import, only indicating in a general way lesser sociological products. Wherever possible book titles are listed. Certain members of the group, however, presented their most important ideas not in books, but in articles, papers, or even (in the case of Mead) through lectures. Figure 2 allows for this. Excluded are non-sociological works, such as Spencer's momumental exploration of

FIGURE 1 The Earlier Sociologists: Chronological Order

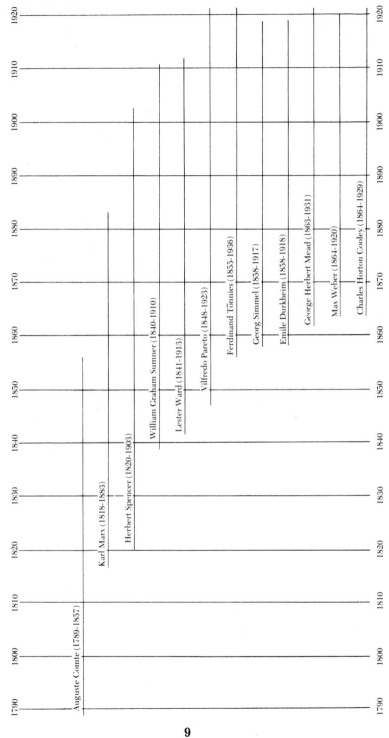

Auguste Comte (1789-1857)

Karl Marx (1818-1883)

Herbert Spencer (1820-1903)

William Graham Sumner (1840-1910)

Lester Ward (1841-1913)

Vilfredo Pareto (1848-1923)

Ferdinand Tönnies (1855-1936)

Georg Simmel (1858-1917)

Emile Durkheim (1858-1918)

George Herbert Mead (1863-1931)

Max Weber (1864-1920)

Charles Horton Cooley (1864-1929)

FIGURE 2 The Earlier Sociologists: Chronology of Their Important Works

	1830-1859	1860-1879	1880-1889	1890-1899	1900-1909	1910-1919	1920-1940
Comte	*The Positive Philosophy* 1830-42; *The Positive Polity* 1851-54						
Marx	*German Ideology* 1846; *The Communist Manifesto* 1847	other works → *Capital* Vol. 1 1867 → other works	Engels' continuation of Marx's work				
Spencer	*Social Statics* 1850	*First Principles* 1862; *The Study of Sociology* 1873; *Principles of Sociology* 1876	revised editions of *Social Statics* and *Principles of Sociology* until 1896				
Sumner			essays during 1880s, 1890s		*Folkways* 1906		
Ward			*Dynamic Sociology* 1883 — other works		*Pure Sociology* 1903		
Pareto						*General Treatise* 1915	
Tönnies			*Gemeinschaft und Gesellschaft* 1887	revised editions for remainder of lifetime			
Simmel				essays and articles	*Soziologie* 1908		
Durkheim				*Division of Labor* 1893; *Rules of Sociological Method* 1895; *Suicide* 1897	other works	*Elementary Forms of Religious Life* 1912	
Mead					lectures and papers at University of Chicago		
Weber					essays, articles, papers 1900-1920		
Cooley					*Human Nature and the Social Order* 1902; *Social Organization* 1909		

the natural sciences and Pareto's important contributions to economics. It is, of course, somewhat artificial to tie the development and communication of a man's ideas to the publication of a *magnum opus*. Ideas may incubate for years, even decades, and they may be communicated through conversation, teaching or private correspondence long before their appearance in published form. Nevertheless figure 2 is a better guide to the chronological profile of sociology's development than is figure 1.

Figure 2 shows that the definition of the sociological task occurred rather slowly over a long period in the nineteenth century, and then entered a phase of far more intense elaboration at the turn of the century. This period of quickened definitional activity coincides with a period of organization and professionalization in the field. Figure 2 also reinforces the impression already given by figure 1 that Marx and Spencer serve a bridging function on the time dimension between Comte and the later sociologists. Their early works are contemporaneous with Comte, their latest efforts—if Engels' elaborations on Marx are counted—occupy the same time period as the younger group. However, figure 2 alters some of the implications of figure 1: Tönnies, despite his longevity, made his contribution rather early in the period; Pareto, though older than many of the men being studied, published his important work late in the period. It is obvious from this chart that the major definitional work of the field has a rather narrow time base. The important group effort at definition begins in the 1890s, reaches its most intense level in the first decade of the twentieth century, and begins to diminish in the period between 1910 and 1920. Only Mead's work extends beyond that date, but this is probably more apparent than real. Mead worked out his ideas early, and tended to restate them year after year without major modification.[1] The major dimensions of his system had probably been developed by 1920. Figure 2 not only provides a justification for the choice of our closing date in this study; it also underscores the point that, despite the important pioneering work of Comte, Spencer, and Marx, the elaboration of sociology's belief system was the work of a single crucial generation.

Another meaningful arrangement of our alphabetical list is into national groupings. The result is as follows:

Britain	Spencer
France	Comte, Durkheim
Germany	Marx, Simmel, Tönnies, Weber
Italy	Pareto
United States	Cooley, Meed, Sumner, Ward

Nationality is an important clue to socialization experience. The university systems of the different countries were characterized by different systems of philosophical assumptions, as we shall see in chapter 4, and this had a profound effect on the world views of the earlier sociologists. Not only did the half-realized assumptions of different national university systems vary, but the particular blocs of philosophical writings which their academics debated also differed. Hegel's influence was central in German scholarship, for example, while French academics related to the works of Montesquieu and Rousseau, and Americans confronted the pragmatism of Peirce and James. Again nationality implies national identification by the individuals being considered, and that in turn means variations in the significance they would give to sociopolitical events occurring in this period. To some events (usually those in their own nation) they would relate strongly and emotionally; other things would awaken only a less intense cognitive curiousity. For example, Pareto's political sociology was strongly shaped by the collapse of liberal constitutionalism and the rise of Fascism in Italy, while Tönnies' typology of social relationship reflected his ambivalence about the rapid industrialization of Germany. The next chapter describes some of these sociopolitical events.

Nationality, because of its relationship to language and to autonomous university systems, also helps in identifying the patterns of greater and less intense communication within our group of sociologists. For example, there was considerable cross-influencing among the German sociologists, and men like Simmel and Weber were both colleagues and friends. Similarly the Americans engaged in often intense debate with each other and with the ideas of Spencer, who also spoke English. In contrast, the profound insights of men like Simmel, Weber and Durkheim trickled only slowly into the American sociological debates, since the availability of their ideas depended on the whims of translation. The effect of national and language barriers was not total. Translation in some cases came quickly, as with the writings of Comte and Marx. Some sociologists were bilingual—for example, Pareto was not quite as isolated from the sociological community as his nationality might at first imply. Travel also served to widen the networks of communication and influence; for example, Durkheim and Mead both studied in Germany. Still, nationality is one important index to the patterns of socialization and communication within the group of earlier sociologists.

In this book the twelve sociologists being considered are not treated as holding equal importance. Marx, Weber, Durkheim, and Mead are given the greatest emphasis because they established competing perspectives on sociology which still serve today to divide the discipline into "schools" of thoughts. We still read and draw direction from large portions of their writings. The second level of emphasis is given to Spencer, Comte, Simmel, Pareto, and Cooley. Spencer and Comte played a crucial role in the earlier development of sociology even though their works are not generally studied today. They drew the first "maps" of the sociological enterprise, and men like Durkheim and Mead evolved their sociology in a close relationship to the older men's perspectives, in much the same way as we today relate to Mead and Durkheim. Simmel, Pareto, and Cooley, although they did not bequeath to sociology total theoretical perspectives, contributed a set of concepts and hypotheses which still influence our thinking. Least emphasis is given to Sumner, Tönnies, and Ward. Their theses are inserted in a few specific sections of the book because on a limited number of issues they played a strategic role in defining the sociological perspective.

Finally, in attempting to understand the characteristics of this group of men, it is useful to approach them as active human beings rather than as just a set of names to be slotted into a series of charts. A good beginning is to explore the dimensions of the role or type[2] we today label "the academic" or "scholar." Almost all the men being considered approximated this type, either for all of their adult careers (like Durkheim or Cooley) or for long periods of their lives (like Marx.)

An academic is primarily oriented to an existing body of knowledge with which he struggles to become thoroughly familiar, and which he then acts to preserve and extend in a systematic way. An academic wants to know the "facts," not as a means to some other end (in the manner of a policeman), but because they have intrinsic value for him. He collects facts by reading obscure works which fascinate no one else, by scrutinizing official reports, complicated tables, and long footnotes, or by carefully observing the details of events around him. He makes careful notes to himself about these facts, and generally views himself as a specialist in certain types of information. Often his concern is simply to record, refurbish, and rescue from oblivion these bits of information. At other times he may arrange the pieces into patterns, and describe them as such. And at still other times he adds carefully and systematically to this pool of information.

As one reconstructs the evidence about the lives of these earlier sociologists, most of them emerge as academics. For example, stories are told of Spencer feverishly recording ethnographic data and storing his notes away in his famous filing system; of Cooley carefully recording the details of his own children's early development; of Weber locking himself away in his study for six hours of every day while he steadily explored the histories of major civilizations; and of Marx, somber and shabby, reading and note-taking year after year in the reading room of the British Museum.

One can, analytically, distinguish between intellectual and academic. The best clue to the difference is a difference in style. The academic places more emphasis on synthesis and on relationship to existing information. New ideas may be for him a by-product of his attempt to master a field, and must be legitimized by existing information. For the intellectual the new idea was the original goal. This distinction between academics and intellectuals is not meant to imply that none of the earlier sociologists were intellectuals. But in seeking to recreate the personalities who formulated sociology, it is more important to understand them as scholars or academics.

As a group, academics associate closely with universities. Most of the individuals in the group under consideration earned the degree of doctor of philosophy. This was in an age when the Ph.D. was not viewed as specialized vocational training for a variety of careers (as it has become today in America) but rather as one's formal declaration of choosing the academic role. Moreover, except for Marx and Spencer, all of our group were associated with universities for much of their post-doctoral careers. The type of association varied. Comte was little more than a lowly tutor and examiner. Except for the last two years of his life, Simmel was merely tolerated by the University of Berlin. In contrast, the university system (in this case the University of Heidelberg) was unusually protective of Weber, for many years allowing him the status of professor although ill health made it impossible for him to assume any academic duties. For the most part, members of this group—men like Tönnies, Durkheim, Pareto, Cooley, and Mead— were full professors at universities. Only Marx and Spencer did not have this formal linkage to a university, but in terms of the academic model they did the next best thing: they remained close to a major library (the British Museum Library) where they could at least tap an enormous reservoir of information.

Academics attempt to become specialists in particular types of information. Given our task, it is of interest to discover whether these men viewed themselves as specialists in the newly emerging field. In fact, all but two of the group did identify to some extent with the idea of sociology. For some, like Cooley and Durkheim, it was a complete and lifelong identification. To others, like Weber and Simmel, sociology was only one of the areas in which they claimed technical skills. Another pattern of identification is shown by Pareto, who for most of his life viewed himself as an economist, arriving at an identification with sociology only late in his career. The two men who did not identify themselves as sociologists are Marx and Mead. To exclude Marx and Mead in pursuit of symmetry, however, would result in an incomplete picture of sociology's development. Although he identified as a philosopher and social psychologist, Mead is viewed by comtemporary sociologists as the major founder of an important school (symbolic interactionism) in Western sociology. He cannot be excluded.

Although there is not a large school of Marxist sociology in Western sociology, Marxist influences permeate the sociological belief system. Many of the earlier sociologists explicitly engaged in a dialogue with Marx's interpretation of history and society. They accepted elements of his theses and reacted against other aspects of it. Their views of sociology often emerged from this debate.[3] Later sociologists too have created their theories out of a similar relationship to Marx's ideas.[4] Critics of prevailing sociological beliefs often draw inspiration from Marx's ideas.[5] Finally, important Marxist concepts and hypotheses are incorporated in the Western belief system—notions on alienation, on social classes, and the importance of economic, political, and conflict processes in society are all illustrations of this. Although Marx in his academic role identified himself as an economist and historian rather than as a sociologist, his influence is so pervasive that we cannot ignore him in a book on this subject.

The fact that almost all of these men were academics and not, for example, businessmen, bureaucrats, politicians or priests helps explain the sociology they created. They are concerned with the technical details of theory: careful definition, elaborate classifications, logical continuity, and frequent introjection of carefully collected facts to support an opinion. Academics frequently live apart from the dynamic core of society, and though they may be students of that action they aspire to a degree of detachment from it in their analysis. This *style* of detachment often characterizes the early sociological writings. Of course personal biases and interests do shape their work. But, although imperfect, the academic aspiration for objectivity does act as a partial brake on bias, and something of this aspiration is to be detected in much of the writings under consideration here.

A second role must also be considered in attempting to understand the earlier sociologists. This is the role of the political man of action, political in a broad sense: the man who confronts his society and either aspires or acts to change and direct it. Political and academic roles contrast with each other. The former requires involvement and decisiveness, the latter is founded on detachment and the hesitancy born from an awareness of complexity. A man may play both roles, but he will then be a personality in tension. Certain of our group were at times political in this scene, and the resulting tension is to be detached in the sociology they created.

Marx, of course, is the most obvious example. He is remembered as the political advocate and the social critic who thundered for revolution far more frequently than as the impoverished scholar who studied in the British Museum Library. The markedly academic phase of his life is flanked by even longer periods when he was a journalist and aspiring political organizer. Accordingly, the style of his writings vary from the polemic of the *Communist Manifesto,* through the informed journalistic analyses of political upheavals in France, to the solidly researched volumes of *Capital.* The earlier emphasis given to Marx's scholarly period should not confuse readers into viewing all his writings as the product of academic research and interest.

Others in the group also show this penchant for a political role, though less dramatically than Marx. Comte and Spencer both at times wanted to direct the course of events in their societies, while both Pareto and Weber entertained specifically political career ambitions at various times in their lives. Sections of the writings of the first two men are explicitly polemical. Less obviously Pareto's analysis of political elites and Weber's of charismatic leadership can be related to their political ambitions. In contrast, Tönnies, Durkheim, Mead and Cooley do not have this political side to their personalities, and their writings do not show the contrasts resulting from an inclination both to scholarship and to action.

The Earlier Sociologists; Individual Sketches

The description of the earlier sociologists as a collectivity has been taken as far as it can go. In the following pages, the members of the group are individually described. For each man a short list of pertinent biographical details is given, and wherever it seems relevant or possible a short sketch of the man's personality is also included. This section is intended primarily for reference purposes. The men are listed alphabetically.

Auguste Comte

Born in 1798 at Montpellier, France, Comte is remembered as "the father of sociology." He was educated at the famous École Polytechnique in Paris, where the focus was on mathematics and the natural sciences, rather than on social phenomena. Before completing his formal education, however, Comte was expelled for participating in a student insurrection against the school's administration. He then became secretary to Henri Comte de Saint-Simon, an influential political leader and proponent of a pre-Marxist version of socialism. The influence of Saint-Simon's ideas on Comte is considerable. The friendship between the two men terminated after Saint-Simon accused Comte of plagiarism, a charge always emphatically denied by Comte. From 1836 until 1846 he was an examiner at the École Polytechnique. After losing that position, he lived in relative poverty, supported only by contributions from his friends, until his death in 1857. His major works are the *Positive Philosophy*, 1830-1842 and the *Positive Polity*, 1851-1854.

Well educated in mathematics, philosophy and the natural sciences, Comte also possessed encyclopedic knowledge, as his books reveal. From early beginnings in the radical flank of Parisian political circles, Comte became increasingly isolated and estranged (except from a few friends) as he grew older. There are hints too of an eccentric amount of self-pride. He sent a copy of the *Positive Philosophy* to Czar Alexander of Russia, convinced that reading it would lead him to reform his vast empire along the lines suggested by the book; he hoped that his ideas would lead to a new scientific religion of society in France, in which he would function as a sort of high priest. As he grew older he moved away from his original conception of a science of society towards a proposal for this new religion on which society would be restructured. The image that comes through is of increasing eccentricity, pride, and a certain bitterness as he grew older and experienced disappointment and poverty.

Charles Horton Cooley

Cooley spent almost his entire life in the middle-sized midwestern town of Ann Arbor, Michigan. Born there in 1864, he did his undergraduate work in engineering at the University of Michigan at Ann Arbor. After a short career as a surveyor and a period of travel and study in Europe, he returned to the university to study for his Ph.D. in economics, with a minor in sociology. He then accepted a teaching position at the University of Michigan in 1892, a post which he held for the rest of his life. He served as president of the American Sociological Association in 1918. His writings include *Personal Competition*, 1899; *Human Nature and the Social Order*, 1902; *Social Organization*, 1909; *Social Process*, 1918; and the posthumous *Sociological Theory and Social Research*, 1930.

Cooley was a recluse, shy and retiring in his mannerisms. His inclinations were those of the scholar and academic, and he was contemplative by disposition. Life in a tranquil university town suited him well, and he refused all enticements offered him to move to Columbia and the urban bustle of New York. His values reflect that peaceful setting and the preferences of America prior to her hectic industrialization.

Emile Durkheim

Born in 1858 to a wealthy Jewish family in Lorraine, France, Durkheim was given an excellent French education and also studied social science in Germany. In 1892 the University of Paris granted him its first doctor's degree in sociology. In 1898 he became the first French scholar to hold a chair in sociology, at Bordeaux. In 1902 he returned to Paris to teach social science, and in 1906 he was appointed professor of sociology at Paris. He helped found the first sociology society in the world in 1894, the Institute de Sociology. He also established and for many years edited the prestigious French sociology journal, *L'Année Sociologique*, which first appeared in 1898. He died in 1918. His most influential books have been *The Division of Labor in Society*, 1893; *The Rules of Sociological Method*, 1895; *Suicide*, 1896; and *The Elementary Forms of Religious Life*, 1912. Durkheim also wrote important statements on education and on the relationships between philosophy and sociology.

In terms of his chosen career, Durkheim was a success, receiving every reward that the academic community can give. Moreover, although not religious, he was self-consciously Jewish in an age when success was not easily granted to members of his minority group. France had been one of the first societies to begin easing discrimination practices against Jews, and Durkheim did not take his success for granted. He was proud and grateful to be French, and easily moved to feelings of patriotism and nationalism when French was challenged abroad. He displays the attributes of the academic role described above. He is regarded today as one of the great founders of modern sociology.

Karl Marx

Marx, born in the Rhineland area of Germany in 1818, was also of Jewish origins, but his family had converted to Christianity when he was very young, and unlike Durkheim, Marx did not think of himself as Jewish. His life was a stormy one. After studying law and philosophy at Bonn and Berlin, he received his doctorate from Jena in 1841, and then became editor of a liberal newspaper which was soon suppressed by the authorities. In 1843 he went to Paris where he moved into the socialist circles active in the city, and where he also began his lifelong friendship with Friedrich Engels. In these years he began to study political economics. Exiled from Paris by the French authorities, he went to Brussels, joined the Communist League, and together with

Engels wrote the *Communist Manifesto* in 1847. In 1848 a wave of revolution swept Europe. Marx returned to Germany to publish a radical newspaper only to have it suppressed and himself exiled as the revolutions failed. He moved to London where he lived in relative poverty, supporting himself by articles which he wrote for the then socialist New York *Tribune* and helped by his affluent friend Engels. Until 1864 he devoted himself strictly to research and writing, publishing on the basis of this work the multi-volume *Capital*. In 1864 he returned to political life, becoming a leading figure in the newly founded International Workingmen's Association. He died in 1883. His friend Engels continued to edit his writings and elaborate on his ideas until his own death twelve years later in 1895. The writings of the two men are voluminous, frequently appearing as pamphlets, articles, letters, etc. Short but adequate bibliographies on Marx are to be found in Hendrik Ruitenbeek, *Varieties of Classical Social Theory* and David Caute, *Essential Writings of Karl Marx*.

The chief characteristic of Mark which emerges from an exploration of his writings and biography is his profound sense of moral outrage. He perceived the misery produced for the lower classes by the new industrial order and it sickened and infuriated him. To quote Feuer,

> Marx's identification with the "masses" was as total as a person's can be; free from the ordinary kinds of self-seeking, he looms as a reproach to the acquiescent, the complacent, the place hunter, the trimmer, the smug.[6]

He devoted his life to destroying the conditions which he thought produced such misery. Both his academic work and his political activity were single-mindedly directed to this goal. His influence on modern thinking has been enormous.

George Herbert Mead

Mead's family were New Englanders, strongly religious and academic. Born in Massachusetts in 1863, Mead's early years were spent at Oberlin College in Ohio, where his father and mother both taught. He studied first at Oberlin, later at Harvard and in Germany. His interests were in philosophy and psychology, and he was deeply influenced by the early pragmatists Royce and James. He taught first at the University of Michigan, but in 1893 he moved to the new University of Chicago, where he taught until his death in 1931. He was acquainted and in communication with other influential thinkers like John Dewey, Charles H. Cooley, W. I. Thomas, and Robert E. Park.

Mead's activities were wide ranging: educational reform, settlement work, as well as regular professional duties. He was an excellent teacher, winning a crowd of devoted followers. His chief difficulty was with writing. During his lifetime, he published very little. His books were published posthumously, compiled by some of those dedicated students. As a personality, he appears to have been a humble and gentle individual, with strong values which he could defend strenuously when challenged. His chief publications are *Mind, Self and Society*, 1934; *Movements of Thought in the Nineteenth Century*, 1936; and *The Philosophy of the Act*, 1938.

Vilfredo Pareto

Pareto was born in 1848 in Paris. His mother was French and his father Italian, so Pareto grew up at home in both languages. Moving to Italy in his childhood, he received an Italian education, and by identification also he was Italian, though his tastes were cosmopolitan. His family was wealthy, and Pareto was trained both in the classics and in engineering. For a while he entertained political hopes but they were unfulfilled. After a short career as an engineer, he turned to the study of economics and to a life of study and research. In 1892 his publications won him an appointment as Professor of Economics at the University of Lausanne, Switzerland, with which he was associated for the rest of his career. His contributions to mathematical economics are outstanding. Partly as a counterpart to the extremely formalistic models of behavior which were his specialization in economics, and partly because of his realization that many of the occurrences in actual economic life are to be understood not in terms of processes intrinsic to that institution but as responses to political and other social pressures, Pareto turned to the study of sociology late in his career. He died in 1923. His major sociological work is the *General Treatise on Sociology*, 1915, translated in 1936 as *Mind and Society*.

A curious air of cynicism and bitterness runs through Pareto's sociology. He calls this disenchantment realism, and it is rather difficult to explain. He suffered various disappointments in his personal life, but so did Marx, or Weber, or Simmel, who did not make the same responses. Instead it seems more meaningful to understand him as an heir to the political "realism" of thinkers like Machiavelli, responding to the political anguish and turbulence of Italy at the turn of the century.

Georg Simmel

Simmel was born in Berlin in 1858. His parents were Jews who had converted to Protestantism, and this Jewish background proved a barrier to career advancement for most of his life. Fortunately a guardian left him a considerable financial estate, so he had private means of support. Simmel was associated with the University of Berlin for most of his life. He received his doctorate there in 1881, and taught there from 1885-1914. During all of this time, his position at the university was marginal and he received no pay despite his reputation as a brilliant teacher and writer. In 1914 he was appointed a full professor with pay at the University of Strassbourg, partly through the mediation of his friend Max Weber. He died in 1918. His writings are voluminous and scattered. A full bibliography is to be found in Nicholas Spykman, *The Social Theory of Georg Simmel* (Chicago, 1925), or in Kurt Wolff (ed.), *The Sociology of Georg Simmel* (Glencoe, Ill.: Free Press, 1950).

Simmel's interests were wide ranging, focused on philosophy, but with strong supporting areas in sociology, history, literature and the arts. He taught and wrote substantially in all these fields. Because sociology had only a part of his attention, and perhaps because of the frustration that his career produced, Simmel's style is brilliant and insightful, but it lacks the concern for carefully arranged supporting facts that characterizes the work of men like Durkheim and Weber. His work is consequently often difficult to read. Nevertheless, Simmel's insights and his philosophical viewpoint make important contributions to the clarification of sociology's task. Many of his papers were translated early and helped to shape the pattern of sociological discourse in America. [7]

Herbert Spencer

Spencer was born in 1820 in Derbyshire, England. His family, though not rich, was financially secure, and since Spencer was a frail child he was educated at home or in small private schools. His teachers, responding to his unusual intelligence and curiosity, exposed him to a very wide range of information, but his schooling was unsystematic. As a young adult he worked for a while as an engineer, then as a journalist, but eventually decided to support himself by means of his writing. For the rest of his life, he continued to educate himself without the aid of formal institutions, and to earn a modest income through his publications. His writings cover a variety of fields: *Social Statics* (1850); *First Principles* (1862) in which he developed a synthesizing philosophy which aimed at integrating all the theoretical sciences; *Principles of Biology* (1864-1867); *Principles of Psychology* (1870-1872); *Principles of Sociology* (1876-1896); *Principles of Ethics* (1879-1893); and *The Study of Sociology* (1873). Spencer died in 1903.

Spencer's influence on American sociology and on American social thought in his own time was profound; indeed, though less obvious today, he still has a pervasive influence in both areas. An understanding of his personality is important for understanding his theoretical position. His family was middle class, nonconformist by religion, and a product of the British midlands; they were, in other words, members of a social group long characterized by independent individualism and a defiant insistence that the government (the Anglican, aristocratic, London-based government) stay out of their affairs, letting them alone to pursue God and business in their own fashion. Both the individualistic position and the hatred of state authority were passed on to Spencer. In relationship to the autocratic, partially feudal types of government prevalent in his youth, those attitudes mark Spencer as a classic liberal; in relationship to the incipient welfare state of his old age, those same attitudes make Spencer conservative, indeed almost reactionary. Other meaningful characteristics are his passionate curiosity, a trait noted from his childhood, a curiosity which led him to an omnivorous collecting of facts. His knowledge was enormous. Coupled with this curiosity was an equally strong drive to "tidy things up," everything—objects of daily life or pieces of information—had to be placed and kept in its proper slot in the scheme of things. The result was his ambitious scheme to organize all scientific knowledge. All these traits—individualism, hostility to authority, curiosity about the facts, and the drive to "understand it all"—struck a respondent chord in America and serve to explain his enormous popularity there.[8] He had his greatest influence in America.

William Graham Sumner

Born in New Jersey in 1840, educated both at Yale and Oxford, Sumner's whole career is associated with Yale where he taught from 1868 until his death in 1910. Although originally meant for the Episcopalian ministry (he was ordained in 1869), he decided instead to teach, and his influence on the thinking of many generations of Yale students is important. Sumner wrote a series of semi-polemical essays early in his career such as *The Absurd Effort to Make the World Over*, 1894. His major sociological work is *Folkways,* 1906; a posthumous book, *The Science of Society,* appeared in 1927, edited by his student A.G. Keller.

Sumner's family was precisely the kind of American social group which found Spencer's philosophy most appealing. His father was an emigrant from England, religious and hardworking, who struggled all his life to keep his family up to a lower-middle-class position. Individualism and hatred of state authority, or of any other kind of massive bureaucratic authority, characterize such a man and these traits are to be found also in Sumner. Sumner functioned as the chief American proponent of Spencer's ideas to American social scientists. His book

Folkways, however, contains important ideas which are separate from this function.

Ferdinand Tönnies

Born in 1855 in the Schleswig-Holstein area in Germany to a wealthy family, Tönnies' independent income allowed him to live as he liked for all of his life. His choice was the life of the student, scholar, and traveler. Both before and after obtaining his doctorate in 1877, he studied widely in Germany, at Strassbourg, Jena, Bonn, Leipsig, Tubingen and Berlin, and abroad, in London and the United States. He was associated for much of his life with the University of Kiel, but did little teaching, preferring to write and do research instead. He was a founding member of the German Sociological Society in 1909, a society which was disbanded by the Nazis in 1933. His own criticisms of the Nazis lost him his position at Kiel in the same year. Tönnies died in 1936. His most influential work is *Gemeinschaft und Gesellschaft,* the first edition of which was published in 1887.

Lester Ward

Ward was born in 1841 in Joliet, Illinois, to a poor family. The death of his father forced him to work early, in a variety of manual jobs, but he taught himself science and languages at night and finally obtained a teaching job. Having served with the Union Army in the Civil War, he moved to Washington, D.C. and a job in the civil service. While working he obtained advanced degrees in law and medicine at the Columbian University, now George Washington University. He completed his studies there in 1872. For most of his life he continued with the civil service, teaching parttime at the Columbian University, and during the summers at a number of other schools, chiefly at the University of Chicago. He taught sociology, his interest in that field having developed after he read Comte and Spencer. In 1906 he accepted a fulltime position at Brown University. He died in 1913.

Ward's most influential book is *Dynamic Sociology* published in 1883. His importance to sociology is his repudiation of the iron determinism of Spencer's and Sumner's social Darwinism, and his insistence on the unique importance of man's mind in shaping his history. He was himself liberal, optimistic, a firm believer in the importance of education—a progressive.

Max Weber

Born in Berlin in 1864 to well-to-do parents, Weber received an excellent education in law and economics at the University of Heidelberg, receiving his degree in law in 1886 and his doctorate in 1889. In 1894 he was appointed by the University of Freiburg to teach economics, and in 1896 he received a similar appointment at Heidelberg. Shortly after this, however, Weber succumbed to the severe illness which was to keep him an invalid and recluse for most of his life. His lapsed into a severe melancholia which for years made him incapable of action. By an effort of will, he gradually forced himself back to an interest in life and work, but it was only by maintaining a strict and organized regimen that he managed to keep his equilibrium. Fortunately he could afford to live comfortably and travel despite his inability to work. In 1918 he was well enough to return to teaching and politics, participating in the peace talks which ended World War I. He died of pneumonia in 1920 while at the peak of his intellectual powers.

Despite his invalidism, Weber was a devoted scholar and prolific writer. Of his writings in sociology, the most influential currently available in English are *The Protestant Ethic and The Spirit of Capitalism; The Religion of China: Confucianism and Taoism; The Religion of India: the Sociology of Hinduism and Buddhism; Ancient Judaism; The Theory of Social and Economic Organization;* and *The Methodology of the Social Sciences.*

Weber is regarded as one of the great founders of modern sociology. Much of his own writing was directed towards exploring and modifying the Marxist view of society and history. His technical sociology also sought to reconcile different philosophical positions in order to develop an analytic and methodological basis for sociology. Weber's father had been a prominent liberal politician who passed on both his values and his ambitions to his son. Weber was both a liberal and a German nationalist—a tragic situation in the early twentieth century. Moreover, he was as much attracted to politics as to academia, and seemed on the verge of seeking a position of political leadership at the time of his premature death. These various tensions, together with a remarkable intellect, serve to make Weber's contribution one of the most fascinating in sociology's early development.

NOTES

1. Charles W. Morris, "Introduction: George H. Mead as a Social Psychologist and Social Philosopher," in George Herbert Mead, *Mind, Self and Society* (Chicago: University of Chicago Press, 1934), p.xv.

2. The concept of "type" has considerable status in sociology. A type is a verbal model, purporting to present the essential characteristics and logical relationships of some general category of "thing," e.g., of some general set of ideas or behavior. This concept is explored in some depth in chapter 8.

3. This debate in earlier sociology is beautifully described in Irving Zeitlin, *Ideology and the Development of Sociological Thought* (Englewood-Cliffs, N.J.: Prentice-Hall, 1968).

4. See Alvin Gouldner, *The Coming Crisis in Western Sociology* (New York: Basic Books, 1970), especially his analysis of Talcott Parsons' tension with Marxist social thought.

5. Examples are C. Wright Mills and Ralf Dahrendorf.

6. Lewis S. Feuer, *Marx and Engels: Basic Writings* (Garden City, N.Y.: Anchor Books, 1959), p.xiv.

7. Hendrik M. Ruitenbeek, *Varieties of Classic Social Theory* (New York: Dutton, 1963), pp. 259-60.

8. For a discussion of Spencer's popularity in America see Richard Hofstadter, *Social Darwinism in American Thought* (Boston: Beacon Press, 1955).

3

The Social
Setting

Any man's ideas will be shaped by events occurring in the society in which he lives. And the men we have described, although they aspired to a degree of objectivity and detachment from their social world, were, as social scientists, students of that world. Moreover, we have seen that many of them, feeling the pull of the political role, were eager to confront and change their societies. It is therefore pertinent to ask: what sort of societies did these men live in? What were the distinctive relationships and noteworthy events of these societies, factors that may have influenced early sociological ideas? This chapter deals with such questions. Obviously a full answer would extend to many volumes. In the space of a single short chapter, we can touch only briefly on the major events of this period. Even this short description, however, will help to show the early sociologists in the context of their times.

The Industrial Revolution

All these men had their important formative experiences in the nineteenth century or in the extension of that century's patterns which runs up to the historic watershed of World War I. This period, which runs from about 1815 to 1914, is a distinctive one in the history of

Western societies. From one perspective it is *the* century in the his-
ory of the West: the period in which most nations in that region experienced unparalleled growth and unchallenged power. This growth
was based on a sudden spectacular acceleration of technological innovation and economic potency. These technological and economic
changes, and their ramifying consequences for the societies in which
they occurred, are known as the Industrial Revolution. The label
"revolution" is appropriate: within a few decades a social order which
had existed for centuries vanished, and a new one, familiar in its outlines to us in the late twentieth century, appeared. The Industrial
Revolution was *the* event in the social world of the first sociologists. It
would almost be legitimate to conceptualize early sociology as an effort to comprehend this event. Some of the dimensions of the Industrial Revolution are explored below.

The Pace and Pattern of Change

Although the period from 1815 to 1914 has been designated as the
period of the Industrial Revolution for those Western nations in which
the early sociologists worked, it would be inaccurate to draw the conclusion that the events of the revolution spread evenly through the
century, or that all five of the nations being considered (Britain,
France, Germany, Italy, and the United States) experienced changes
of an identical sort. Over the century, periods of relatively slow
change alternate with spans of steady cumulative growth, and, even
more dramatically, with relatively short spurts of intense expansion.
Moreover, the various nations were differently affected by the tech-
nological-economic changes which are the core of the revolution.
Some were almost totally restructured, others only partially reorgan-
ized, and still others only superficially affected. The pulse of the Industrial Revolution therefore is uneven both over time and over geographic regions. One effect of this on observers like the early sociologists was probably to heighten their awareness of the momentous nature of the change being witnessed because of the intensity of the
contrasts that became apparent between nations, between regions
of a single nation, and between periods in the memory of individuals.
This uneven pattern also produced different perspectives in the group
of early sociologists, reflecting real differences in the situations which
they observed. The most important of these is a clustering on the time
dimension: the world of Comte and of the young Marx and Spencer
differs dramatically from that of the later generation of sociologists.
There are also differences among regional clusters of sociologists. It is
necessary then to get some feel for these variations in the pattern

and pace of the Industrial Revolution. A quick overview of the situation at different points in time may serve to communicate such awareness.

A good time to begin is around 1830, when Comte first began to publish the volumes of his *Positive Philosophy.* If one stands back to survey the European continent and the United States with an image of the late nineteenth century in mind, the impression one receives is of a world in slow motion. We are referring here to the patterns of economic life, and to the overall texture of men's everyday world. Politically there were sufficient upheavals to create in the minds of the minority which analyzes events a sense of social instability. Since change of the scale that was about to occur always rests on an evolutionary base of cumulative small events, sufficient developments in that overall texture were already evident to create in contemporaries an awareness of imminent change. But the nature of that change and its direction were not clear. Much of the everyday routine of economic survival followed a pattern that had endured for generations.

Most men lived by farming. In the United States, a land of sparse population and vast empty areas, almost 90 percent of the population was in agriculture. In the hegemony of small states which was later to become Germany, 70 percent of the population worked the land. The figure is 60 percent for France and for the geographic area which we know today as Italy, and those percentages had not changed for centuries.[1] (In contrast, in 1960 only 6.3 percent of the labor force of the United States was engaged in agriculture.)

Patterns of farming varied somewhat. In much of Europe the age-old feudal pattern endured. Feudalism implied powerful, land-based aristocracies, a peasantry powerless and tied to the land, primitive farming techniques, and a productive system only partly oriented to the market place and chiefly directed to the subsistence of the various strata dependent on a land-based economy. In the United States, where most farmers were small independent land-owners, techniques were also frequently primitive, and the goal was often subsistence of the family unit. In the southern states, a new, even more austere version of the power relations of feudalism was emerging. A religious ethos everywhere permeated these agricultural societies.

A minority of the population lived in cities. In the United States towns were very small. On the European continent the only large cities were the local or national capitals, and no major shift in the urban-rural ratio had occurred for hundreds of years. [2] In these cities men supported themselves in the traditional crafts and professions, or by trade and commerce. The standard division in modern societies of the population into middle and working class had little significance in these societies. It is true that the commercial and professional "bourgeousie" and the "traders and artisans" were increasingly flexing their political muscle in the cities, but on the national scale these work-force categories were still overlaid by the classic feudal distinctions of peasant, lord, and priest.

England is the exception to these generalizations. The future of the West could already be discerned in England. There an urban society had developed, with only 25 percent of the population still in agriculture. Agriculture, moreover, showed few traces of feudalism. It was instead a commercial enterprise, using modern know-how to produce commodities on a large scale for the market. The growing urban population was concentrating not only in the capital, but in a number of new towns growing up around the coal fields of the north and midlands—cities like Manchester, Birmingham, and Leeds. The coal fields were important because of increasing use of the fuel to power machines which could mass produce textiles and iron goods. The factory was becoming the base for the subsistence of a variety of strata, both middle and working class. In this sense it contrasted with the land-based classes of the continent and the United States. Marx's early awareness of the importance of industrialization for patterns of class relations almost certainly springs from the knowledge of English developments he gained through Engels. (Engels belonged to a manufacturing family working out of Manchester.)

Thus the pace of life was already quickening in England by 1830. Yet it would not do to exaggerate the degree of the change. Industrialization was still at a fairly primitive, simple level. Its organization was simple—the family-owned factory. Its products were chiefly textiles and iron goods. Many of the older crafts survived. Everywhere in the regions being considered the horse drawn carriage, the sailing ship, and the terrible roads slowed the pace of communication. Men thought of the world as Europe—and America; or America—and Europe. Asia, Africa, South America, and Oceania did not affect ordinary men's image of the world. And despite interest in the so-called "English method," its implications and ramifications for the world were not grasped.[3] Comte was a product of this period, viewing the world from the perspective of France, where the kinds of changes now being considered were modest, not massive.

A dramatic difference is apparent sixty years later, around 1890. Trains raced across continents, steamships plowed the oceans, and the telegraph linked continents together in instantaneous communication. Britain stood at the center of the world-wide commercial system, investing in major undertakings on all the world's continents, drawing raw materials not only from America, but also from Asia, Africa, Oceania and South America, and selling her manufactured products in all those markets. The world had shrunk to a size at which men could comprehend it as a unit, or at least as a single economic area in which Eruope's influence was entrenched and dominant.

Although Europe's economic predominance seemed unchallengable, Britain's no longer was. For an economic miracle had occurred in both the United States and the new nation of Germany. Germany had become urban by 1890, with over 50 percent of its population located in cities. The United States already had over one-third of its people living in cities and was to pass the 50 percent mark in little more than a decade. Whole clusters of new industrial towns had sprung up on coal fields and strategic waterways. In the United States this urban explosion was in process on the Pennsylvania coalfields and in the young midwestern states. In Germany, the industrial complex of the Ruhr had developed in less than two decades. The United States now outstripped Britain in steel production; Germany had overtaken Britain in the ramifying new chemical and electrical industries.[4] Britain was still the leading industrial nation, but she now had challengers in the two younger giants.

What had happened was that the small nucleus of technological and economic change discernible in 1830 in Britain had elaborated itself several times over, and had simultaneously spread outwards to the corners of the region being studied. Textile factories could be found everywhere, including Italy and France. New industrial towns had sprung up in France too, around the northern coalfields. Factories now produced the full range of commodities and were soon to enter upon the first arms race, helping to push the world into World War I. The family-run factory had been replaced by complex corporate structures, the hated "trusts." The complexity of the class system dependent on this mode of production had multiplied, ranging from the "robber barons" through the different ranks of middle and working class. Concomitantly the old rural-based social systems were shrinking to the vanishing point as agriculture too became part of the large-scale commercial system.

The pace of change was not the same everywhere. Italy was as yet hardly affected. France had reached her industrial capacity, but was still extensively agricultural. Britain's changes had been steady and developmental. It was in the United States and Germany that the transformation was so rapid as to appear revolutionary. Up to 1870 Britain had still been the only important heavy industrial nation, producing half the world's coal, seven-tenths of its iron, and almost all of its steel. Germany and the United States were rapidly overtaking Britain, and their industrialization had occurred within the space of twenty years.

Men living through such changes must have been impressed by the great vitality and power of their societies. Yet there seemed also to be basic instabilities in the foundations of the impressive new economic structures. Bouts of extraordinary expansion alternated with periods of severe overproduction and depression, when tens of thousands would be thrown out of work and the fortunes of families would suddenly vanish. This mysterious sequence of boom and crash affected many of the first sociologists, and runs like a theme through their writings. It is a major variable in Marx's prognosis about capitalism, but it also figures in the thinking of men like Durkheim, Pareto, and Weber.

This world—expansive, transformed, unstable—was the world of most of the sociologists in our group. They viewed it from the various vantage points of the different nations, and with the memory of a slower past still alive in men's minds.

Migration, Urbanization, Social Problems

Paralleling these economic changes were sharp changes in population characteristics. The population of the region was growing far more rapidly than it had in earlier periods. The accelerating population growth rate had begun in the later half of the eighteenth century (for most of the countries being considered) and was probably a consequence of the declining incidence of famine and plague.

More important, however, than the sheer increase in population was its spatial relocation. The loci of increase was the countryside, just at the time when the growing mechanization and commercialization of agriculture began decreasing its potential to support a large rural work force. This excess rural population moved across oceans and national frontiers, primarily to America,[5] and from the countryside to the expanding labor markets of the towns. In this period three of the five countries being studied were transformed from rural to urban societies. In England this happened during the first half of the nineteenth century; by 1900 over 61 percent of the English population lived in towns of more than 10,000 people. In Germany and the United States the transformation occurred in the last half of the nineteenth century. For the region as a whole, urban populations multiplied by 300 percent during this period. Everywhere men were on the move, swarming to the cities.

This migration provided the labor force for rapid industrialization. It also resulted in severe social dislocation. National and municipal governments were unprepared for and unskilled in handling such situations. The migrants crowded into appalling slums, sanitary systems collapsed under the pressure, disease was everywhere. Infant mortality rates in the slums were astronomical.

Subjected to the instability of the economic market (which brought frequent massive unemployment) and to the appalling work conditions of an unregulated factory system, the first generation of industrial workers began to grow up in the urban slums. Cut off from tradition and community, confronted with intolerable living conditions, they turned frequently to violence or crime.

Nowhere did the movement of people and the resulting stress on the society seem clearer than in the United States. Here the migrants to the cities were not just peasants, they were the peasants of other cultures. As the century progressed the migrants seemed increasingly different. They came now not just from the religiously and culturally similar Northern European states, but from the religiously and culturally dissimilar Mediterranean and Central European societies. More and more they chose to seek refuge in the cities rather than in the countryside. Here they became foci for all the new stresses and instabilities of the emerging urban order—people obviously different, alien even to the language of their new society. Table 1 gives some figures on this migration.

TABLE 1 :   Immigration from Europe to the
United States 1831-1920 (in thousands)

	Europe	Great Britain	Ireland	Germany	Italy
1831-1840	496	76	207	152	2
1841-1850	1,598	267	741	435	2
1851-1860	2,453	424	914	952	9
1861-1870	2,065	607	436	787	12
1871-1880	2,272	548	437	718	56
1881-1890	4,737	807	655	1,453	307
1891-1900	3,559	272	388	505	652
1901-1910	8,136	526	339	341	2,046
1911-1920	4,377	341	146	144	1,110

SOURCE: Conrad Taeuber and Irene Taeuber "Immigration to the U.S.A." in C.B. Nam, *Population and Society* (New York Houghton Mifflin 1968), pp. 314-32.

All the early sociologists confronted and interpreted these phenomena. They did this even more frequently than they tried to explain industrialization. Their judgments of the social stress and tension vary.

Some saw it as transitional and sought to hasten the transition. Others feared that society as they knew it would be destroyed. Others accepted as permanent the new phenomenon of a society in tension but sought ways of reducing its worse features. And still others were torn by ambivalence, rejoicing in the vitality of their societies yet yearning for the quieter times that were passing or gone. Yet all judged social stability to be both desirable and problematic. They all set themselves to explore its foundations. This is one of the major themes of early sociology.

New Social Classes

Industrialization resulted not only in new spatial allocations of men, but also in new social allocations of power and prestige. In other words, the Industrial Revolution radically altered the arrangement of social classes.

From the preceding description of burgeoning urban populations what must seem most obvious is that this period produced a large urban working class. During much of this period, this new class seemed to lack both power and prestige. The members of this class had sought new opportunities in the cities. They found work conditions as harsh as those they had known in the countryside, income and employment circumstances which still kept them at the bleakest subsistence levels, and the intolerable living conditions of new urban slums. The new tyrants in their lives—industrialist, landlord, merchant, and state—were distant, impersonal, ruthless, and detached from that tradition of obligation and personalism which had softened the edges of the older agricultural tyrannies. Yet their dependency on these new powers was as great as ever. They had exchanged the familiar tyranny of feudal controls for the new exploitations of an unregulated industrial order.

Yet the working class was a numerous class, collectively indispensable to the new industrial order. These were its potential reserves of power. By the latter part of this period, the working class had begun to realize this power. Organizing into unions, associations, and parties, they began to hammer out of the system some measure of greater comfort: shorter working hours, higher wages, various pieces of protective legislation to regulate the work situation, and even the right to vote. Although they had a few allies, on the whole they fought their own battle, a fierce and often bloody one against the hierarchy of privilege. This new class of men, exploited, volatile, unpredictable, and increasingly militant, was something that had to be interpreted and accounted for by the earlier sociologists.

Even more influential in the development of sociology was that aggregate of groups which is labeled the urban middle class. There were middle-class groups before the industrialization of the Western nations —commercial classes, professionals, master craftsmen. But prior to these economic changes, they had been a small group, lacking in power and prestige. Industrialization altered all this. The organizational and technical talent that produced the Industrial Revolution was middle-class talent. As a class its numbers multiplied and its structure elaborated: new orders and ranks of commercial and financial groups, a network of professionals and technicians, and, above all, a new generation of men who worked in industry, at all levels of supervision, management and ownership. As national economies shifted to industrialization, the societal gravity center of power and privilege shifted to this class of men. Part of this triumph was economic. But all members of the class were not equally affected, and the economic fate of its component groups ranged from the vulgar affluence of Veblen's "leisure class" to the precarious marginality of Marx's "petit bourgeousie." Part of their triumph was political. But this victory was never total. Everywhere in Europe compromises had to be made with the old aristocratic classes, and by the end of the period new compromises were to be made with the militant working class.

Total victory came in the area of attitudes and values. During the nineteenth century, the middle-class value system became the value system of the West. With modifications, it endures to the present. It was an outlook that had evolved slowly in the centuries-long struggle for social recognition which the preindustrial, embryonic middle class had waged against the feudal order. Although subject to cross-cultural variation and internal ambiguities, there was a common core to this culture. Because of its pervasive influence the middle-class culture which came to dominance in the nineteenth century deserves some brief description.

The middle-class value system places supreme value on economic man. The requirements of the marketplace are its sacred principles: hard work, property, economic achievement and success, "usefulness." The normative standards which guide life emphasize practicality and a pragmatic rationality. This is not a self-interested materialism. Rather these standards represent the good or desirable; they are values to be treated with reverence, and never with frivolity or cynicism. The economic ethos spreads outwards to some very general propositions: man should be judged by what he does, each man should be judged separately, and the judge should not let his personal emotions enter into his decisions. As such it contrasts with the feudal belief that a man's position in society determined the criteria by which he was to be evaluated.

Yet this economic ethos has been accused of reducing men to the status of all other objects, to be judged, like an object, in terms of instrumental worth. Certainly this viewpoint deemphasizes man's other roles—man as artist, theologian, politician, even as scientist (though science has important secondary status since it produces economically salient information). The economic value system has no room in it for assessing the total richness of a man's life or the morality of his intentions.[6] In its nineteenth century version, this view of the world was cloaked in a sense of formal propriety and of conventional religiosity, though neither of these attitudes was essential to it. This complex of values conquered industrial and industrializing society. It is the backdrop against which sociology evolved its first schema.

The older social arrangements, whose origins were in agricultural economies, did not wholly vanish. The remnants of feudalism and of the various rural patterns of the American continent could still be discerned in the late nineteenth century. It was of course most visible in the countries or regions least affected by the economic revolution. This superimposition of one pattern of status and power on another produced a complex system which was to tax the interpretative powers of many of the first sociologists.

Overseas Expansion

The nineteenth century marked the zenith of the West's direct penetration of other areas of the globe. Settlers flowed out not only to the United States, but also to Canada, South Africa, Australia, New Zealand and South America. There they forced local populations into submission, harvested crops from virgin soil, and shipped back mineral riches to the original homelands. Western commercial enterprises extended to all the corners of the globe, purchasing commodities which could not be found at home, selling the products of the new industrial system, and investing its profits in even more profitable ventures abroad. Various means were used to handle local recalcitrance. Much of Asia, Africa, and the Pacific was simply partitioned into colonies and territories "owned" by the various Western states. When a society appeared too long established for such annexation, a hostile ruler might be replaced by a more sympathetic rival, as frequently happened in South America or the Middle East. As a last resort there was always force, based on a superior technology: Egypt, Japan, the Philippines, and China illustrate this type of control. Sometimes too the Western States squabbled with each other over the spoils, as the United States did with Spain. Eventually this hostility would help produce World War I. Meanwhile the traditional cultures of the rest of the world weakened under the impact of the West. Out of the partial collapse of those cultures came the situation of the present century, when Western dominance finally faces challenge.

A great deal of the motivation behind this expansion was directly economic, and the underpinnings of this type of impulse was the same technical-economic revolution which we have labeled the Industrial Revolution. There was, however, more to this expansion than direct economic self-interest. There was population growth; a new militant nationalism which sought the symbols of power in the ownership of territory; missionary zeal; a sense of adventurous exploration; and humanitarian concern for the situation of native populations. The basis of many of these moods was an underlying self-confidence, an unwavering belief both in the righteousness and the superiority of Western culture which can also be traced back to the sense of power and vitality produced by the Industrial Revolution.

Overseas expansion had consequences for sociology. The assertion of control over non-white populations was controversial even in times of such self-confidence. Social scientists could be found in both camps, creating theses which either justified or attacked those involved in colonial expansion. The question of racial differences and their implications found an early place in the sociological belief system. Even more central to early sociology, and often fused in the racial argument, was awareness of cultural variation. Explorers, traders, missionaries, administrators, and anthropologists recorded and reported more or less accurately the details of life in the multitudes of new social groupings which they encountered. Westerners were deluged with the flood of ethnographic information. Never had man more evidence of the variety of answers which his species could produce in response to the problems of living. This knowledge was built into the foundations of sociology—indeed, one impulse behind the emergence of the field must surely have been Western man's need to interpret this evidence of cultural variation.

Political Instability

Despite the upheavals of territorial expansion, 1815-1914 was a century of peace between Western powers. Peace was not absolute by any means, but the international wars of this period were short, and frequently softened in their impact by their distant locations. Not until the last decade of the century did there exist a standoff atmosphere of armed confrontations between strong blocs of nations. In this sense the period is one of peace. In contrast to the long, bitterly destructive wars of the preceding century, it impressed contemporaries this way. The optimism created by this awareness, and the disillusionment that came in the last decade when Europe was obviously racing into the irrationality of World War I, both have an impact on early sociological thought. It affects the views that men held about the basic nature of man in industrial society. Assumptions of this type are important foundations in the development of sociology and are explored in chapter 6.

During the same period the societies being studied experienced much internal political instability. Although the long-term consequences for social life wrought by the economic revolution were ultimately more pervasive both for society and for sociology, this political instability is also important in its consequences, and, in the short term, more dramatic in its impact. It is true that at the most general level much of the political turbulence of this century may be viewed as an out-growth of the economic revolution, specifically as the attempts by classes produced by the revolution to assert political dominance. The mesh between economic changes and political unrest is not perfect. For one thing some of the more significant political events occur prior to the extensive industralization of a society. For another, classes which found themselves in positions of economic power did not necessarily obtain equivalent political power, despite their efforts to do so. Other social groupings showed remarkable political resilience. And again, even when a measure of political power was gained by one or other of the new classes, there proved to be no necessary correlation between economic acumen and political effectiveness. The image of clearly delineated economic classes self-consciously and efficiently working for control of the state apparatus, ruthlessly pushing aside economically "less relevant" social groups, and using new political strengths to further their economic interests—the image, in other words, which Marx draws at his most polemical—is not the one presented here. Instead economic and political institutions are viewed as complexes of social relationships, interrelated yet partly autonomous. For a variety of historical reasons, some of the Western societies experienced in this period profound technological and economic changes which produced in these societies tensions, attempts at accomodation and rejection, and a series of adjustments, compromises, and deadlocked confrontations. Such a situation lends itself to political turbulence.

More specific to the task at hand, many of these political events appear to have significance in shaping the outlook of the earlier sociologists. Some of the more important of these are discussed below.

The French Revolution

The French Revolution does not really fall into our time period. The revolutionary and Napoleonic eras end in 1815—our starting point—with the restoration of the French monarchy. Of the early sociologists, only Comte could have had any personal experiences of those years, and those would have been childhood memories.

But the French Revolution profoundly affected the thinking of Europeans for decades after the defeat of its last symbolic defender at Waterloo. It affects the development of sociological thought as a motif in a pattern of ideas, not as a set of events directly experienced by earlier sociologists. The intention here is to look at the features of the motif.

The French Revolution was *the* revolution in European thinking at least until the final quarter of the century. It survived in men's thoughts as a model and symbol of what a revolution was, what revolution could be. Depending on personal preference, some reacted to this symbol with revulsion, others with exhilaration. As such the French Revolution features importantly both in conservative and radical thought in this period. The Revolution was remembered as a time when the "people" (or the "masses," depending on one's ideological position) rose against a traditionally entrenched dynasty and a traditionally hallowed social system, striking out for a more equalitarian social order. It was a society convulsed, a time when men tried to make their world over, willing to endure and inflict terrible pain in order that noble but abstract principles be woven into the fabric of their everyday lives; principles like "liberty," "equality," "brotherhood," "justice," "reason," and "democracy." The French Revolution was the destruction of feudalism by political means, the successful mobilization of feudalism's exploited or marginal classes, the intellectuals' challenge to established authority. During the Revolution, as men recalled it, the principles of liberalism had fused with the decisiveness of radicalism.

Ultimately, the French Revolution was crushed. But in the years that followed, as one instance of political instability or social unrest followed another, men repeatedly recalled the Revolution. Some recoiled in horror at the possibility and sought at all costs to halt such a recurrence. Others would hope anew that here at last was the combination of circumstances that would finally destroy the "forces of reaction." Of our group Comte is the purest example of the former. Durkheim too, stays pretty close to the "romantic" conceptualization of revolution. For others at the end of the century, though, the romantic image begins to be overlaid by the class war model which Marx and others delineated. This is true of Pareto, and of the German thinkers. The Americans as a group were least affected by these traditions. Their society had its own revolutionary tradition, and had been least affected by the military and political consequences of the French Revolution. If only as an influence on Comte, Marx, and Durkheim, the French Revolution deserves this brief discussion. But it has another role in this narrative. It is of symbolic significance in the story of liberal political frustrations to which we now turn.

The Frustration of the Liberals

Liberalism is a label both for a set of political beliefs and for a series of political movements in nineteenth-century Europe which sought to implement those beliefs. In both forms liberalism drew its support from the middle classes. As a belief system, liberalism had been evolved by the middle class of earlier centuries as a protest against its social marginality, its political subordination and its frequent experience of autocratic arbitrariness in a feudal system. As a political movement, its thrust came from middle class groups of the industrializing societies who had moved to the center of the economic sphere and who sought equal political importance.

There were three major themes in the liberal platform. The first was a set of guaranteed or "constitutional" personal freedoms from feudal autocracy: freedom of speech, of assembly, of movement, of the press; trial by jury; an end to the formal union of Church and State with its implications for ideological persecution; and so on. The second theme reflected the fact that the middle classes were, among other things, an economic interest group. They demanded that the state act in their economic interest. Initially these economic demands were for a *laissez-faire* governmental policy on economic matters, for free trade and an unregulated market place. Later as various national groups began to feel the pinch of competition, the cry became one for protection, and an increase of the state's role in the economy. The third demand grew stronger as liberal experience and sophistication grew over the decades. Basically this was a wish for political mechanisms which would function to block arbitrary repeals of the various freedoms which liberals wanted. This crystallized into a demand for elected assemblies which would represent the middle class and be responsible to it, and which would have real power in the political process. The cry for "freedom" evolved into a cry for "power" as the only lasting guarantee of freedom. The legitimating principle for these demands was the principle of individualism. Stressing the unique and autonomous status of the human individual, as well as his potential for perfectability, the liberals made their bid for freedom and power in the name of all mankind. All our sociologists related to these beliefs. Some like Marx and Pareto delighted in exposing liberalism's basis in an interest group. Most of the others, with more or less enthusiasm and qualification, believed in it.

The century of liberal political agitation is the nineteenth. Association with the French Revolution gave France great symbolic significance as the dynamic center of the liberal political movement. (This is so even though Britain proved to be the state in which liberals quietly made the greatest political gains.) Paris in particular was the focus of liberal attention. Paris seemed always to be in the midst of some sort of liberal agitation, and whenever this intensified into open confrontation tremors of hope ran though the liberal ranks in Europe. Moments like these occurred in 1818, 1824, 1830, and 1848. Each period witnessed liberal uprisings in Paris and in a number of other European cities.

On the surface, however, the record of liberal political activity appears to be a record of frustration. Again and again the liberals, after momentary successes, would find themselves beaten back by elements of the older feudal order: the monarchs, the military, the aristocracy, the Church.

The intervals between the dates listed above and the years after 1848 were all periods in which "reaction," with varying degrees of harshness, prevailed. For in a revolutionary confrontation with traditional political groups the middle classes lacked the necessary "countervailing" force. This they might have obtained by alliance with the urban working class or the peasants, which would have vastly increased the numbers on their side. Time and again middle-class liberals attempted such an alliance, but these always proved short-lived. Basically, the middle class groups distrusted both workers and peasants. They feared for their property. They were frightened by the radicalism of their allies. In the end they chose protection by the traditional political groups rather than face the more fundamental dangers which a working class alliance promised. The record of 1848, the largest and last of liberal uprisings, illustrates this well.

Yet below the surface the situation was not quite so bleak. Liberals found that their alliance with the older political powers brought some returns, for they were useful to those groups. They brought skills and financial resources to the alliance. They won influence, and in a gradual way this brought them certain gains between 1815 and 1870. Certainly they gradually won their way on the economic plank in their platform. Over the decades a strong economic alliance was forged between middle-class interests and the traditional authorities: well-to-do industrialists and financiers replaced the old aristocracy as economic advisers to the rulers; the apparatus of taxation and fiscal administration gradually "modernized"; and the middle class obtained *laissez-faire* or protection to suit their needs. Moreover, the constant demands of liberals with regard to the "freedoms" plank in their platform gradually won concessions from the ruling groups. Over the period, one by one, many of the demands were met: legal reforms, jury trials, religious freedoms, freedom of movement and of speech. But these principles were granted, they were not seized. These rights could be revoked in any crisis, and it was the old ruling groups who defined "crisis." The frustration of the liberals down to 1870 stems from their failure on the third plank in their platform, the failure to win direct political power. Everywhere this continued to elude them, except in Britain, and in Britain the victory was obtained at the cost of a symbolic fusion with aristocratic interests and values so complete that it remains difficult to this day to say whose was the victory.

In 1870 a series of political events finally gave extensive power to continental liberals. In France, power had passed to a legislative assembly. In Italy, a constitutional monarchy was established with a liberal constitution which vested much power in the elected assembly. Liberals at last seemed to have won their long sought power. This time they did not fail to hang on to power, yet they did not develop into effective rulers. Strong parties failed to develop, coalition government followed coalition government, weak vacillating direction was the norm, and crises and scandals succeeded each other in rapid succession. Meanwhile the threats to their power increased. Liberals increasingly found themselves attacked on the one hand by a reactivated conservatism, on the other hand by an increasingly militant working-class socialism. Even in Britain these new threats were real, while internal ideological feuding weakened liberal ranks. In Germany the liberals remained as they had been before 1870, completely subordinated to aristocracy, monarchy and army. If frustration is created by a record of modest gains, which feed but increasingly fail to keep pace with a rising curve of expectations, then this is the experience of European liberals in the nineteenth century. This was more intense on the continent and less so in Britain because of the different records of failure and success. It is not at all the situation in America, where a feudal order never existed, where liberal aspirations for freedom and power were written into the constitution and steadily realized during the nineteenth century. The situation served to create a constant political restlessness in Europe, particularly in those circles in which the first sociologists moved, and it led those sociologists to a curiosity about power and politics which permeates their sociology and differentiates it from that produced in the same period by Americans. This difference has only begun to break down in the last decade.

The Rise of Nationalism

Nationalism implies passion. It is an intense identification of self with the nation-state or with a cultural grouping. The nationalist's primary interest is in promoting his state or group. Its interests must take precedence over any other group or organization. Minimally, it must be independent of all such others, and, optimally, it ought to be dominant over them. Nationalism is one form of ideology, and ideology, though secular, has the emotional overtones of religious fervour. Moreover, nationalism links to politics: it can be roused for political ends and it must translate into political activity. In both respects nationalism contrasts with patriotism. The latter means a love of and devotion to country, but has nothing of nationalism's aggressive assertion of superiority and power; it implies a deeply personal emotion, but not necessarily political involvement.

Nationalism is a relatively new phenomenon in man's history. It spun off from the French Revolution and from revolutionary statements about "the people's" right to rule themselves. Carried by French armies to the corners of Europe, these ideas took on new meaning for cultural groups long subordinated in large polyglot empires, or dominated by foreign princes.

For decades after Napoleon, nationalism remained fused with and subordinate to liberalism, a simple translation of the liberals' demand for political enfranchisement into the claim that a people—a historically and culturally distinct group—had the right to self-government. After 1848 it emerges as a separate and potent political force. Part of the explanation lies with the frustration of liberal ambitions for political power and the ideological splintering that resulted from this. The right of a people to self-government took on an independent status. In this period the rhetoric moved beyond claims to self-government, and developed new mystical conceptions of homeland, race and folk, as well as beliefs in the nationality's destiny for power.

In 1870 nationalism experienced two major triumphs with the emergence of the new states of Germany and Italy. The continuing

embarassment of liberalism in the subsequent decades thrust nationalism into greater and greater prominence. Its only rival for the loyalties
of men was socialism. But socialism united all the established social
powers against it, a fact which gave the edge to nationalist beliefs.
In France and Italy nationalism was represented by an impatience with
the day-to-day mediocrity of government, and a wish for power,
prestige and *la gloire* in the international arena. Emotions like this
made Pareto seek to rationalize the growing might of Mussolini, and
turned Durkheim into an ardent Francophile as the catastrophe of
World War I approached. In England and the United States tenents
like those of "manifest destiny" electrified men, rallying them behind
jingoistic and expansionist foreign policies, and behind conflicts abroad
which seemed to be a defense of national honor. In Germany the
quest for national power meant an eager search for areas of colonial
expansion, a search motivated not only by economic interest but also
by the wish to demonstrate German power and civilization to the
world. Indeed the colonial expansion of this period, which we have
described earlier in this chapter, with its accompanying claims for
racial and cultural superiority has important roots in the militant nationalism of this period. The rush for colonies and the jockeying for international prestige created inevitable hostilities between the western nations. By 1900 they were already arming themselves and moving sus-
piciously abroad, although it was not until 1914 that the conflict finally
broke out.

Most of the early sociologists were liberals. Their response to the
rise of nationalism was on the whole one of dismay. Around the turn
of the century one finds serious questionings of man's potential for
rationality and a new curiosity about his "inherent" emotionality. Yet
nationalism pervaded their situation and subtly affected their outlooks
and interests: the shift from Comte's urbane and cosmopolitan conceptualization of society to the later sociologists' easy assumption that
the nation state was the natural unit for analysis; the absorption with
historically distinct cultures; and the arguments on the pros and cons
of racial superiority all have some roots in the mood and political developments of nationalism.

Summary and Conclusions

This chapter has been built on the assumption that the ideas of earlier
sociologists were in part shaped by the social and political events of
their day. It has consequently attempted to sketch in a few of the most

important of those events. The decision of what was important was shaped not only by the consensus of historians of this period, but also by extrapolation from the themes and content of the sociology written in it. Great emphasis has been placed on industrialization with its implications for the pace and patterning of life, for urban growth, and for the distribution of power and prestige. Consideration has also been given to political events: the impact of the French Revolution, the liberal uprisings, the growth of a militant nationalism.[7] Western overseas expansion has been looked at on more than one occasion.

The intention has been to create a "feel" for the period. It was a dramatic era. In it occurred one of the most massive restructurings of society that the West has experienced. The earlier sociologists were witnesses of the actual transition: they saw an old order pass away and a new one emerge. With the benefits of hindsight we today can speak with confidence of what was happening. To men living through the stages of change, the situation contained far more uncertainty. Sociology can be viewed as one of the desperate attempts made by the new men of influence to comprehend what was happening to their world, as change followed change, and as the older systems for understanding collapsed.

The events described affected different sociologists in different ways depending on their location in time and space. Industrialization was one thing for Pareto and another for those experiencing it in Germany or in the American midwest at the turn of the century. Nationalism too was different for the German and Frenchman. Our only intention here has been to sketch in the minimal details, not to describe the specific experiences of individual sociologists. The student who is curious about a particular man's experiences can follow the clues and piece together the picture to gain a fuller insight into that man.

NOTES

1. See R.M. Hartwell, "Economic Change in England and Europe," in *The New Cambridge Modern History* (Cambridge: Cambridge University Press, 1965), vol. 9, *War and Peace in an Age of Upheaval*, ed. C.W. Crawley.

2. Ibid.

3. Marx is an exception to this statement; this is perhaps one mark of his genius.

4. See Charles Wilson, "Economic Conditions," in *The New Cambridge Modern History* (Cambridge: Cambridge University Press, 1962), vol. 11, *Material Progress and World Wide Problems,* ed. F.H. Hinsley.

5. To illustrate this dramatic pace of trans-Atlantic migration one has only to look at the population figures for the U.S. over the period 1750-1900: 1750—2 million; 1800—7

million; 1850—26 million; 1900—82 million. J. Durand, "The Modern Expansion of World Population," in *Population and Society*, ed. C.B. Nam (New York: Houghton Mifflin, 1968), pp. 108-20.

6. Alvin Gouldner, *The Coming Crisis in Western Sociology* (New York: Basic Books, 1970).

7. No separate treatment of political radicalism has been given in this chapter, though this theme has been touched on at several points with discussions of working class militancy, socialism, etc. On the whole the group of sociologists under consideration here were more influenced by liberalism than by radicalism. The exception to this statement is Marx. For an excellent and dramatic treatment of radical thought in this period, and of Marx's place in it, see Edmund Wilson, *To the Finland Station* (New York: Doubleday, Anchor Books, 1953).

4

The Intellectual
Background

This chapter attempts a brief survey of ideas prevalent in the circles
in which the early sociologists moved, ideas which they fed into the
new discipline, sociology. This may be the most important cluster of
variables in the shaping of sociology.

The concern here is with the *weltanschaung*, the world view, of the
first sociologists. We are curious about the ideas of the period which
shaped their emphases, their choices among alternatives, and their
views on what was problematic. Some of these ideas have already been
explored in the preceding chapter: the middle-class value structure,
the liberal belief system, and the mood of nationalism. These were
general cultural themes.

However, these men came into contact with more specialized ideas
and beliefs as members of the scholarly community. On the whole
these are the phenomena on which this chapter will focus. The first
concern will be with some of the major philosophical alignments of
the time. Sociology is an offshoot of social philosophy, and in this
period the connections between the new field and the various complexes of philosophical assumptions which dominated different university systems are particularly clear. No general descriptive survey can
be attempted in the space available. Instead the attempt will be made
to convey with a brief sketch the answers each philosophical system
gave to the following questions:

47

(1) What is reality like? What are its most important characteristics, its crucial relationships, its central processes? We label this the metaphysical question.

(2) How does one know reality? What processes can we trust as reliable modes of enquiry? We label this the epistomological question.

It is easy to see how the assumptions a man might have along these lines (assumptions acquired through education because they were the assumptions of those who taught him) would fundamentally affect both his general frame of reference and the type of sociology he developed.

In the light of these questions, two of the major philosophical alignments of modern Western thought, empiricism and idealism, will be considered first. Next, and still in terms of these questions, a brief look will be given to two major manifestations of developmental thought in this period—Darwinism and historical materialism. Darwinism is symbiotically related to the type of sociology developed by Spencer and his disciples; historical materialism is similarly linked to Marx's social science. As such they are approached again and again in the main part of this text. The last philosophical school to be described will be pragmatism, an important development in late nineteenth-century thought. The next concern will be with a few of the technical, scientific developments of the period which were generally influential on the academic community, and on early sociology. Finally, we return to the prevailing ideological systems. Liberalism has already been described. It will be contrasted here with both conservatism and Marxist socialism.

Postivism (Empiricism)

This description is of a model or "ideal type"—it is far more pure and simplified than the outlook of any particular individual. But though in this sense unreal, it is not a fantasy. Any type is distilled from a number of empirical cases, in this case from the beliefs of a number of individuals. Each individual probably qualified some of the dimensions of these beliefs, or blended in themes from different ideational systems, or allowed certain inconsistencies. But the type is generalized from the beliefs of many individuals. It disallows the qualifications and inconsistencies, making instead the logical or plausible connections between the various themes. It is therefore both real and unreal. Certainly it is real in the sense that many of the early sociologists worked within the context of some modified version of this belief system.

In choosing a label for this outlook, preference is given to the term "positivism" over that of "empiricism." Empiricism is the appropriate name for the more general philosophical orientation from which positivism developed. Positivism is an extreme or radical version of the empiricist philosophy. The radical variant of empiricism was in fact adopted by some of the founders of the discipline. In this book the term positivism does not just refer to the technical system developed by Comte. Instead the term is applied to a more general set of beliefs of which the Comtean system was a manifestation. [1]

In dealing with the epistemological question of how one knows, and particularly how one can be certain that what one knows is indeed the truth, positivists furnish a straightforward answer, one that at first glance seems completely convincing. Accurate information, they say, results from application of the methods of inquiry developed by the natural sciences, the so-called logico-experimental method. Only this mode of inquiry is productive of truth, and properly used it will lead one to the truth, in any practical sense of the word.

Underlying this principle is an article of faith for positivists, namely that there are no ideas, no processes of thinking, no knowledge of any kind which is intrinsic to or autonomously produced by man's mind. Man at birth is a blank page, Locke's *tabula rasa*. All his knowledge develops from his experience of the world: experience is the source of all ideas and of all knowledge. Nor is the word experience to be mysteriously interpreted: experiences are the stimuli which feed through the senses of sight, touch, hearing, taste, and smell. Experience is sensory data.

The techniques of natural science are refined and controlled ways of processing sense data. Science, as conceptualized by positivists, begins with data that is material and observable, and builds through processes of careful observation and experimentation, classification and analysis, to the discovery of the general principles which underlie the area of experience about which one is curious. These principles allow one to explain, to oneself and others, the phenomena about which one was curious. Such explanatory principles are truth. Their final enthronement as such comes if they can be successfully used to predict and perhaps control the processes one observes. Positivists reject all knowledge which is personally arrived at by intuition, introspection, revelation, and so forth. All knowledge must be subject to public standards of testing, to verification by members of the scientific community. No concept or statement is valid unless it successfully weathers such testing.

The positivist realizes that man's mind operates on sensory experience, that human consciousness is a factor in the processing of experience. But they seen no need to dwell on this. Mind or consciousness is assumed to be a mechanical processor of information. For sociologists of a positivistic inclination, the fact that sociology's realm for exploration is human beings poses no distinctive problems. Social life is just another sector of the material world which will yield like any other to the techniques of scientific investigation. The scientific method is the means to knowledge.

It is obvious that this faith in science must rest on a system of metaphysical assumptions, that is, on a system of beliefs about the characteristics of reality. In the first place, positivists do not doubt that there is a reality, a universe of discrete material objects which exists apart from us, and despite us. Individual men, each equipped with a mind and senses, are to be numbered among the discrete objects which make up the real world. Moreover, man stands in a relationship to the rest of his universe and he is tied to it by necessity. Reality impinges on him, works on his life at every stage, forces itself upon his senses. Man, if he is to survive this onslaught, must struggle to comprehend reality, and to exercise some measure of control over it. Indeed in some form or other man has always done this; science is only the latest and most effective of his techniques.

A second article of faith for positivists is that the universe (reality) is orderly, whatever its appearance to the untutored eye. Order consists of a system of fixed relationships or modes of association between classes of objects in the real world. These relationships are given in the nature of things, or result from the nature of the process that created them, which in itself was orderly. These relationships are the "laws of nature." Man, particularly in his role as scientist, can discover the laws of nature, at which point they can be renamed "scientific laws." Natural or scientific laws are constant: they exist forever. Any relationships observed between particular objects will be determined by these general principles. A good example of such a principle, frequently referred to by positivists, is the "law of gravity." There are no exceptions to the application of such laws, unless some other general principle is at work. Even change is governed by external principles of change, and is orderly. The positivists' faith in a system of natural laws that govern all the activity in our universe is a secularized version of the religious belief in a Divine plan which is eternal and to which all things are subject. Everything that positivists said about nature in general they felt would hold true of society in particular.

This viewpoint so easily persuades us (apart from its intrinsic merits) because it fuses with the general middle-class value structure described in chapter 3 and was in this way transmitted to us. In earlier centuries middle-class groups in Europe had existed in a relationship of tension with the more powerful social groupings derived from feudalism: monarchy, aristocracy, church. These latter groups moved in a cultural system based on religious precepts. As part of their battle with the "establishment," middle-class groups challenged this world view, opposing it with an alternative perspective distilled from the scientific mentality and the scientific successes of the sixteenth, seventeenth, and eighteenth centuries. Apart from incorporating positivism's metaphysics and epistemology, the nineteenth-century middle-class ethos has another point of affinity with positivism. Logically extended, both define man as object. Positivists do this by insisting that man is just one type of object in a mechanistic universe, and that he is, like everything else, open to scientific investigation. The middle-class economic ethos conveys something similar by insisting that all men be judged instrumentally, in terms of their usefulness in the marketplace. The cultural triumph of the middle class in nineteenth-century society implied the triumph of positivism as a world view. So entrenched did this become that today most people would have great difficulty thinking of any other answer to the epistemological and metaphysical questions. But in the period being investigated, the period in which the middle class ethos was just coming into ascendancy, men did still question this perspective. We now turn to an alternative perspective of the period.

Idealism

If the positivists' viewpoint seems familiar to us, that of the idealists now appears very strange. Yet it is historically the older viewpoint, and in the nineteenth century and even more in the eighteenth century it found itself in combat with perspectives like those of the positivists. Idealism eventually lost the battle, hence its strangeness to us today. Again this description is a model or type, and again the term is applied to a general set of assumptions rather than to a technical philosophical system.

If the holy words of the positivist are "science" and "natural law," those of the idealist are "consciousness" and "ideas." The crucial point in their argument is precisely the one to which positivists give short shrift: man can never directly confront a "real world" because the phenomenon of mind always intervenes between man and reality. Mind is their label for man's sensory mechanisms and intellectual processes. Mind acts as a screen or filter in all the knowledge-producing activities. Nor can one be certain as to how much of a role mind plays in these activities. If positivists, on faith, dismiss the importance of mind's role, idealists do the reverse; they insist that mind and particularly intellect is the crucial knowledge-producing instrument, and cannot be treated simply as an automatic processor of incoming stimuli.

Since mind is crucial but its role is undefined, there is no simple answer to the question "what is reality?" One cannot be sure how much one's view of reality really reflects a material world and how much it is a product of mind. There is no certainty even that there is a material world. One can only be sure that one has ideas about such a world. Ideas then become the key to everything. They are in fact the only reality of which one can be certain.

What happens if one takes as one's data about reality only the various forms of consciousness that man has had about the world? What disappears almost immediately is the positivists' image of an aggregate of discrete or separate objects eternally linked together by a set of lawlike relationships. Logically one is left with only the infinite conceptualizations of the world which the species man has had. Since this is so elusive and unmanageable as to defy any attempts at further analysis, idealists adopted certain conventions. Particularly, they rooted their analyses in history and in the islands of consensus which have emerged in different periods and regions. One has then a large but finite aggregate of states of "collective consciousness."[2] Further, if one restricts one's analysis to a single region which has experienced some historical continuity (such as Western Europe) one has a changing but evolving "reality." Since the zenith of idealism precedes the nineteenth century when the globe became a meaningful conceptual unit for Western men, it does on the whole focus on Western European consciousness. This theme of evolving ideas is therefore a strong one in it.

The image of reality as varying consciousnesses destroys the positivists' assumption of natural laws, except for some general principles about how ideas change.[3] Idealists regarded most of what positivists termed natural laws as creations of a particular period in consciousness. They pointed out that the image of what was lawlike has varied over time and space.

Similarly the image of a universe of separate identifiable objects vanishes. Ideas do not have the fixed boundaries of material objects. Nor does an idea have an elemental unity; it is instead a fusion of opposites, the thing and its negation. Again, an isolated idea has very little significance. Ideas exist in complex configurations and can only be understood as such. The description of consciousness must build upon all these beliefs.

It is obvious that from this perspective the only way to really know, or to discover ultimate truths, is by disciplined persistent scrutiny of the process and content of ideas themselves. And since one is most certain of one's own ideas, the analytic process should both begin and end with scrutiny of one's own consciouness. The processes which positivists' most disdain, such as introspection and contemplation of one's own thoughts in process, are crucial to the idealist, and truth for them is that moment of insight when one finally "understands" how some process occurred. It is a highly personal and private understanding, imperfectly communicable. The goals of explanation and prediction and the criteron of verifiability have no important place in such a perspective.

Idealist relegated empiricism, as a research process, to a minor place in the truth-producing process. They ranked the study of the process of thought itself higher. From this last type of study they produced the idea of the dialectic, the process of thesis, antithesis, synthesis, which they held was the process of the evolution of consciousness itself. Realizations of this type are the closest approximations to an ultimate truth that idealists would allow.

From this perspective the study of societies presents a unique set of problems. Societies are basically aggregates of minds and their relationships. Understanding such a pehnomenon requires the development of a special set of analytic techniques. The suggestion that any profound understanding of a society could result from the "mere empiricism" of the positivists was untenable to them.

Idealism's historic roots are in the world view of medieval Europe. Its basis is religious. It needed as an ultimate unifying principle the concept of God. This gave an explanation for the mysterious immanence of mind. It also provided a source of stability in reality which even its adherents felt must be, despite the logical implications of absolute fluidity resulting from the view of a world existing only in the ephemeral consciousnesses of human beings.

The confrontation between idealism and positivism had been sharpest in the seventeenth and eighteenth centuries. This was when the classic statements for both approaches were made, with names like Locke, Berkeley, and Hume ranging on the side of the scientific viewpoint, and Kant and Hegel defending the tenets of idealism. By the nineteenth century, and particularly its latter half, the battle had largely been won for the scientific perspective. An increasingly secular outlook deprived idealism of its most basic principle. Yet it lingered on as a series of philosophical predispositions in academic circles. Idealism's counsel was primarily that mind and its product were unique. Its influence in the period under consideration was greatest in German academic circles, where Hegel's influence long remained a central motif. Consequently the group of German social scientists most clearly show these philosophical assumptions in their work. This is particularly true of Simmel and Tönnies. Weber is also importantly influenced by it, though he was self-consciously trying to work out his own compromise between the two points of view. And in an odd, deliberately inverted way, one can trace the impact of this view on Marx's thinking.

But the thesis about mind reached out more widely to affect sociology. Not even the most doctrinaire of positivists could absolutely deny the importance of this variable, particularly in the study of man and society. Of the group being considered, the most undiluted positivism was found in the views of Comte, Durkheim and Pareto. Yet none of these can be accused of discounting mind and ideas. Each spent much of his time trying to deal with these concepts. For Durkheim in particular the tension between the two orientations was very consuming.

Developmental Perspectives

During the nineteenth century, positivism gained two powerful new allies in the battle with idealism: the views of historical materialism and social Darwinism. Although vastly different in content and ideology, there were certain similarities between the two views. First, both were essentially philosophical arguments which sought legitimation by militant claims to being rigorously "scientific." Second, both incorporated and made "scientific" a theme which was prominent in idealism, was of minor importance in positivism, and which seemed to have considerable support from the evidence of history: the theme of developmental progress.

The linked notions of progress and development appear in the seventeenth century.[4] During the decades of bitter fighting between idealism and empiricism it remained almost exclusively the property of the idealists. Until the nineteenth century, the argument about progressive development was an argument about cultural change, about knowledge, wisdom, and morality; that is, about ideas. These were the things that were cumulative, indestructible, and steadily improving. As a consequence of such development, all the rest of man's lot would steadily be bettered.

This argument, which meshed so well with existing feelings about the thrust of history, and which at the same time argued for the supremacy of ideational variables, was triumphantly seized upon by the idealists. Herder, the German philosopher-historian, attempted to trace a collaboration between God and nature in the record of progress. Kant sought to prove the reality of moral progress from the evidence of history. Hegel's discovery of the dialectic revealed the actual mechanics of ideational development. This argument for the supremacy of mind and ideas over experience of the material, supported as it was by extensive historical data, could not be undermined by the positivists. Even so doctrinaire a positivist as Comte saw progress as a fact, and its essential dynamic as ideational. It was left to historical materialism and to social Darwinism, both nineteenth-century constructs, to expropriate this theme for empiricism.

Historical Materialism

This perspective is inextricably linked to the name of Karl Marx. The description that follows is essentially of the philosophical underpinnings of his social thought. Historical materialism almost literally turns Hegelian idealism inside out, refuting its basic premise, using its major weapons and building the important strengths of idealism into its own alternative perspective.

> The ideal is nothing else than the material world reflected by the human brain and translated into forms of thought. [5]

With these words Marx abandoned the ambivalent stance of the positivistic social scientists on the role of mind and decisively denies it any independent status in shaping man's life. The material conditons of life shape man's ideas, and never *vice versa*. Ideas are merely epiphenomenal to experience.

Historical materialism goes on to specify what material experiences are most crucial. Man's elemental distinction is that he produces the things he needs for survival. Man does not merely take from nature what he needs for survival as do all other animals; instead he manipulates nature, working upon her to procure what he needs. This is the source of his uniqueness. This nexus of experience fundamentally shapes him, his ideas, and all his social relationships. This is the economic variable, the "mode of production," if by economic one means all those activities clustering around the manipulation of one's physical environment.

The relationship between man's life and the mode of production is a dynamic one. All social change of any importance springs either directly from developments in the mode of production, or, one stage removed, from the conflicts that occur between men because of the mode of production. Moreover this change is in every sense developmental and ultimately progressive. The mode of production becomes increasingly complex, increasingly capable of efficiently providing for the growing list of man's material needs. Social conflicts in any social epoch evolve from the almost insensible experience of tension to moments of total and massive confrontation. Each major confrontation produces a new form of social relations, a new "stage" in man's advance towards that final period when all his needs are met and conflict between men disappears. This progressive development is not a normative statement of ideals but a sequence grounded in history; it can be traced throughout the historical record of man's life in society. These developments occur dialectically. Each new stage in social relations inexorably creates, out of the logic of its pattern of relationship, an alternative to itself. The conflict between the established pattern and its alternative ultimately produces a new form of social relationship. But, at the most general level, all these changes and processes arise mechanically from that locus of material experience, the mode of production. Ideas have little to do with it in any fundamental sense.

This perspective was strengthened by devastating attacks on idealist thinkers and by astute use of historical data, particularly that drawn from recent history, since modern history lent itself particularly well to such interpretation. Marxists could claim with pride to have "stood Hegel on his head."

Social Darwinism

Social Darwinism is closely associated with Herbert Spencer, whose views were as influential on American sociologists as Marx's were on the Europeans. Where Marx used history and logic, Spencer went directly to the natural sciences. As the name implies, this perspective derived status from associating intself with Charles Darwin's momentous thesis about biological evolution. But Spencer did not hesitate to formulate his own scientific views:

> Evolution is an integration of matter and a concomitant dissipation of motion; during which matter passes from an indefinite, incoherent homogeneity to a definite, coherent heterogeneity; and during which the retained motion undergoes a parallel transformation.[6]

This law was deduced from certain ideas then current in physics. It was to be applied to all aspects of the material universe. Everything could be conceived of as matter and motion, structure and energy, permanently in dynamic interaction. For any entity or class of entities there were only two alternatives: either to cease to be, or else to elaborate structurally to the point where energy could be channeled and contained. This was the general principle behind all evolutionary development. It pertained to the emergence of the physical earth from a nebular cloud of gases, to the appearance of life from a chemical mass, to the development of increasingly more complex species of life forms which Darwin had documented, to the stages passed tnrough by the human fetus and by the maturing individual, and finally to society. The different types of evolution were continuous, each building upon the preceding kinds of development, each producing more complex phenomena. Social evolution was the final and ultimate state, which Spencer called super-organic evolution.[7] Society itself was in the process of developing, from the earliest stages of simple tribal units to the complexity of modern industrial society. The evidence for such change was abundant in the ethnographic literature. The final outcome and the climax of all development would be the perfect society, adapted fully to its environment, meeting all the needs of its members.

Despite the differences in content, there are marked similarites in the form of these two arguments. Both historical materialism and social Darwinism claimed to advance positivism's faith in natural laws by actually discovering such a law. In both cases the law was essential to an understanding of society. Both viewed conflict if not as an ultimate good, at least as a instrumental good for development. (This was done in social Darwinism by an uneasy fusion of notions of *species* evolution through "survival of the fittest" with the more prevalent theme of *typological* evolution, such as the evolution of "society." Conflict is incorporated in the species evolution model.) Both perspectives deny mind any important status, basing all the important social dynamics on man's material nature, either his economic or his biological nature. The acceptance of either perspective required one to abandon notions of free will, for each preached determinism by natural law. Yet both promised a utopia as the reward for such submission, and further, predicted that the utopia was almost at hand.

Pragmatism[8]

This perspective was developed in America. The term itself appeared in the late nineteenth century in the writings of C.S. Peirce, but as a general outlook pragmatism did not become popular until its exploration in the writings of William James during the first decade of the twentieth century. Pragmatism was a response to the various outlooks already described. It adheres to positivism's advocacy of science, yet it confronts idealism's concept of mind, avoiding the brash materialism of Spencer and Marx.

On the epistemological question, pragmatism came out strongly for the positivists' position. Knowledge was obtained by using the research procedures developed by the natural sciences. Ideas were ultimately derived from experience of the environment. Controlled experience, or scientific procedure, was the only proper tool for inquiry.

Pragmatism differed from positivism in its views on the nature of reality and man's relationship to the material world. Positivists seemed to envisage a material universe rather similar to our present concept of the solar system: a set of discrete objects linked together in eternal relationships which are determined by universally applicable natural laws. Moreover they made the easy assumption that man related almost automatically to this world, that his senses fed him essentially patterned information about his essentially orderly universe. Pragmatists reject the latter notion, and at the same time restrict their own image of reality to man's experience of it.

The world as man experiences it is a deluge of unpatterned sensory stimuli in which nothing appears fixed, permanent, or ordered. This is the material universe, "a booming, buzzing reality."[9] Yet man has to survive in this apparently unstable environment; he has to evolve techniques for adaptation or control; he has to order or make sense of it in his quest for effective survival. In this adaptive struggle mind plays the vital role. It is mind that interprets and shapes man's environment, creating order out of non-order. The idealists are correct in placing supreme emphasis on mind. They may even be correct in suggesting that there are multiple interpretations which mind may make of reality and that no single one of these is necessarily the only correct one. Truth as man knows it is not an absolute, but a process of fleeting moments when he is conscious of a mesh between his anticipatory ordering of his environment and his subsequent experience of it. Pragmatists leave it an open question whether such moments can result from varying interpretative schema.

While pragmatism supports the idealists' thesis that man's uniqueness lies in his possession of mind, they reject the latter's other position that mind is not amenable to empirical study. They argue that thought is a natural process like breathing or digestion; that it is biologically based and physiologically capable, through training, of reason; and that it uses concepts which are acquired through socialization or developed directly from personal experience. As such it can be scientifically studied. Indeed, scientific truth consists of understanding and explaining the relationships between man, mind, and environment (whether physical, social or cultural). Mind, far from being beyond science, must become the major focus for empirical investigation.

The world as described by pragmatists is an extraordinary fluid and ambiguous phenomenon, even more so than the idealists' image of multiple patterns of evolving consciousness. It is little more than a flickering barrage of stimuli. Society is simply one general category of stimuli: those emanating from other human beings and their relationship to self or ego. Man is the only point of certainty in the whole picture: a biological creature uniquely endowed with intellect, adaptively and constantly oriented to the immediate future which he struggles to "control" through interpretation and anticipation.

American sociology in the period under discussion was chiefly influenced by the alternative perspectives of Darwinism and pragmatism. This meant that it had no ideological doubts about the role of science in the pursuit of sociological information, in contrast to some European thinkers. Instead it divided on the question of the role of mind, and the extent to which close scrutiny of the individual was essential to sociological analysis. Of the individuals whose ideas are to be discussed here those most influenced by pragmatism's perspective were Cooley and Mead.

Technical Developments

This section briefly describes certain scientific or technical developments of the period which were influential in the academic circles in which the early sociologists moved.

Essay on the Principles of Population

In 1789 Thomas Malthus published, in England, the first form of the *Essay*. In 1803 a second version appeared. Its thesis was that all animal species tend to multiply faster than the rate of increase possible for their food supply. In particular the human population increases at a geometric rate, while its sources of sustenance grow only arithmetically. Malthus supports his theses with much statistical data, and made statistical projections into the future. He predicted that the time would come when migration would no longer be able to mitigate the tension. The two possible outcomes of this inevitable tension were either the regulation of population growth through voluntary birth control, an alternative which Malthus for a variety of reasons viewed as both impracticable and ill-advised, or the occurrence of "natural" catastrophes like poverty, famine, epidemics, and war which would painfully provide checks to further population increase. Historically, and probably in the future too, the latter aggregate of disasters was the effective regulator of population growth.

The *Essay* was widely influential. This was a period of rapid population increase and, more important, of massive population movement from the countryside to the very visible centers of very high population density, the cities. Moreover, as a correlate of these social changes, much poverty, sickness, and other evidence of "natural" catastrophe was present. The *Essay* seemed to mesh well with visible trends in society, and its bleak interpretation of these trends consequently gained in status.

The implications of *Essay on the Principles of Population* for sociological thought were various. It gave new emphasis to the demographic variable, presenting this as the substructure of societal processes and historical events. Correlatively, it took a quantitative view of man, treating him as an aggregate of similar objects, a species which could be effectively studied by statistical means. It painted a picture of competition or conflict for scarce values as an essential and eternal social dynamic. Finally, it took a deterministic position on the relationship of material conditions to man's life. There is a direct chain of influence from Malthus to Darwin's principle of selective survival, and to Spencer's "survival of the fittest." The shadow of Malthus's interpretation can be seen too in Marx's images of social conflict, in Sumner's *Land Hunger* and even in Durkheim's early tendency to trace social change back to the factor of varying population density.

The Origin of Species

In terms of the questions which motivate this book and the academic circles which interest us, Charles Darwin's *Origin of Species* (1859) was almost certainly the most influential single publication of this period. Its thesis was that biological species were mutable, capable of structural and functional change. The mechanisms producing these changes were the pressures on a species for adaptation to its hostile and fluctuating environment and the phenomenon of selective survival (the survival and reproduction of those variations in the species which maximized chances of survival in the environment). The long-term consequences, from the moment when life first appeared on the globe, had been the survival of only the most adaptive life forms and the emergence of increasingly complex biological species. Mammals in general, and man in particular, were among the latest products of this process. The argument was supported by elaborate data from fossil records and from botanical and zoological observation.

The book received enormous publicity. This was partly because of the blow it struck at the religious principle of man's divine origins. The book also became well known because it seemed to climax a whole series of themes already present in both scientific and philosophical writings, summarizing and substantiating them. A few of these have already been mentioned: idealists' theses about cultural progress, Malthus' image of grim competition, Spencer's theme of the "survival of the fittest." Darwin acknowledges the influence of both Malthus and Spencer on his thoughts. But because of the publicity and its impressive empirical substantiation, *The Origin of Species* also acted as an independent influence on the academic community. It provided another important bulwark to positivism, demonstrating the material roots on all life forms and vindicating the utility of empirical investigation. It gave an enormous boost to developmental and deterministic theses. It legitimizes with a cloak of scientific rigor the model of fierce but creative competition as a primary dynamic in the life process.

Evolutionary assumptions permeate the social thought of this period. Of the group that concerns us only Pareto deliberately fought against the application of these assumptions to social history. For some, like the earlier thinkers and the later German sociologists, the idealist image of cultural development explains to a considerable extent their evolutionary ideas. But for others, particularly for Spencer and the Americans, Darwin's book on biological evolution is the chief influence.

Adolphe Quetelet and Social Statistics[10]

Comte had originally intended to call his proposed new field of study "social physics." In *Positive Philosophy* he says that he had to call the new subject "sociology" because his first preference, "social physics," had been preempted by a "Belgian statistician." The Belgian in question was Adolphe Quetelet (1796-1874), a man of prodigious talent, who by age 23, after initially dabbling in the arts, had become a doctor of mathematics and a professor at the Athenaenum in Brussels. Among other things Quetelet was indeed a "statistician." Attracted to statistics in the 1820s, he had become intrigued by the possibility of analyzing society statistically. To this end he persuaded the Belgian government to establish a Central Statistical Commission in 1841, and he was a major influence in the establishment of an International Statistical Congress in 1853, the successor to which (the International Statistical

Association) persists to this day. From some of his writings on statistics certain ideas emerged which were to irritate Comte, deeply influence Durkheim, and pervasively affect the climate in which sociology developed.

These ideas appear in three influential publications in the 1830s: *Research on the Law of Human Growth* (1831); *Research on the Propensity to Crime at Different Ages* (1831); and *On Man and the Development of his Faculties* (1835). In these he pointed out that certain social characteristics, if calculated as rates, existed with remarkable stability in a population over time. Among these were various factors associated with the life cycle, and such "moral" phenomena as a societal propensity to crime, to suicide, and to marriage at different ages for the different sexes. He substantiated these claims with numerous tables. So stable were these rates that they could be considered material facts, implying that society possessed certain traits which mark it as a material "thing" accessible to empirical study like any other aspect of the material world. He goes on to reject the idea that any divine or mysterious power explains these social constants. Instead they must result from other social characteristics of the group, characteristics equally available to empirical analysis. Although naiveté of data collection in his time never allowed him to quantify any other social characteristics than those that appear in these early writings, he never wavered in his belief that this problem was a problem of technique only, and had nothing to do with the particular character of society. The affinity between these attitudes and those expressed in Durkheim's writings in the 1890s is remarkable.

Quetelet stressed the importance of quantification as a methodology for the study of societies. The statistical analysis of large numbers seemed to him to be the key not only to describing society in terms of its "factual" points of stability, but also to explaining those facts by means of other social facts with which they might correlate. In later writings he explored in a simple way the implications of statistical means and variations around the mean, the concepts of random variation and probabilistic statements about such variation, and the possibility of causal connections between social facts as revealed by fairly elaborate cross-tabulations. Quetelet was insistent that sociology's hope for becoming an exact science lay in its ability to utilize mathematics.

All these ideas are not unique to Quetelet. To some extent they are simply indicative of developments in the field of statistics during the nineteenth century. But Quetelet was an unusual man and a original thinker. He tends to have been neglected by chroniclers of sociology so that it is difficult today to determine exactly the channels of influence from his ideas to sociology. Certainly both Comte and Durkheim were personally familiar with his writings. It is also tantalizing to speculate on the links between him and Weber. At a more general level, developments such as these in the field of statistics served to reinforce the influences for quantification and demographic analysis already observed in Malthus's writing and strengthened the positivist's emphasis on the empirical analysis of societies. These developments are another illustration of the mood that asserted a deterministic thrust from material variables to man's life in society.

Anthropology

Social statistics was one source of data, research methodology, and concepts for sociology. Another such source was anthropology, and its data collection arm, ethnography.

Territorial expansion in this period gave a tremendous boost to the recording of the details of life in non-Western societies. During the century there was a vast output of published ethnographic material. But one general limitation of such data was that it was on the whole not collected by trained ethnographers. Instead, the material was collected by amateurs of varying degrees of skill—missionaries, colonial administrators, travelers, explorers, and a variety of others who through various types of chance contact surveyed and reported on the life of "exotic" cultures. Although a number of research directives and manuals were written in this period, ethnographic data was of variable comprehensiveness and reliability. Sociologists thus drew on an extensive and half-assimilated mass of comparative data, but occasionally built their theoretical postulates on shaky foundations. Spencer and Sumner are particularly good examples of such dependency.

Anthropology first placed a heavy emphasis on the concept of "culture" and on the utility of a comparative methodology. Anthropology also reinforced sociology's tendency to assume a unilinear evolutionary dynamic for societies in general and various institutions in particular. E.B. Tylor's *Primitive Culture* (1871), which works out in detail the evolutionary progression of religion, is a classic illustration of this theme in anthropology.

However, some of the first reactions against these assumptions began to appear in later anthropological studies. In the 1880s the emphasis began to shift to detailed historical analyses of particular cultures, and to the use of concepts of diffusion and migration for explaining cross-cultural similarities. The earlier theme of cultural evolution is echoed as late as 1912 in Durkheim's exploration of religion. Later emphases on history, distinctive cultures, diffusion, and migration meshed well with the assumptions of idealist philosophy and are evident in the writings of Weber and Simmel.

Psychology

A third influential source of data, research techniques, and concepts for sociology was psychology. The sociologists who concern us in this book all explicitly related in various ways to psychology. Spencer and Comte both spent considerable time exploring its ideas and felt that a knowledge of psychology was important in the education of any sociologist. In contrast, the later generation represented by Durkheim and Weber seemed to go to unnecessary lengths, from our perspective, to deny the continuity between psychological and sociological perspectives. Later, Cooley, Mead, and Pareto once again drew close to psychology, building some of its assumptions into their images of the social process.

Some of the reasons for this lie with sociology's own internal development: the early view of a unitary science with sociology as its latest and most magnificent product; the later zeal to establish a separate professional status for the field. But some of the reasons are with psychology and its own changes in this period.

Psychology, like anthropology and sociology, experienced its first major developments as a social science in the nineteenth century. Deeply influenced by positivism, its concerns were both with the physiological bases of thought and sensation, and with the elemental structure of those experiences, which it sought to map and measure. Beginning with Gall's attempts to locate the various faculties in specific sections of the brain in 1810, subsequent decades witnessed explorations of the physiological structure of the nervous system, linkage of capacities like speech with the operation of some sector of the brain, experimentation with sensations like touch or color perception, the measurement of reaction times, and so on. Theorizing concentrated on analyses of the elements which entered into human experience: the proportions of emotion and cognition in thought, for example, or the proportions of hereditary and environmental influences in personality. The concern then was with creating a fairly static model of the structure of individual experience. There was less interest in the complex functioning of experience, the blending of multiple factors into such behavioral complexes as problem solving, perception, or self-control. Similarly there was a neglect of social-psychological variables and an emphasis by default on the dominance in individual experience of elemental physiological processes located in the individual organism. Not until the beginning of the twentieth century did the shift to these hitherto neglected topics begin with psychologists like William James turning their attention to complex behavioral sequences, with the development of *gestalt* theory, and the rise of psychoanalytic theories. Throughout the period, however, psychology remained firmly committed to the empirical tenets of positivism, painstakingly searching for accurate techniques for observation, measurement, and experimentation. Psychology was, on this particular criteron, a model for emulation to the positivists in sociology.

Sociologists' reactions to psychology vary with their academic ideologies and with the nature of the task at hand, as well as with developments in the latter field. Comte and Spencer, anxious to legitimize sociology by showing its continuity with the rest of science, stressed that a knowledge of psychology—precisely of the elemental and physiological basis of personality and experience—was a preliminary for the sociologist in his efforts to understand man in the group. Later sociologists like Durkheim, Simmel, and Weber, while acknowledging this basis of personality, were anxious to show how their field differed from psychology because of its emphasis on the complex, socialized, behaving social actor, in contrast to the latter's interest in basic reflexes, and elemental sensations and faculties. Mead and Cooley, familiar with turn-of-the-century developments in psychology, once more drew close to the field, adopting many of its new perspectives, seeking to emulate certain of its techniques, and refusing to acknowledge any but the most permeable of boundaries between sociology and psychology.

Ideology and Sociology

The concept of ideology is introduced into this description of the intellectual background of early sociology because prevailing ideologies seemed to have permeated the academic community of the period in varying degrees, providing values or biases in the work of the early sociologists, and building some of the emotional thrust that underlies their work.

The concern here is with fairly explicit belief systems shared by a number of individuals, capable of translation either wholly or in part into directives for action in the political arena. Such actions may range from a simple cognitive orientation towards politics to direct participation in political life. We distinguish between two levels of ideology: "pure ideology" or the general, rather abstract, values providing ultimate legitimation for the belief system, and enduring relatively unchanged over long periods; and "practical ideology," the norms of the belief system, directing the adherent to particular forms of behavior, more subject to change in response to situational particulars, and, though legitimated by the pure ideology, not necessarily a logical translation of the general values.[11] The three ideological systems which seem to have worked in this way during the period are labeled liberalism, conservatism, and Marxist socialism.

Liberalism

At the level of pure ideology, liberalism focused on the human individual, on his potential for development and fulfillment, and on his right, derived from such potential, to freedom for the "pursuit of happiness." Liberals also believed in the creative force of human rationality, and in a progressive direction in history which resulted from the steady unfolding of this creative dynamic. They saw man as an active agent working in history to shape his own future, and looked forward to the day when he would create a state of both freedom and justice, but they did not incorporate an image of revolutionary change as a *necessary* variable in this process of change. The possibility of revolution was not precluded, especially in the earlier nineteenth century, but more fundamental to progressive change was the existence of a group of enlightened individuals concretely and responsibly working for the betterment of their society. Individuals were therefore change agents, but the pattern of change was as often incremental as it was revolutionary. At the level of practical ideology, nineteenth century liberalism focused on the protection of property;[12] the extension of constitutional rights; enfranchisement; and an early claim that the state ought to diminish its role in the workings of the society, which was later replaced by demands that the state increase this role. This last shift resulted, among other things, from the accession to power of those middle class circles from which liberalism derived its greatest support.

Conservatism

If liberals rallied around a faith in the ultimate value of the individual, conservatives were similarly oriented to a belief in the sanctity of society, or culture, holistically conceptualized. To conservatives society was a miracle, distilled from aeons of random experimentation by generations of men, in which everyone had his place, in which potential contradictions were mysteriously absorbed and effaced, and in which the range of human needs were satisfied. Society was a unity, rooted in the traditions and assumptions of everyday life.

Phrased in terms very similar to sociology's contemporary concept of unanticipated consequences, conservatives predicted that only disaster could result from piecemeal meddling with parts of the culture.

In place of a value on change, conservatives stressed the importance of order, stability, and the unquestioned beliefs and traditions of the group. They were oriented not so much to the past as to the immediate present, the *status quo*, which they viewed as containing the last vestiges of a glorious and more stable past, and which they hoped to preserve from the encroachments of the future. Caught in the pressures of both eighteenth and nineteenth-century developmental thought, conservatism could not absolutely deny the fact of social change nor denounce all the consequences of those changes as harmful. Conservatives at least partially accepted the thesis of progress, but in contrast to liberals they ascribed this not to the rational plans of individual men, but to the massive evolutionary dynamics of an unfolding cultural system. The best way to guarantee future progress was to leave this process alone, allowing it to work itself through in its full complexity. This was conservatism viewed at the level of pure ideology.

At the level of practical ideology, the content of conservatism shifts over the period. In a century of rapid changes an ideology concerned with preserving the immediate present had to change. In the period of Comte, European conservatives defended the survival of feudalism against advancing industrialism. Somewhat later Americans argued for the preservation of a rural republican system against similar changes. By the end of the century, the effort was to preserve the *laissez-faire* system of the early industrial period from the growing centralization and "welfare system" of the government. But whatever the platform there was continuity in the pure themes of the value of tradition, the sanctity of the present social order, and the dangers of rapid change.

Marxism

Since Marx's sociology and Marxist socialism are so closely related, and since the former is intensely analyzed in the main sections of this book, the description of Marxist ideology given here will be brief.

Marxism was oriented neither to individual nor to society but to that segment of society (or aggregate of individuals) which it called a social class, and in particular to the proletariat class, the wage earners of industrial society. This class is conceived as a truly revolutionary group bearing those virtues and values which make possible the ultimately just society. Although (like liberalism and conservatism) incorporating a theme of developmental social change, Marxism's image of such change contained, as essential ingredients, overt conflict and revolution. The active agents for change were classes of men. The final confrontation, when a society would emerge which had eliminated the sources of exploitation and conflict, was almost at hand. At the level of practical ideology, Marxism concentrated in this period on intensifying the revolutionary potential of the working classes by educating them, heightening their class consciousness, organizing them into economic and political units, and attempting to form them into an international movement.

Effects of Ideology on Sociology

Sociology fuses with practical ideology only in its earliest stages: in the writings of Marx, Comte, and Spencer. Comte specifically sought with his sociology to create a blueprint for social stability. Spencer directed his efforts to ensuring a *laissez-faire* governmental policy. The expression of these views in the earlier nineteenth century mark Spencer as a liberal at the level of practical ideology. But his continuing defense of such a position late in the century mark him as a conservative, anxious to preserve a passing order. Indeed, since Spencer's practical ideology was always justified in the name of society and its slow, natural evolution, he is better characterized as conservative, despite some debate on this. [13]

Later sociologists, more anxious to gain academic status than general popularity for their field, drew away from explicit linkage of sociology and practical ideology. They struggled for proper academic detachment and objectivity. Ideology finds its way into their writings at the level of pure ideology—as values and goals in their work. It has become customary to identify earlier sociology as conservative at the level of pure ideology.[14] Certainly some of this earlier group were moved by a deep concern for social order in the midst of their own perceptions and experiences of rapid and often violent change, and their sociology is oriented to this question. Such a value is apparent in the works of Durkheim, Pareto, Tönnies, and the social Darwinists. But the discipline has roots almost as deep in the basic liberal concern for the individual and his rights or needs for freedom and rationality: this is explicit in Simmel's writings, and almost as clear in the orientation of Weber, Ward, Mead, and Cooley. Order and freedom—this seems to be the crux of the ideological tension in academic sociology.

Regarding the beliefs and values of Marxist socialism, there is no one in this period who directly extends this perspective in his sociology (except Marx, of course). Only Pareto, for his own purposes, borrows its motifs of rigidly stratified societies, power, and conflict. Yet there is a close relationship between sociology and Marxism, one of creative tension which would have delighted Marx, the philosopher, had he analyzed it. Men as different as Weber, Durkheim, and Pareto are keenly aware of the Marxist thesis and devote their work, in part, to confronting and answering it.

Summary and Conclusions

This chapter has described some of the ideas which were influential in academic circles, and which had an impact on the thinking of some or all of the early sociologists. It described the metaphysics and epistemology of positivism, idealism, and pragmatism. It looked at developmental thought in general, and more closely at two nineteenth-century variants of this: historical materialism and social Darwinism. Certain technical developments of the period were briefly reviewed: the ideas of Malthus and Darwin, and the orientations of social statistics, anthropology, and psychology. Finally certain political ideologies—liberalism, conservatism, and Marxist socialism—were discussed in terms of both their abstract values and their practical platforms in the nineteenth century.

Some general themes emerge from all this. The most important is the triumph of positivism as an epistemology. Not only does it have its own proponents in the nineteenth century, but it also wins vocal and powerful allies in social Darwinism, historical materialism, and pragmatism. It gained an enormous triumph in Darwin's writings, and as far as sociology was concerned, positivism's epistemology was further reinforced in the Malthusian thesis and the perspectives of social statistics and psychology. It was as though a sudden convergence of unexpected factors served, in this period, to tilt the balance in favor of one of the combatants in a long war. It was probably necessary that such a surge of confidence in the scientific technique should accompany the first beginnings of sociology, a field which purported to study social life scientifically.

There is less consensus, however, on the metaphysics of positivism. The old concern with mind, as the medium through which man experiences reality, remained strong. Hegel's ideas lingered on in Germany's universities, and neo-idealists elaborated anew on the thesis of mind. These events were reinforced by pragmatism's orientation and anthropology's emphasis on culture. Against the implications of such perspectives ranged the positivist's belief in a mechanical universe governed by eternal omnipotent "natural laws." Sociology could not avoid the influences of these diverse themes. Despite the growing faith in the scientific method, its area for investigation overlapped closely with the territory of the proponents of mind. The conflictful triangle of scientism, mind, and natural laws shaped the field from its beginnings. Much of this book will be affected by it. The same points of tension are still in modern sociology.

Another dominant theme is the popularity of developmental imagery, and its nineteenth-century variant, evolutionary thought. Except for an ideal-type positivism, everything else described above has contained some element of this theme, and in practice committed positivists like Comte accepted the developmental model. The belief system of early sociology is similarly permeated by this idea of social change. Only at the most general level, however, is this a common thesis. When one gets down to specifics there are several variants of the developmental model, ranging from Marx's image of social revolution, through German theories of change in unique, historical cultures, to conservatism's thesis of massive yet almost imperceptible evolution.

A less emphasized but still important pattern in the preceding description has been the fragmentation of social philosophy into a series of social sciences. Sociology was not the only discipline to experience its initial and important definition in the nineteenth century. Indeed, part of sociology's belief system was shaped by the need felt by early sociologists to distinguish themselves from the other new social sciences, and thus to justify their own existence and claims to privilege. A final theme has been the emergence of ideology in this period and the impact of various ideologies on sociology. Again this is a problem that also affects modern sociology.

Although the ideas described are important influences, it would not do to assume any simple and mechanical extension of these themes into earlier sociology; as though, depending on time and spatial location, each man was exposed to some particular selection of these ideas which then fit together like the pieces of a puzzle to assume the sum and form of his sociology. In the first place, a vast number of other notions, not described here, also affected these men. Second, the various ideas meshed with their experiences, both entirely personal and of the general type described in chapter 3, and only then fed into an ideational product. And third, there are a variety of other factors which one may never be entirely able to isolate which shape a man's responses to some idea presented to him. All these qualifications taken together mean that the descriptions in this chapter give only a moderate amount of predictability to any particular man's sociology. Nevertheless, this intellectual background is the best single cluster of variables for understanding the themes and interests in early sociology. We turn now to those themes.

NOTES

1. H. Stuart Hughes, *Consciousness and Society* (New York: Vintage Press, 1958), uses the term positivism in a similar way.

2. The fact that Durkheim, an avowed Positivist, used this term (see chapter 5) is indicative of how thoroughly elements of idealism permeated sociology and were melded into its basic structure.

3. The principles of dialectic change are important here.

4. This whole thesis is elaborately worked out in Robert Nisbet, *Social Change and History* (New York: Oxford University Press, 1969).

5. Karl Marx, *Capital* (Moscow: Foreign Languages Publishing Company, 1954) volume I, p. 19; as quoted in Irving Zeitlin, *Ideology and the Development of Sociological Thought* (Englewood Cliffs, N.J.: Prentice-Hall, 1968).

6. Herbert Spencer, *First Principles* (New York: Appleton, 1898), p. 407.

7. Richard Hofstadter, *Social Darwinism in American Thought* (Boston: Beacon Press, 1955).

8. This section draws heavily on H.S. Thayer, *Meaning and Action: a Critical History of Pragmatism* (New York: Bobbs Merrill, 1969).

9. This is William James's phrase.

10. This section draws on David Landau and Paul Lazarsfeld, "Quételet, Adolphe" in *International Encyclopedia of the Social Sciences,* edited by David Sills (New York: Macmillan and Free Press, 1968).

11. This analytic approach to the concept of ideology is suggested by Franz Schurmann, *Ideology and Organization in Communist China* (Berkeley and Los Angeles: University of California Press, 1966).

12. The regard for property may in fact be so central to nineteenth liberalism as to be "pure ideology;" in any case the concern for both individual rights and for property are an inherent source of tension and change in liberal ideology.

13. For example, Talcott Parsons, in his introduction to Herbert Spencer's *The Study of Sociology,* (Ann Arbor: University of Michigan Press, 1961) categorizes Spencer as a liberal.

14. Robert Nisbet is well known for this opinion; see "Conservatism and Sociology" *American Journal of Sociology* 58 (September 1952): 167-75.

Part Two

Definitions of Sociology

5

The Subject Matter
of Sociology

With some knowledge of the personalities of the early sociologists, and of the social and intellectual settings in which they wrote their pioneering statements, we turn to the main task—an analysis of their efforts to describe the boundaries and concerns of sociology. As a necessary preliminary to these efforts, the early sociologists had to say what it was sociology studied, and, at a general level, what perspective ought to be maintained in these studies. The early sections of most of the sociological works produced during this period, and on occasion, extensive, separately published statements, are devoted to this definitional issue.[1]

This chapter is divided into four main sections. The first looks at the consensus among earlier sociologists on the point that sociology was to be a science. Next various definitions of sociology's subject matter will be described. Following this is a review of some of the conceptual strategies that were advocated as ways to begin analysis of this subject matter. Finally, we look at the various images of society which earlier sociologists held.

Sociology as Science

In this early period there were many differences of opinion about precisely what sociologists studied, and how they should approach such study. But it is also important to recognize that at a more general level there was a high degree of consensus about sociology's *raison d'etre*. Without exception our sociologists held that the new discipline had as its task the *scientific* study of man's social experience. This view is of course expressed by the positivists. We hear from Comte that

> in the class of organic sciences there are only two sub-categories: there are the sciences which study the individual organism, and there are the sciences which study the species, especially when it is gregarious. Sociology is the study of *man* as a gregarious species;[2]

and from Durkheim,

> We . . . wish to establish the science of ethics . . . to treat the facts of moral life according to the method of the positive sciences.[3]

But we also find this view expressed by those most influenced by idealism. Simmel, for example, stated that, "like every other exact science, [social science] aims at the immediate understanding of the given;"[4] and Weber is explicit that, "the type of social science in which we are interested is an empirical science of concrete reality."[5] The same views are to be found expressed in the writings of both Darwinists and pragmatists.

This level of consensus is not trivial, for by asserting that sociology was the scientific study of social experience these earlier sociologists were making two important and related points. First, they were stating formally that sociology was not to be viewed as a direct extension of philosophy, the field which had hitherto exercised a virtual monopoly in the study of man's social experience. Sociology, Pareto said, with his characteristic acrimony, must "eschew entirely the science of the metaphysicians."[6] Weber more elaborately made the same point: in seeking to understand social "reality" the sociologist should *not* be viewed as seeking

> the meaning which is "true" in some metaphysical sense. It is this that distinguishes the empirical sciences of (social) action, such as sociology, from the dogmatic disciplines such as . . . logic, ethics and esthetics, which seek to ascertain the "true" and "valid" meanings associated with the objects of their investigation.[7]

One can trace this formal awareness of the distinction between social philosophy and sociology through the writings of all the men being studied. It is true that sometimes this formal acknowledgement did not seem to act as a restraint on speculations about absolute truth and goodness, but this is more evident in the earliest writers, Comte and Spencer. By the turn of the century, when the sociological output of our group was most prolific, the distinction between social philosophy and sociology was not only formally recognized but, for the most part, actually practiced.

Second, by defining sociology as the science of social experience, the new field was from the start seen as operating under the constraints of scientific investigation, however those constraints were interpreted. For the strict empiricists this meant a commitment to the "logico-experimental method," as Pareto repeatedly described it. But even those most wary of applying the techniques of the physical sciences to the study of social life, like Weber, explicitly recognized that their linkage of sociology to science means that the former is constrained to be concerned with the empirical, that it must strive for accurate observation, for clarity, and for verifiability in its conclusions.

Man has always speculated about his group experience. Some of his earlier writings on the subject may be categorized as history or ethnography, but most of the memorable writings on this subject in earlier periods are philosophical. If we wish to focus specifically on the emergence of sociology, however, we have to say what distinguishes it from these earlier statements. The differentiating factor seems to be that sociology is insistent that social experience can and ought to be studied scientifically, that one can treat social experience as part of the empirical realm, and that one must initially look outwards, not inwards, for the material with which to build an explanation of social life. The consensus that emerged in the late nineteenth and early twentieth century on this point is a fact of considerable importance in tracing the emergence and development of the field.

"The scientific study of social experience"—at this very general level there was consensus on the definition of sociology. The problem, however, was to say more precisely what "social experience" was. and then to determine what the "scientific study" of this phenomenon would entail. Conflicts of opinion in the group become apparent at these more specific levels, conflicts which have important implications for the emerging structure of sociology.

The Study of "Society"

One obvious way to translate "social experience" is to equate it with "society" and to argue from this perspective that sociology has as its essential task the study of human society, *in toto*. The earliest sociologists took this approach in defining sociology's subject matter. For Comte, sociology was the study of man as a gregarious species. This means, he goes on to specify, the study of all the complex phenomena of social life: associations, institutions, and "civilization." Spencer, very similarly, described sociology as the science of incorporated human nature. Starting with human beings,

> the science of sociology has to give an account of all the phenomena that result from their combined actions.[8]

Marx also intended his social science to analyze and explain the unfolding chronicle of man's life in groups, and the multitudes of relationships and events that have been recorded in his history as a separate species. To this huge array of factors they gave the name "Society."

The earliest sociologists thus assumed responsibility for studying a very wide ranging, perhaps disparate, aggregate of phenomena. They had to attempt to impose order and seek enduring relationships in this aggregate. This is Comte's explicit intention: sociology must study all the facets of civilization (which is Comte's term for shared ideas, beliefs, etc.); all the principles of organization; all the entities we call institutions. "Society," he said, "is a systematic relationship of institutions, social manners and ideas, a unity of physical, moral and intellectual processes."[9] Every aspect of man's life in the group is sociological material. From this perspective, Comte put sociology at the apex of his hierarchy of the sciences, as the climax of all scientific investigation, as the ultimate, subsuming field.[10] The same ambitious views are clear in the writings of Spencer and Marx.

Of the later sociologists, however, only one continued to define sociology at the science of society as a total phenomenon. To Pareto,

> Human society is the subject of many researches. Some of them constitute specialized disciplines: law, political economy, political history, etc. Others have not yet been distinguished by special names. To the synthesis of them all, which aims at studying human society in general, we give the name of sociology.[11]

The similarity of Pareto's view of sociology's subject matter with the views of Comte and Spencer gives rise to some intriguing similarities in their approach to an analytic strategy for sociology.

But, in the later generation of sociologists, Pareto's was a minority position. Many members of this group insisted that so wide ranging a field of concentration prevented systematic analysis, and began to seek more narrowly defined areas which were the "peculiarly social" aspects of group life, the particular subject matter of sociology. Simmel argued this viewpoint most tersely: "Nothing is gained by throwing everything into a pot and sticking a new label on it, sociology."[12]

Society, Simmel argued, is an abstract concept which can be articulated and interpreted in a thousand ways. There is, in fact, no science of man which could not be viewed as a science of society. Sociology ought not to try to replace all the disciplines which study man, but should develop its own particular questions about society. Durkheim also pointed to the generality of the term society and argues that sociology's concerns are more specialized, less wide ranging. Weber developed this theme further. By insisting that sociology adopt a limited set of interests and stick to these in its study of society, he said, we are admittedly exposing the field to criticisms of óne-sidedness, but this one-sidedness is essential to disciplined inquiry. An understanding of society in its entirety is impossible: one must narrow one's perspective in order to ask questions precisely and develop a conceptual apparatus. From the overlapping of such limited answers a wider understanding of society will come.[13]

The earliest period in the definition of sociology is characterized by far-reaching claims for the scope and potential of the new field. To Comte, sociology represented the climax of the development of science; to Spencer, sociology studied "superorganic evolution," the climax of the evolutionary processes of the universe. The relationship they proposed between sociology and other academic disciplines is essentially one of dominance. Sociology subsumed other, earlier developed fields of inquiry, incorporating their strategy for investigation and utilizing their information in order to make sense of the most important, most complex phenomenon of all: man and his life in the group. The sociologists who succeeded Comte and Spencer, however, redefined the nature of sociology's relationship to other academic fields. Sociology as they saw it was only an equal of other disciplines. The "social" was simply one aspect of that wider reality with which all disciplines are concerned. In its use of a scientific method, sociology had something in common with all sciences. In its concern with human experience, it would claim affinity with both the humanities and other social sciences. The overlap of method and subject matter argued for a closer relationship between sociology and the other social sciences. This is still the attitude in contemporary sociology.

In rejecting the view that sociologists studied an undifferentiated aggregate of phenomena labeled simply "society," the second generation of sociologists had to specify what their more specialized area for investigation was. In reviewing the various statements on this point, two sets of answers, not entirely unrelated, seem to emerge. To some sociologists sociology was the study of what we today call culture; to others it was the study of association between human individuals. Out of these two clusters of response emerge much of contemporary sociology's rather complex definition of its subject matter. In order to explore some of the features of these two sets of answers, we will now focus on the views of four sociologists: Durkheim and Weber, who both propounded the "culture" viewpoint, and Simmel and Mead, who stressed the "association" approach.

The Study of Culture

Durkheim's sociology was primarily concerned with the body of rules which human relationships generate over time, however spontaneous those relationships might be initially. Sociology investigates all aspects of the process by which a "moral" system becomes superimposed on a relationship which may originally have developed out of needs or interests. Sociology studies that dimension of society by which the group is seen to exert moral or emotional control over its members.[14] Sociology then is not concerned with the study of society in general, but with one aspect of social life: the emergent system of constraints on the individual which comes out of the association between individuals.

During his career Durkheim repeatedly changed the label he gave to this phenomenon, and each change of label is associated with an increased awareness of the range of factors which operate as socially derived constraints. In his first book, the *Division of Labor in Society,* he seemed to equate these constraints with morality: sociology is "the science of ethics," and he repeatedly talked of moral forces, moral law, or a moral system. In the *Rules of Sociological Method,* he called these constraints institutions; sociology is the study of institutions, and the term "institutions" refers to "all the beliefs, all the modes of conduct instituted by the collectivity."[15] In his later books the most frequent term used for this phenomenon is "collective representations." Elsewhere he listed the following group products under the label of collective representations: religion; law; morals; customs; pedagogical practices; architecture and avenues of communication; currents of public sentiments; and public opinion.[16] In other words, sociology is the study of how culture (as it is currently defined) functions to constrain the behavior of man.

It is clear from Durkheim's statements that "social" consists of systems of shared ideas. These shared ideas, however, have a character distinct from the particular ideas of the individual. Moreover, though collective representations are ideas, they are not, as the idealist might claim, ideas which only exist in the mind of the observer (the sociologist). Durkheim was adamant in stressing that collective representations are natural phenomena. Collective representations, he said, are

> part of nature, indeed its highest representation The social realm is a natural realm which differs from others only by a greater complexity.[17]

Collective representations exist; they are a collective reality, living active forces, as real as natural cosmic forces in their effect on the individual. And since they are material and real, collective representations are amenable to the techniques of empirical science.

To Weber also sociology was the scientific study of culture:

> If one wishes to call those disciplines which treat the events of social life with respect to their cultural significance "cultural sciences" then social science in our sense belongs in that category.[18]

Like Durkheim, Weber argued that culture was not only ideational but it was also real and concrete:

> The social-scientific interest has as its point of departure the real i.e. the concrete, individually structured configuration of our cultural life, and its development out of other social-cultural conditions . . . we are concerned with psychological and intellectual phenomena.[19]

However, the two men did have some differences in their approaches to the concept of culture. Whereas Durkheim's emphasis was on culture as a system of constraints on the individual's behavior, Weber's stress was on culture as a system of meanings which the individual brings with him to a situation, which confers significance on that situation, and which thus in large part makes sense of the individual's behavior.

> Culture is a finite segment of the meaningless infinity of the world process, a segment on which human beings confer meaning and significance . . . we are cultural beings, endowed with the capacity and the will to take a deliberate attitude towards the world and to lend to it significance. Whatever that significance may be it will lead us to judge certain phenomena of human existence in its light . . . this significance alone is of scientific interest.[20]

The broad consequences of either approach are the same in that one arrives at knowledge about the institutionalized idea framework in which men operate, a framework which both Durkheim and Weber saw to be particularly characteristic of man's social experience. But the Durkheimian approach seems to imply much more—a duality between man and his cultural products, a relationship frequently characterized by resistance on the one side, constraints on the other. One can from this perspective presumably arrive at knowledge of the idea frameworks without knowledge of the individual; and on the basis of this knowledge one can predict the behavior of the individual. The Weberian approach, in contrast, fuses man and his ideas, makes knowledge of one inextricably interwoven with knowledge of the other. Arriving at such knowledge means that one understands a particular pattern of behavior rather than that one can predict future outcomes.

Another difference between Durkheim's view of the subject matter of sociology and that of Weber's stems from Weber's greater concern for the Marxist view of the social process. To Weber social science studied culture insofar as it appears to be related to socioeconomic behavior, and socioeconomic behavior is broadly defined to mean all the "planful provision and work, struggle with nature, and the association of human beings" generated by the fact that man must manipulate his environment if his material and ideal needs are to be met.[21] Sociology is concerned with patterns of cultural meanings which either directly or indirectly relate to this central congery of human activity. Sociologists should either study structures of meanings which relate to strictly economic activity, like the ethics of the stock market; or meaning structures in other institutions which influence economic activity, such as the ethics of ascetic Protestantism which generated a "work ethic" conducive to western capitalism; or meaning structures in other institutions which result from economic activity, such as increasing bureaucratization in western organizations. Weber in his definition of the subject matter of sociology both accepted the broad Marxist focus on the economic institution and pointed out the analytic complexity involved in such a focus. Throughout his own career he stayed close to the economic issue in his concern with meaning structures.

The long-range goals each man had in his study of culture present us with yet another difference between them. Durkheim felt that sociology must approximate the other sciences: its long-term goals are explanations of group behavior couched in general lawlike statements. Weber, in contrast, was emphatic that sociology must not seek to approximate the natural sciences. The point about cultures, as he saw it, is that they vary so widely in time and space. Sociologists sought to see historically real cultural configurations in their uniqueness, and to understand why a particular culture was the way it was. Such understanding would come from analysis of the particular constellation of factors which preceded and generated it. General statements about social life *per se* could never be more than trivial. They may have a role in the first stages of sociological investigation, but the sociologist must then move beyond general statements to a patient, meticulous analysis of the particular case.[22] Both men, one might say, were interested in the "big picture," but they had different "big pictures." Durkheim seemed to concentrate on much narrower, specific relationships between particular cultural variables, but he wanted to find relationships of this type which are universal to all societies. Weber eschewed the study of universal social processes, but he wanted to grasp not just single relationships but the whole pattern of relationships in particular cultures.

The Study of Association

Contrasting with the emphasis on culture is the stress on human associations as the subject matter of sociology, although this latter view did not exclude a concern for much of the same material that Durkheim and Weber focused on. To Simmel the uniquely social was embodied in the processes of interaction that go on between people, interaction involving a sense of mutual orientation, or awareness of the other person. For example, two strangers may collide in front of a ticket office, apologize and then go their separate ways. But for a brief moment, they have been aware of each other, reacted to each other, and in that moment the social existed. There was interaction, or association. It is a misleading convention, he argued, that makes us identify the terms "society" or "social" with the major organizations and institutions of our experience. This is a dangerous simplification holding us back from a true appreciation of the nature and complexity of society. For society, from the sociological perspective, consists of an intricate, ever-changing web of human interaction or "sociation." Taken singly, each sequence may appear inconsequential; taken jointly we have the fabric of social life.[23]

> Sociation continuously emerges and ceases, and emerges again. Even where its eternal flux and pulsation are not sufficiently strong to form organizations proper, they link individuals together. [Sociation] accounts for all the toughness and elasticity, all the color and consistency of social life . . . one should properly speak not of society, but of sociation. Society is merely the name for a number of individuals connected by interaction. It is because of their interaction that they become a unit.[24]

For Durkheim sociology studied the gridlike system of normative constraints within which the individual acts; for Weber the concern was with the shifting spectrum of perspectives and interpretations through which man relates to his environment; and to Simmel sociology focused on an enduring, yet ever-varied interlocking system of relationships between individuals.

To understand Simmel's many and varied writings, one should hold fast to this knowledge of his concern with the process of interaction itself. He explored situations of recurring interaction: power, competition, gratitude, reconciliation. He studied the life sequence of a group, from initial unity, through conflict, to new forms of unity, in a concern for interaction as a developmental sequence. And he focused on social positions or statuses (the aristocrat, the stranger, the poor) in an attempt to explore the way in which interaction itself defines or creates what the layman sees as personality types.[25]

It is also important to understand that Simmel saw social interaction as always incorporating a subjective element. Social interaction is not merely behavior, but behavior characterized by awareness of the associative link to others. The fact that one is aware of the other person, aware of the associative bond between oneself and that other, concerned for, appreciative of, or at least conscious of the experience of linkage to the other is essential to Simmel's definition of sociation. For him the social ceases only when one is indifferent to the other actor, when one sees him strictly as an instrument or means to some end, when an awareness, however transient, of the intrinsic aspect of the social bond does not occur. Simmel saw the experience of sociation to be in itself rewarding, apart from the more concrete rewards which cooperative activity might achieve. The experience of the social bond satisfies some deep seated need in all of us, and because of this a social element emerges in almost every type of interaction between human beings. Because of this, too, man frequently creates situations which have no exterior, material ends, which exist purely for the experience of sociation—the party, the ritualized game, or courtship.

The psychological element is even more pronounced in Mead's definition of association. In fact, Mead saw his field as a logical extension of psychology, labeling it "social psychology." Whereas Simmel concentrated on interaction patterns, and assumed the individual's awareness of interaction, Mead was as much concerned with the nature of that individual awareness as he was with associative patterns. He argued that the two were inextricably connected.

As Mead argued it, sociology studies the relationship between the human individual and his social environment. The human individual is characterized by intelligence, which means that he is capable of actively relating and adjusting himself to his environment. The social environment is that set of relationships that arises when an aggregate of human individuals engage in cooperative activity. The sociologist studies two types of association: the association between an individual and his social environment, and the patterns of association between a group of human beings, that is, the social environment. These relationships at both levels are characterized by mutual determinism, mutual dependency.

What is the nature of these relationships? If we first consider the relationship between a single individual and his social environment we find that it has two components: the overt behavior of the individual *vis-à-vis* that environment, and his subjective experience of the relationship (his "covert" activity). Both components must be analyzed. If we stand back and look at the wider pattern of group associations, we observe, simply, overt behavior, interaction among the many individuals in the social environment. But this interaction is primarily of one type: it is communication, the exchange of meaningful symbols by individuals. Interaction in the human group is to a large extent symbolic. The transfer of these symbols triggers individual behavioral sequences. The sociologist's task is the study of these symbolic networks and the way in which the group and the individual are linked by this communication. Accompanying this study is the requirement to study the individual's "covert activity" to the extent that it originates and responds to such communication.

To Simmel the social was interaction, behavior between individuals; to Mead that interaction was usually of a particular sort—communication. Weber argued that the social scientist studies the shifting perspectives and interpretations which the social actor brings to his situation; Mead also focused on the subjective processes of the social actor, but he emphasized the interdependence between the actor's meaning structure and his social situation, in which each constantly affects and reshapes the other. There are thus connections between the ideas of Simmel, Mead, and Weber, and Weber's theories show a linkage with Durkheim's. Although wide ranging and complex, the responses of this important group of second generation sociologists to the question "what does sociology study?" are not unrelated.

Strategies for Analyzing Social Experience

From the above statements about the nature of the social, the earlier sociologists then went on to develop various strategies for its scientific study. In part these strategies involve the development of particular techniques for sociological investigation, an issue to which we will turn in a later chapter. These research tactics, however, are derived from more abstract statements about *where* the sociologist must look for his clues to the nature of social experience, statements which are so closely related to the theoretical definitions of sociology's subject matter that they are described at this point.

Deduction from Known Principles

One general tactic adopted in the approach to the study of social experience was to look outside the discipline for assistance. This involved turning to the more established natural sciences for insights, general principles, or useful analogies which might be of assistance in studying sociological materials. This was the tactic used to some extent by Comte, Spencer, Marx, and Pareto. It seems that these men, who gave sociology the obligation of studying all of society, most felt the need to seek outside assistance in their task.

In terms of the material presented in chapter 4, the most predictable imports from general science to sociology are the developmental and evolutionary principles best publicized in Darwin's works. It is commonly acknowledged today that evolutionary thought antedates Darwin's *Origin of the Species;* that in fact Darwin's works come as a climax to and a final vindication of many earlier scientific and intellectual developments. This is substantiated by Comte's use of evolutionary analogies prior to the publication of Darwin's famous book.

Comte's insistence that his new discipline must begin with and focus its attention on the complex amorphousness of society in general rests on his positivistic faith in natural laws. One such law the existence of which he never doubted is that society has evolved and continues to evolve. Indeed Comte went so far as to say that sociology was the study of society in evolution, "the science of social development." He was certain that as sociologists studied actual historical societies, they would find them to be all single cases illustrating the fact of the development of "society," the more general, abstract phenomenon. As was described in chapter 4, Spencer developed an even more elaborate rationale for his belief in society's evolutionary development. He then grounded many of his analytic procedures for social science on the assumption that development was a scientific law.

Another principle to which both Comte and Spencer were attracted originates not in the scientific principles of the day but in its more general intellectual mood. This is the principle of organicism, the tendency to interpret whatever aspect of the natural universe attracts one's curiosity in terms of an analogy to an organic entity, frequently mammalian in general characteristics. The structure of an organic entity provides a map to the structuring of another aspect of reality which one is investigating: this too is "alive" or vital, and the relationship between its parts are like the relationships between the parts of a living organism. The roots of organicism are in religious thought and in philosophical idealism: the impulse behind the popularity of this principle in early nineteenth century thought is the conservative reaction to the Enlightenment and to revolutionary thought.

Running through Comte's writings on society is the view of society as "the social organism," of which the basic "cell" is the family, and the "organs" are the major institutions of government, economy, religion, etc. As organs in the healthy biological entity exist in harmony with each other and with the cumulative vital needs of the organism, so harmony among institutions and between each institution and the particular society's needs is the necessary and "normal" state of society. Societal disturbances are "maladies" of the social organism, the proper study of social pathology. From organicism too comes Comte's famous analytic distinctions between "statics" and "dynamics," between the fixed structure and the dynamic functioning of the social organism. And the assumption of organismic structuring underlies Comte's emphasis that society must be studied *in toto,* as a single unit, without any prior attempt to understand constituent elements. For the essence of the social organism is in its complex internal dynamics: it is impossible to understand these by focusing on the cells alone, or on any particular organ.

Herbert Spencer's reliance on organicism is even more explicit and more well known. "The permanent relations among the parts of a society," he said, "are analagous to the permanent relations among the parts of a living body."[26] And, as if this were not emphatic enough, he proceeded in a now famous chapter of the *Principles of Sociology* to trace step by step the likeness between society and organism.[27] Both entities display growth, increasing structural complexity, increasing functional specialization, increasing interdependence of organs. Both entities contain tiny elemental units or cells out of which all the greater units are fashioned. Spencer's social "cells" are individual persons. In each case the entity outlives any of its particular cells, though in sudden catastrophe the cells can survive the entity. True, the cells of society are discrete, but communication binds them into a whole resembling the concrete whole of the biological organism. The only important distinction, really, is that sensation or feeling is limited in the biological entity to one subsystem, the nervous system, but in the social organism it is diffused among all the elemental units.

Spencer's views on the structural evolution of society have to be related to his more general beliefs in evolution as the dynamic process of the universe. Society's development occurred, he believed, simultaneously with the continuing evolution of the physical and biological world, with the evolution of the human species through such mechanisms as "survival of the fittest," and even with the continuing evolution of man's beliefs and ideas. Evolution goes on at many different levels. Each level changed partly because of the dynamics intrinsic to it, but each level also affected the developments occurring at other levels. Society's development could be partly explained by the evolution of other aspects of the universe. At the same time society affects those other evolving aspects of the universe. Spencer's sociology is like an intricate mobile sculpture, in which a series of rotating spheres "nest" one inside the other. A good measure of his popularity with his contemporaries probably has to do with the fascination of such a complex model of reality.

The organismic statements of the earliest sociologists seem bizarre and archaic today. Yet it is important to look at them seriously for two reasons. First, although organicism was formally renounced quite early in the history of sociology, some of its assumptions, like those of natural order and pathological disorder, structure as distinct from process, and the uniqueness of wholeness are still very much with us. Second, it might prove valuable to pause for a moment and ask ourselves what it was they were really trying to say. If we look beyond the now dated language and the exotic illustrations, is there anything more there? Were there any particular insights about the nature of society which they struggled to articulate?

To answer these questions we will turn to another sociologist who felt that sociology studied society as a total complex phenomenon: Vilfredo Pareto. Pareto too looked initially to the more developed sciences for insights which might help to organize the complex of data he had delineated as the area of primary sociological concern. He drew, however, not so much on the organic sciences which inspired Comte and Spencer, but on the mechanical sciences which were part of his own educational experience. Against this background he began to describe society as a system, the Social System. It seemed to him that each of the major categories of scientific investigation is really an area of distinctive relationships or processes. From this perspective society is a cluster of distinctive processes. If we think about a society, Pareto argued, we will realize that it is nothing but a complex pattern of behavioral sequences. Nor are societies areas of randomly fluctuating behavior and constant chaotic change: they are complex, but they are patterned. It is not the nature of the human beings, *per se*, which distinguishes societies as a separate class of phenomena; rather it is the kinds of relationships which those beings generate with one another.[28] The influences on those relationships are several. There are factors like the soil, climate, flora, fauna, geological, and other conditions of the natural environment in which the society is embedded. There is the influence of other societies and the historical experience of the society itself. There are characteristics of the social members, their sentiments, interests, and attitudes. There is the state and type of knowledge prevalent in the particular society.[29] But the outcome of all these facts in aggregate is a complex of relationships between individuals, relationships which may be viewed as processes. These processes interlock, constantly affecting other areas of the social process, and in turn are influenced by these other areas. Because society presents the scientist with a distinctive, fairly self-contained, elaborately interlocking set of processes, it is legitimate to describe society as a system, the Social System.[30]

This description of society is quite consistent with contemporary descriptions of society as a system. One is, in fact, immediately aware of the "modernity" of Pareto's approach in contrast with our reaction to the organicism of Comte and Spencer. Yet it would be unfair to give Pareto all the credit for originating in this period the social system notion because it is impossible to discount the efforts both Comte and Spencer were making to reach exactly this conclusion about the nature of society. Indeed they used the term the social system repeatedly and naturally throughout their sociological writings, and they were constantly impressed by the relational interconnections in societies. Moreover, Spencer elaborated at least as fully as Pareto the question of the social system's relationship to its analytic environment. However, both Comte and Spencer, after gaining this insight about systemic relationships, then turned to the prevalent organic analogy, and got trapped in the dead-end of detailed comparisons of cells, vital processes, organs, etc. Pareto can take credit for overcoming this problem. Pareto emphasized that while the social system was a system of human relationships, the components and structure of these relationships were still unknown to sociology. Thus there is room for building up inductively from an analytic scrutiny of social relationships to a general theory of society, despite the deductive thrust of his social system model. He advocated and practiced both modes of sociological analysis. Comte and Spencer, while advocating induction, in fact limited their own investigation of society very much to the deduction of specifics from known general principles and laws.

Marx's approach resembles that of Pareto: it blends deductive and inductive strategies. As chapter 4 described, Marx derived his sociological theory from a more general system of philosophical assumptions which has been labeled historical materialism. This stressed the importance of economic activity, the ubiquity of conflict centered on that activity, the dialectic tensions for change in societal arrangements, and the developmental thrust in human history. All these emphases may be regarded as general principles or laws of society which Marx brought to the study of history, and from which he proceeded deductively in the analysis of events. From these principles he arrived at his concepts of class and class relations.

Economic life has several facets, Marx pointed out. For example, a series of cooperative activities in society are a consequence of the demands of the economic institution. One of the most crucial facets of the economy, however, is a divisive rather than an integrative dynamic. This centers on the *means of production,* the resources essential to the productive effectiveness of economic life (such as land, physical plant, and money). In complex societies men do not all relate in identical ways to the means of production. In particular, men can be divided into two categories: those who own the means of production, and those who, while dependent on those means, are nevertheless non-owners. This basic variation produces social classes. The two fundamental classes, eternally in tension with each other, are those of owners and non-owners. Each class is internally differentiated into subcomponents of a class. For example, in modern society, small-scale peasants, large landowners, industrialists, merchants, and financiers are all elements of the "owner" or capitalist class.

In his practice of sociological investigation, social classes and their relationships to each other are Marx's major analytic variables. His concept of classes, and some of their most general characteristics (like the tension in their relationship to each other), were deduced from his general laws of social life. The details of class and class relationships in particular societies or particular historical epochs are not, however, specified by the general theory. These details remain a matter for empirical investigation, and on the basis of such investigation one can then proceed to build up inductively to "middle-range" explanations of particular events.

Comte, Spencer, Marx and Pareto all wished sociology to bring a scientific perspective to all the recorded data about man's life in society. Their confidence in such an ambitious scheme rested first on their belief that societies operate in terms of natural laws, the discovery of which would greatly simplify the task of sociology. Second they had faith in the continuities between scientific fields, and felt that they could use existing scientific truths as a means to understand societal organization. Organismic or mechanical imagery led all four men to view societies as "social systems." Comte, Spencer and Marx drew on evolutionary theory to create theses about social development. Marx used his own "scientific" theory of historical materialism to derive concepts of social class and societal conflict. All four men felt that sociologists could proceed deductively from such general scientific "truths" to the development of sociological theory.

The Search for Empirical Indicators

A different tactic was adopted by those who felt that sociology should take a limited focus, either on culture or on association. To these men culture or association had empirical referents. The sociologist must initially concentrate on these. Accurate knowledge of these referents would then facilitate a more extensive development of sociological theory. Durkheim, Simmel, Weber, and Mead all subscribed to this approach. Each man had a different unit on which he felt one must initially concentrate: Durkheim spoke of social facts, Simmel of social forms, Weber of social action, Mead of the social act. A somewhat different approach to research strategy is associated with each term. But the more general tactic is the same. One must first know the unit, then build to knowledge of the more complex. They stressed an inductive approach in contrast to the deductive emphasis of the thinkers described in the last section. Briefly, we will now look at what each man meant by his particular "crucial variable." Since Weber and Mead must closely overlap on this point, we will look at them first.

The Study of Action Weber's definition of social action, and his conviction that sociological explanation starts with knowledge of social action, are natural developments out of his focus on culture and his belief that culture operates primarily in the world view of the actors in a situation. The unit of analysis, he felt, is a simple unit of social action, that is, a simple behavioral sequence carried out by an individual. Behavior is broadly defined to include both internal and external processes, passive acquiescence, and even the failure to act. But essential to the definition of social action is a requirement that the behavior have some subjective significance to the person initiating it— it must *mean* something to the actor. The sociologist is not interested, empirically, in the pure reflex. Weber believed that in the meanings which actors attach to their behavior lie a major explanation of that behavior; this part of the explanation of behavior is precisely where the sociologist is to be the expert. Action must also have another characteristic if it is to be studied by the sociologist: part of its subjective dimension must involve the actor's awareness of and adjustment to other acting individuals. This is what makes the action social. The unit of analysis on which the sociologists must concentrate as he begins his interpretive task is a unit of social action, involving the individual, his behavioral sequence, the meanings he attaches to that sequence, and his perception of other individuals. In this knot of primary variables lies all the clues for understanding culture and major cultural epochs.

Mead also wanted social science to begin its analysis by concentrating on units of behavior—"acts" is his term. "The act" he said, "is the fundamental datum in social science."[31] He too defined behavior broadly to include both overt behavior and subjective experience, or as he termed it, covert behavior. "(The act) has both an inner and outer phase, an internal and an external aspect."[32] Like Weber, his chief concern was with the explication of the internal processes of an act, with the meanings and symbols manipulated by the actor. And even more than Weber, Mead's subjective dimension of behavior must include awareness of other acting individuals, for the social scientist studies the relationship between the actor and his social environment, i.e., the group.

The differences between Weber's "social actions" and Mead's "act" are, however, as important as the similarities. Weber's image of the acting individual rests on the assumption of a straightforward mean-end paradigm: the behavior of an actor is prompted by some goal which he has in mind, and involves the selection of behavioral tactics for achieving that goal. This assumption is very evident from the categories which Weber developed for classifying action in terms of its subjective significance. One kind of action is rational action, which seeks to maximize one's chances of achieving as many desired ends as possible, and which selects means that balance the greatest amount of efficiency possible with the least amount of costs. Another category is value-based action in which the actor pursues a single goal, regardless of other possible goals; means are chosen which maximize the actor's chances of achieving that end, regardless of costs. Then there is traditional action which rests on the conviction that certain established behavioral sequences are legitimate or sacred; repetition of this sanctified and customary sequence becomes the goal of the actor. Finally, there is emotional action, which is his residual, least explored category, the category in which the means-ends pattern does not operate clearly and the actor's behavior is propelled by some emotion seeking release.[33]

The study of social action in terms of its subjective significance is, as Weber interpreted it, primarily a study of motivation. What does the actor want? Why does he go about things this way rather than some other way? If we can understand these things from the actor's point of view, we can understand a behavioral sequence, and by aggregating and elaborating on these types of understanding, we can evenutally begin to know a particular culture or historical epoch.

Mead was much less interested in motivation than Weber was. Mead's concern, after all, was not so much with culture as with the relationship between actor and group and the consequences of this association for subjective experience and overt behavior. Weber gave awareness of the group a part in his analysis of social action; for Mead this awareness of the group and relationship to the group became central. The actual motivation behind an actor's behavior becomes secondary or is assumed to be generated by and evolved through this relationship. Mead's questions are: How does the actor perceive his social environment? What are the cues it sends out to him? How does his experience and behavior evolve in this ongoing exchange with his group? Just as Weber concentrated on motivation, Mead focused on communication as a many-faceted, dynamic, and constant process of overt behavior and subjective experiences. In Weber's basic unit of social action, the actor is highlighted, admittedly against a backdrop of other individuals, in a somewhat solitary quest for some future goal. In Mead's social act, the actor is emmeshed in a pulsating network of symbolic communication. His behavior evolves and his future goals pale before his concern with effective relationships with his social environment, here and now.

The Study of Facts Despite these differences, both Mead and Weber were emphatic that the initial building block of sociological explanation must focus on an individual's *subjective* processes. By so doing they created a problem which has continued to bedevil the field. The wish to develop an empirical basis for sociology motivated Durkheim's statements about "social facts," his basic analytic unit. Although Durkheim, like Weber, believed that sociologists must study culture, he was insistent that "collective representations" (as he labeled it) are real and eminently study-able. As a scientist, one has to seek the empirical referents of these group ideas. One must and can locate material "things" which are particularly social and embody these shared ideas. For convenience these things are called social facts. In order to learn about the nature of social reality, the sociologists must collect, classify, measure and analyze these facts.

But how does one isolate such facts from the vast aggregate of material things available for study? In his *Rules of Sociological Method,* Durkheim tried to lay down guidelines. One must first of all look for things which influence the individual's behavior, factors which coerce or constrain him to follow a particular sequence of action. These things exert their influence regardless of the individual's particular wishes or whims. For much of his life he may accept these constraints and appear to act spontaneously along a particular line. But one ought not to be deceived by this apparent spontaneity. There are social or group-generated reasons for the choice of one kind of behavior over another, and one can always find situations where the individual attempts to resist these constraints, only to find himself forced to conform by society. Some material constraints of this type may be biological or physical, given by the natural environment: a particular climate or terrain, a sudden storm or earthquake. These are not the sociologist's data. Nor is he concerned with strictly psychological processes: the constraints exercised by the mechanics of perception or learning, for example, or some particular interest or emotion unique to an individual. Social facts are ultimately exterior to the individual; that is, there is no need for these constraints to be built into the consciences of each group member. In the case of any particular member, a social fact may only be part of his environment, something he has to come to terms with, whether or not he personally accepts them. One is looking for "ways of acting, thinking, and feeling external to an individual, and endowed with a power of coercion by reason of which they control him."[34] Take, for example, the legal system of a society, both its civil and its criminal laws; or the religious precepts of a group which enjoin certain rituals, or more fundamentally, make one either a part of an ongoing community or an isolate in search of a personal God. Look at the rigid routines of military life, or the pervasive effects of particular pedagogical practices. All these are social facts which Durkheim himself analyzed and studied. He mentioned others: customs, beliefs, symbols of communication, moral maxims, and social currents of enthusiasm or anger which periodically sweep a society.

Durkheim, the positivist, felt far more urgently than Weber or Mead the need for sociology to approximate the empirical precision which the natural sciences were already achieving. This urgency prompted his emphasis on social facts as the building block of scientific sociology, and the social facts do indeed present us with entities which are more discrete and "material" than the social action or social act variables.

The Study of Forms Finally we come to Simmel's stress on "social forms" as the building blocks of sociological analysis. Something of Durkheim's concern to avoid consideration of individual motives, interests, and drives is also to be found in Simmel's articulation of the "social forms" concern. Simmel, however, was prompted not by Durkheim's desire for "hard data," but by the conviction that society is to be found only in the interactions *between* individuals, and that it is possible to isolate and analyze these interactions apart from the particular motives and interests which bring individuals into association. Together with all the variables aggregated in historical societies, we have the fact that men are constantly in interaction; sociology is distinguished by its particular perspective which seeks to isolate interaction *per se* and to describe, classify, and explain it. Amid the flux of interaction the trained sociological eye will be able to detect certain patterns, sequences of interaction which recur in countless situations. These are the social forms, the "hardest" substances in the fluctuating interactional net, and this is where the sociologist must begin his empirical work. A form is a recurring interaction sequence.

From Simmel's perspective, identifying forms only with major institutions like religious or economic organization is extremely limited and static. Far more fascinating are the fixities of interaction on which society is not so well informed: patterns of domination and subordination, competition, imitation, or the formation of cliques and parties. These one can find in all organizations—families and friendship groups, communities, business organizations, and churches. These repeated processes are the dynamic core of sociological interest. Whatever the motives that bring men together—survival, salvation, affection, greed—these interactional forms emerge again and again. And as they emerge they absorb men's energies and interests into the perpetuation of the interaction sequence itself: over and above the energies and interests directed to specific individual goals. Social forms are characterized by reciprocal orientations in the actors, though the amount of reciprocity varies, providing an important criterion for classifying forms. Some forms are bound up with the real individual interests of daily life, other forms are simply play, ritualistically pursuing association in and of itself.

Simmel was never really comfortable with the concept of social forms. He said frequently that an abstract description of them is unsatisfactory, and his own such descriptions were clumsy. But what he was reaching for was a concept of structures in interaction, structures which, since they are behavior, are dynamic, structures which though frequently unremarked as such by those involved in the behavior, explain much of the tough resilience of social life. The sociologist must begin here with his study of the social. By forcing the sociologist to think about *behavior* as it actually occurs, Simmel was presenting an idea which contrasts with Durkheim's interest in *social conventions* which influence behavior, and also with Weber's and Mead's concern with man's *subjective orientations* to social life. Each of these factors has a place in present-day sociology's conception of its subject matter.

Images of Society

What images of society did these early sociologists really have, if we assemble all the bits and pieces? For Comte and Spencer, there was Society, the distilled essence of all actual historical societies, ideal yet real, and a product of Nature. Society is the phenomenon of man's existence in an aggregate. All actual societies are subsumable by Society, they each illustrate aspects of Society; yet Society in fact emerges as something very much like Western society and its history. Society has a clear time dimension. It appeared at a particular moment in the history of the universe, it has slowly and marvelously developed, and it moves towards a time, now not too far distant, when it will achieve its perfect state, the happiness of all its human members. The details of this development are there in the record, clear if one knows how to interpret the facts. Society has an internal structure, has had and will have it throughout its development. It consists of an intricately interconnected set of institutions—family, politics, religion, and so on—each of which supports and relies on all the others. The further Society has developed, the greater has become this interconnectedness. Marx's image of society is broadly similar, but the motifs of conflict and tension, and the centrality of the economy and social classes give a different texture to his picture of society.

Pareto saw many societies, historically and geographically dispersed, each apparently very complex; a huge aggregate of behavior and ideas, infinitely variable. And at the center of it, or at least at the center of his concern, is Western society in its various historical phases, and Italian society, again varying over time. But behind the facade of chaotic variation, Pareto perceived a degree of sameness. There are certain constant factors—environment, time past, other societies, and above all human nature. The relationships between these constants, though numerous, occur universally, and the resulting processes in social life also occur universally. The sociologist has as his task discovering these universal processes and relationships and describing the system which lies behind the superficial variation of historical societies.

Weber's view contains many societies, also located through time and space, but he had no belief in an underlying sameness. In fact, he saw the thrust behind sociological curiosity as residing in the endless variety of societies. Everywhere one looks one sees variety. Everywhere one finds men behaving differently (and sometimes from our modern Western viewpoint, bizarrely). Scrutiny of the facts can show endless ways of dealing with the problems of survival, and an infinite wealth of ideas. The sociological problem is to make sense of this variety, first of all to oneself, and then to one's audience in the West. To wish for some overall standard pattern to it all is futile: man is extremely capable of finding different answers to common problems, and problems can vary widely.

Weber listed only a few universals of which we can be sure. One is that in all societies men act in the pursuit of goals; another way of phrasing this is to say that wherever they are and whatever they may be doing men's behavior generally makes sense to them. Another certainty is that within each society things will be related (to a degree). That is, something that appears mysterious in an unfamiliar society will be the result of other, perhaps equally mysterious, processes in other areas of life in that society, and the overall picture will, once we can decipher it, have a degree of consistency (though never perfect consistency—societies are never closed, perfectly self-renewing entities). The sociologist is just an outsider looking in on the wide variety of behaviors in a culture. The key to understanding the culture is to find out why people within it act the way they do. What goals do they see themselves pursuing? Why do they decide to pursue those goals in certain ways? How do they perceive their environment and what effect does this perception have on their other ideas and behavior? Their behavior makes sense to them; the sociologist must find out what sense. Once he does this he will be able not only to see the pattern in the behavior of a society, but also to understand it.

Durkheim, like Comte, Spencer, and Pareto, had a certain common image of all societies, though not the societal prototype of Comte and Spencer, nor the constants in concrete social relationships of Pareto. Rather he felt that, in all societies, behavior will have some of a common pattern because all men have to conform to certain constant pressures. Some of these pressures are given by nature, others by the human psyche, but most important are the pressures generated by aggregated living itself, rules for behavior which the phenomenon of group life spontaneously generates. From one perspective society might even be viewed as a network of such rules. Knowledge of these rules gives the scientist considerable predictive ability in regards to human behavior. The sociologist has as his task the discovery of these rules. There will be many material cues to the rules in a society. Durkheim saw both the varied complexity of historical societies, and the skeletal underpinnings in each of a network of socially generated rules for behavior; his concern was with the latter.

Simmel and Mead had images of society which are similar and fairly easy to envision. Both saw numerous, initially undifferentiated individuals bound together by invisible but very numerous threads of interaction—behavior which is oriented to the other actors. These networks are constantly changing, yet the more general fact of elaborate interconnectedness is a constant. For both, the sociologist's task was to "see" those invisible but real linkages: Simmel wanted to discover the patterns in those threads of interaction, while Mead's focus was on the links between those patterns and the individuals originating them. For both, the social process, while it has internal developmental sequences, was something considered without sharp historical time or geographical space referents. Yet one has the impression that their unconscious referents were the Western societies they knew well.

Summary and Conclusions

This chapter has explored some of the most general positions and assumptions of earlier sociologists as they outlined the nature of the sociological task. Table 2 summarizes the major points of the chapter, showing clusters of agreement and points of disagreement in the discussion of sociology's subject matter. Certain key words and phrases have been italicized. The chapter dwelt at some length on these. The student should remember them and understand their place in the first definition of sociology's subject matter.

Although the material reviewed here is of too general a nature to relate easily to the sociopolitical events described in chapter 3, it is very easy to link the substance of this discussion to the information in chapter 4 about the intellectual climate of the period. The impact of positivism is evident at several points: in the general consensus that a scientific study of social phenomena was possible and in the commitment to empirical procedures; in the quest for universal generalizations, which only Weber avoided; and in the belief in a social system of enduring structures and relationships which Comte, Spencer, Pareto, Marx and, to a lesser degree, Durkheim, all espoused. Equally apparent is the influence of developmental and evolutionary thought, particularly, but not exclusively, in the perspectives of the earliest members of the group. For Comte and Spencer this blended with the conservative belief that society, which has miraculously developed over the ages, should not be altered in a piecemeal and abrupt way. The relationship between pragmatism and Mead's view of sociology's subject matter is also very clear.

Most fascinating of all is the effect of idealism on these thinkers. Weber, with his concern for configurations of meaning, for historically unique situations, and for the individual's perceptions, most obviously showed the influence of this philosophical school. But in Simmel's view

TABLE 2 : Views on the Subject Matter of Sociology

I. Sociology attempts a/the scientific study of social life— Comte, Spencer, Marx, Durkheim, Weber, Simmel, Mead, Pareto	
II. 1. Sociology is the climax of scientific development—Comte, Spencer, Marx	Sociology is a new and aspiring science—Durkheim, Weber, Simmel, Mead, Pareto
2. Sociology will draw on and synthesize date from many other scientific fields—Comte, Spencer, [Marx]°, Pareto	Sociology's task is primarily to be analytic of the social data it collects—Durkheim, Weber, Simmel, Mead
3. Many sociological principles can be deduced from known scientific and philosophical truths, e.g., evolution, materialism—Comte, Spencer, Marx, [Pareto]°	Most sociological principles will be derived inductively from the empirical study of *social facts* (Durkheim); *social forms* (Simmel); *social actions/acts* (Weber, Mead)
III. Sociologists study all the manifest characteristics of society and their relationships as a *system*—Comte, Spencer, Marx, Pareto	Sociologists study only certain, distinctively "social" characteristics of society; these are *cultural-normative* phenomena (Durkheim); *culturally determined perspectives* (Weber); *interactional patterns* (Simmel); interactional patterns, especially *communication* patterns (Mead)
IV. Sociology's primary concern is with objective or manifest social processes—Comte, Spencer, Marx, Pareto, Durkheim, Simmel	Sociology's concern is equally with *objective*-manifest and *subjective*-psychological processes, so long as they are related to social life—Mead, Weber
V. Sociology seeks to generalize from sociohistorical data to (a) the evolutionary development of society—Comte, Spencer, Marx; (b) the universal characteristics of social life—Durkheim, Pareto, Mead, [Simmel]°	Sociology seeks to understand 'historically real' social situations —Weber

[   ]°—these individuals do not fit neatly into one or other category of the particular dichotomy. but tend to bridge or span both viewpoints.

99

of sociology as a perspective in its own right, and in his and Mead's interest in the subjective orientations of social actors to each other, we have other evidence of the impact of idealism. Nowhere are the consequences of this viewpoint for sociology more strange than in Durkheim's views on sociology's subject matter. Durkheim was torn between his positivistic conviction that sociology must study material objective phenomena and his idealistic belief that the meaningful aspects of social life are products of mind: consensus on norms. This explains the curious problem that surrounds his concept of "social facts," which appears so clearcut in its formal definition but which in actuality is a most elusive guideline for sociology. Yet Durkheim's difficulty is only a microcosm of the general difficulty which emerged in this early effort to clarify sociology's subject matter. Most of the later members of the group reviewed here were attempting an uneasy fusion of positivistic techniques and the idealist concern with mind. None of them satisfactorily resolved the problems inherent in this fusion. Instead the problems were passed along to later sociology.

A detailed comparison of the ideas of these earlier sociologists with those prevalent in contemporary American sociology is beyond the scope of this book: indeed it is subject matter for a book in its own right. At this point, however, it seems appropriate to compare the two periods briefly. The impressions we get from a quick overview of the two situations is that none of the earlier points of view have really completely vanished. Instead one sees different emphases: the retreat and blurring of some of the older notions, and the advance of others to positions of greater dominance. Predictably, the explicit evolutionary and organicist extravagances of Comte and Spencer have disappeared, though many of the implications of these analogies are still with us. Less predictably, perhaps, one finds a retreat from much of the Weberian position—from his stress on economic-related phenomena, on cultural uniqueness, on seeking the "whole picture" by historical and comparative analysis. In contemporary sociology we find instead the dominance of the positivist position, best illustrated in the preceding discussion of Durkheim's stance. We find the same quest for universal relationships in social data, and an aspiration towards lawlike statements, systematic theory, and, ultimately, prediction.

One finds that the position that sociology must limit its initial analysis to something peculiarly social has become the more usual stance in recent sociology. But the critics of this "academic sociology," those who wish sociology to return to the primary concern with society in all its complexity, are a numerous group both within and outside the discipline. One peculiar inversion, however, has been the acceptance by many present day "academic sociologists" of the social system notions evident in the writings of Comte, Spencer, and Pareto. The view that we must now build from our "peculiarly social" elements—roles, information flow, etc.—to a grasp of the "social system" is very prevalent today. And the critics who wish sociology to return to a primary focus on actual social events criticize social system notions as artificial —and academic.

The old divisions between the stress on cultural factors and the stress on associational processes have again, on the whole, been formally abandoned. In practice, however, one tends to find that many of the differences between "schools" in contemporary sociology spring from the same differential emphases on cultural or interactional variables. One finds almost everywhere an acceptance of the role of subjective or covert processes in either the cultural or the associational aspects of social life. Sociology has, in other words, relinquished the more dogmatic Durkheimian claims of exteriority, and accepted what both Weber and Mead stressed—the crucial role of social psychological variables in sociological explanation. This has not made the task of investigation any easier, especially since sociology at the same time has moved toward Durkheim's positivistic stress on "hard data." But the criterion of exteriority proved to be both empirically and theoretically unworkable; as we shall see, even Durkheim gradually though unwillingly moved away from it.

One could go on with this comparison, pointing out the survival, almost intact in some circles, of the Meadian approach, the pervasiveness of Weber's means-ends paradigm, the new labels for the old concepts of social action, social forms and social facts, but the detailed comparison of the two epochs is not our main task here. Our concern is, rather, with the earlier period, and we now turn to another aspect of early sociology.

NOTES

1. In the former category see the early chapters of Auguste Comte, *The Positive Philosophy* (London: Chapman, 1853); Herbert Spencer, *Principles of Sociology* (New York: Appleton, 1890); Vilfredo Pareto, *The Mind and Society* (New York: Harcourt, 1935); in the later category there is Max Weber, *The Methodology of the Social Sciences*, trans. Edward Shils (New York: Free Press, 1949); Georg Simmel, "Grundfragen die Soziologie," published as Part I of Kurt Wolff, *The Sociology of Georg Simmel* (New York: Free Preee, 1950); and Herbert Spencer, *The Study of Sociology* (Ann Arbor: University of Michigan Press, 1961).

2. Comte, *Positive Philosophy*, volume I, p. 27 Italics added.

3. Emile Durkheim, *The Division of Labor in Society*, Trans. ed. (Glencoe, Ill.: Free Press, 1964), p. 32.

4. Simmel, in Wolff, *Sociology of Georg Simmel*, p. 23.

5. Weber, *Methodology of the Social Sciences*, p. 72.

6. Pareto, *Mind and Society*, p. 16.

7. Max Weber, *The Theory of Social and Economic Organization*, trans. Talcott Parsons (Glencoe, Ill.: Free Press, 1947), pp. 89-90.

8. Spencer, *Principles of Sociology*, p. 53.

9. Comte, *Positive Philosophy*, p. 77.

10. Comte's thesis on the hierarchy of the sciences is still well remembered. Sciences can be categorized either as applied, or as theoretical, and the theoretical sciences further subdivide into descriptive and abstract types. The abstract sciences can be hierarchically arranged so that each stratum draws part of its knowledge from the strata below it, but at the same time deals with more complex phenomena. By these criteria astronomy comes at the bottom of the hierarchy, dealing with the most simple phenemenon. Above it can be ranked the various physical and natural sciences, with biology placed highest. At the apex of this pyramid is the new field of sociology, drawing on all the earlier sciences but at the same time dealing with the most complex, most concrete phenemena. *Positive Philosophy*, volume 1, chapter 2.

11. Pareto, *Mind and Society*, p. 3.

12. Simmel, in Wolff, *The Sociology of Georg Simmel*, p. 4.

13. Weber, *Methodology*, p. 71.

14. Durkheim, *Division of Labor*, pp. 338, 350, 368.

15. Emile Durkheim, *The Rules of Sociological Method*, trans. Sarah Solavy and John Mueller, ed. George Catlin (Glencoe, Ill.: Free Press, 1950), p. vi.

16. Emile Durkheim, *Suicide*, trans. John Spaulding and George Simpson (Glencoe, Ill.: Free Press, 1951), pp. 313-18.

17. Emile Durkheim, *The Elementary Forms of Religious Life* (New York: Free Press, 1915), p. 31.

18. Weber, *Methodology*, p. 67.

19. Ibid., p. 74.

20. Ibid., p. 81.

21. Ibid., p. 64.

22. This difference between Weber and Durkheim is discussed more fully in chapter 8.

23. Simmel, in Wolff, *Sociology of Georg Simmel*, pp. 9-11.

24. Ibid.

25. For a more detailed discussion of these characteristics in Simmel's work see Donald Levine, "The Structure of Simmel's Social Thought," in *Essays on Sociology, Philosophy and Aesthetics by Georg Simmel* et. al., ed. Kurt Wolff (New York Harper Torchbooks, 1959).

26. Spencer, *Principles of Sociology*, p. 436.

27. Ibid., pp. 436-50.

28. Pareto, *Mind and Society*, pp. 1433, 1448, 1456, 1543, 1567, 1624.

29. Ibid., p. 1433.

30. Ibid., p. 1435. For a detailed discussion of Pareto's social system ideas see Joseph Lopreato, *Vilfredo Pareto: Selections from his Treatise* (New York: Cromwell, 1965). The reference is to Lopreato's introduction to the book.

31. George Herbert Mead, *Mind, Self, Society* (Chicago: University of Chicago Press, 1934), p. 8.

32. Ibid.

33. Weber, *The Theory*, p. 93.

34. Durkheim, *The Rules*, p. 3.

6

Man and
Society

During the process of delineating sociology's subject matter, the early
sociologists repeatedly struggled with a particular conceptual problem.
Whatever they chose to focus on—society, culture, or interaction—
they believed that their concern as sociologists was with something
other than an aggregate of human beings. Yet they saw themselves
either generalizing from the behavior of such beings, or using their sociological perspective to explain that behavior, or both. Conceptually,
men (or man) stood in some relationship to sociology's subject matter.
The problem was to specify the nature of that relationship. This problem was made acute for them because they lived, as we do, in a culture which treats individual human beings as the self-directing, dynamic core of social and historical events. Did they choose to accept
this belief? On what basis might they question it? Again and again they
come back to the cluster of questions which this general problem implies.

This chapter reviews the early discussion of the relationship of man
to sociology's subject matter. It is organized around three themes
which recur in the debate: (1) Does man have any traits which are
not socially derived, and if so what are they and what do they imply
for social life? (2) In what way does society influence man, and
vice versa? (3) What status does the individual, as a discrete and
unique unit of the human species, have in a system of sociological
explanation?

In the process of answering these questions, the earlier sociologists clarified even further their definition of sociology. They developed certain concepts and hypotheses which have come down to the present. They explored with great thoroughness a problem which still exists for sociology, and which continues to interest students of the field. Both because of its importance to these earlier thinkers and of its relevance to us, the general question of the relationship of man to "society" deserves our attention.

Human Nature and Society

Are there any traits of behavior or personality common to the human species, yet not developed out of their experiences of society? What might such traits be? These are the questions to be explored here. In contemporary society the chief source of such assumptions has come from Freud's explorations of the human libido, but in recent years there have been an increasing number of competing theses such as the argument about man's innate aggressiveness, his basic impulse towards proprietorship (the "territorial impulse"), his physiological intolerance for high densities of spatial crowding or for saturation by sensory stimuli, and so on. All these ideas, except those of Freud, have only recently become considerations for sociologists. Even Freud's ideas were not available to early sociology. Instead they were affected by two other competing interpretations of basic human nature.

Background to the Discussion

The first input was the inheritance from eighteenth-century thought. The seventeenth and eighteenth centuries were characterized by a particular type of optimism about man and his future. This is when some of the major developments in scientific knowledge occurred, and when the belief in progress (both in knowledge and in wisdom) first developed. The period has been labeled the Age of Reason because of the intensity of its faith in man's intellectual powers. The Age of Reason reached its apogee in the eighteenth-century Enlightenment in France and England, when an intensely productive output in the general field of social philosophy directed itself towards criticism of the existing social situation and development of ideal models for social organization. This criticism provided the basic philosophical underpinnings of both the American and the French Revolutions, and garbed thus in revolutionary rhetoric, it reached the period that concerns us.

The Age of Reason takes a definite position on the question of innate human nature, a position shaped by the transitionary status of the period between the earlier "ages of faith" and the secularism of industrial society. While denying the divinity of man's origins, and the effects of such origins on his basic character, thinkers of this period could not completely abandon the belief that there was an elemental kernel of inalienable human nature, mysteriously derived and pervasively influential on man's individual behavior and on his history. Enlightenment thinkers placed their concept of "natural man" against the image of divinely created man, and their belief in man's potential rationality in opposition to the religious belief in man's soul.

The eighteenth-century image of "natural man" weaves through nineteenth century sociology almost as clearly as Freudian man has a place in twentieth century social thought. A great deal of energy went into refuting or qualifying the theme of "natural man." Yet thought about man's basic characteristics was inescapably influenced by the thesis. Natural man is potentially a rational being, capable of elaborate personality development and self-sustaining stability. These qualities are given him by nature, and can emerge and survive outside the existing elaborateness of society and culture. Indeed, the elaborateness of society and culture as it presently exists blocks man's basic drive for self-fulfillment, foisting on him an unnatural servility and irrationality. Enlightenment thinkers argued for an elaborate system of innate human traits, derived from "nature" rather than from society. Chief among these qualities was the potential for rationality. To date the relationship between these traits and society had been one of tension and conflict, with social conditions operating to thwart man's basic nature. But human nature might yet triumph over society, working in it to create a social situation more congruent with man's innate qualities.

The second input into the sociological perspective is a nineteenth-century one, derived from both biology and psychology. The nineteenth century witnessed pioneering and major explorations of man's physiological structure in both fields. Nineteenth-century psychology was for a long time primarily oriented towards mapping out this structure. In the field of biology, the most outstanding example of this interest is to be found in the theory of biological evolution.[1] The thrust of such work was to stress not the higher and mysteriously derived intellectual capacities of man, but rather the elemental mundane traits which were rooted in his biological structure: the sensations, drives, needs, and instincts which originated in his animal nature, and which showed his relationship to the other animal species from which he had evolved. This more diffuse input does not lend itself to the terse summarization possible with eighteenth century "natural man." It emerged piecemeal from the separate researches of many scien-

tists; in many cases it was only the preliminary stages of work that
would be continued in the next century. But the general direction is
clear enough. Man has an elemental nature which has physiological
roots. This nature is displayed in the areas of feeling and emotion. If
this perspective has an ancestry, it is earlier social philosophies about
man's structure of "sentiments." The major strength of the position,
however, was not its philosophy but rather its substantiation by detailed
scientific work.

An Evolutionary Thesis

Of the men whose ideas concern us, only one, Herbert Spencer, argued that men, at the basic non-socialized level, are not all alike, and
the variations between types of men may be greater than any common
characteristics. This thesis springs from his own unconditional acceptance of evolutionary theory, and in particular of the Larmarckian
belief in fairly specific and (from the time perspective of evolutionary
change) fairly rapid modification in the structure of organisms in response to particular discrete environmental pressures.

> Faculties and powers of all orders grow by exercise, dwindle when not
> used; and that alteration of nature descends to posterity . . . . the evi-
> dence of hereditary is overwhelming. The Hindu and the Englishman,
> the Greek and the Dutchman have acquired undeniable contrasts of
> nature, *physical and psychical,* which can be ascribed to nothing but the
> continuous effect of circumstances, material, moral, social, on their ac-
> tivities and therefore on their constitutions.[2]

This was basically an argument for racial variation in human nature,
though the concept of race is imprecisely worked out, and tends to
fuse with evidence of cultural and national diversity. Spencer argued
that within any single historical society "innate" traits were to a considerable degree similar. There might be some class, sex, and individual
variation, but the similarities between members of a single society
would be more important than these differences. By way of contrast
the innate characteristics of the members of different societies varied
widely. Spencer went on to argue that the types of innate characteristics evidenced in different societies could be ranked on a continuum
from primitive to civilized. Basic human nature was an evolving phenomenon. Racial differences in "physical and psychical constitutions"
marked stages in this evolution. These mutations were observable in
both emotional and intellectual character.

The mental development of the human animal . . . becomes increasingly special and complex. Though this chiefly exemplifies intellectual prog-- ress it is equally the law of emotional progress . . . . Primitive man is deficient in complex emotions. His consciousness differs from that of the civilized by consisting more of sensations and the simple representative feelings directly associated with them, and less of the involved feelings. [3]

It was an ingenious approach to the debate on human rationality; a "yes" and "no" answer. Primitive man was constitutionally incapable of either the intellectual or emotional states associated with rationality. But civilized man, that is modern Western man, had evolved physiologi- cally to the point where he did have such capacities. In the future his descendants might be wholly rational.

Within the group of sociologists whom we are studying there was little support for a thesis of currently evolving human nature. Only Comte allowed for it, and he denied both the scope and importance of the process. Although he admitted that "there seems to be a gradual and slow improvement in human nature" he felt that this improve- ment occurred only "within narrow limits." [4] In most respects man's physiological evolution was complete, so that one might conceive of a general nature common to the species. For all the others in the group this was a theoretical starting point: elemental human nature was ev- erywhere the same. The "psychical" differences observable among men of different societies had other roots than in genetic structure.

Modifications on "Rational Man"

Only Lester Ward picked up the eighteenth century belief in man's rationality almost unaltered. His views, however, did not arise out of a deliberate acceptance of Enlightenment philosophy, but rather from a conscious effort to qualify Spencerian sociology. Spencer's position led to highly deterministic conclusions. Only long-term genetic trans- formation would produce a truly moral man and a fully good society. It was foolhardy to rush into programs of reform and change. The only probable outcome of such plans would be to slow the processes of evolution, with disastrous consequences for man's future. Ward, re- formist in outlook and optimistic about his society's chances for rapid social amelioration, could not accept such a requirement for passivity and submission. Nor, with his training in and respect for the natural sciences, could he reject the evolutionary thesis entirely, though he did not view man as currently evolving. His way out of this quandry was to modify the Spencerian thesis of evolution.

Ward felt Spencer overlooked a process Ward called *creative synthesis*. The evidence on evolution seemed to show that at various moments in the overall process existing elements suddenly combined in such a way as to produce some wholly new factor or structure in the biological record. At such moments the evolutionary process shifted gears, bursting suddenly into a whole new phase. Evolution was not simply a linear progression, but a steplike series of stages, each new step marking the appearance of one of these new phenomena. One such crucial leap forward had occurred when an organism possessed of intellect had appeared. This was man. The implications for evolution were that whereas all previous species had adapted blindly through natural selection, the moment had finally come when adaptation and the advancement this implied were possible through deliberate action and strategy. The pace of evolution had quickened. The implication of creative synthesis for the sociologist's concern about human nature was that man was an organism physiologically possessed of intellect, and intellect was very much like the Enlightenment notion of rationality: it implied powers of cognition and reasoning, and the potential for ameliorative planning and action.

Variants on the theme of rational man appear at other strategic points in early sociological thought. Marx used certain features of this thesis in his own model of basic human nature, even though he saw himself as opposed to the eighteenth-century stress on the importance of ideas in shaping man's history. Marx saw as fundamental in human nature the fact that man is a producer. Man was the only animal species that deliberately worked on his natural environment to procure the things he needed for his survival. Although this did not imply anything at all about man as a contemplative or philosophical being, it did mean that man was a problem solver, endowed with those faculties which allowed him to wrestle with his environment in pursuit of what he defined as his needs. There was not much distance between this and Ward's image of the organism possessed of intellect and capable of deliberately adapting to the problems presented by his situation. The difference was that Marx set narrower limits to the range of this problem solving ability, placing it within the context of economic action, and avoiding the link between the specific problem-solving faculties involved in such action and the more general implications of intellect.

Another variant on the rational man image is found in Max Weber's writings. Instead of the problem-solving, environmentally-oriented economic producer, Weber built into his sociology the assumption of a more diffuse "social actor," one whose behavior ranged over a wide institutional area—religion, recreation, politics, etc. as well as economic life—but who always had reasons for what he did. Man was rational for Weber not in the eighteenth-century sense of doing what was logical or scientifically correct, but in the sense that he pursued goals deliberately. The goals might from the strict scientific sense be pure nonsense, but man was not a mindless automaton. He knew what he wanted, he acted in pursuit of his goal and he selected means which in the context of his life seemed to enhance his chances of getting him where he wanted to go.

> The acting individual weighs the conditions of future development which interests him, which conditions are objectively given as far as his knowledge of reality goes. He mentally rearranges into a causal complex the various possible modes of his own conduct and the consequences which these could be expected to have. He does this in order to decide, in terms of the mentally envisaged possible results, in favor of one or other modes of action appropriate to his goal.[5]

Man was by nature purposive. He acted with more or less explicit conceptualizations of means and ends. The variations in behaviors which one observed were shaped by the varying meaning contexts in which men acted. In this lies the importance of the sociologist's task of investigating real, historically based structures of meaning.

Something very similar was assumed by the symbolic interactionists Mead and Cooley. Man was essentially a creature with a mind, and their view of the mental process was very similar to Weber's. Mind is man's ability to anticipate the future, to weigh alternative courses of action, to envisage the alternative outcomes, and to make decisions accordingly. In contrast to Weber, and more like Ward, Mead was anxious to assert that the phenomenon of mind or intellect was physiologically based. He elaborated on the capacities of the human brain. Man was an actor endowed with mind because he was an organism possessed of a particularly complex brain. Again more like Ward than like Weber, the symbolic interactionists linked the functions of mind generally to the adaptive need rather than to the specific, culturally determined goals of Weber's model. And finally, true to pragmatism's orientation, Mead and Cooley conceived of mind as a complex but unitary process, to be analyzed as such, in contrast to Weber's paradigm of fairly discrete goals and means, and his primary interest in the *content* of those factors. But despite the variations, eighteenth-century rational man in his various guises as producer, purposive actor, or minded organism entered the mainstream of sociology from several points, and became part of sociology's conception of reality.

"A Creature of Sentiment"

Out of the group who concern us here the most violent and elaborately stated rebuttal of rational man is to be found in the work of Pareto. Pareto's prime target was rational man, particularly the eighteenth-century and the Marxian versions of rationality. He drew on the alternative theme of biological, animal-like, impulsive man.

Pareto started by asserting that man was by nature nonrational. Most of the time man did things which he knew, in the light of information available to him, could not possibly get him where he wanted to go. Much of the time he did not even know where he wanted to go, acting with no explicit knowledge of the purpose of his activity. Man was propelled not by cognition but by what Pareto called *sentiments*. Man's sentiments provided the underlying dynamic of his personality and behavior. A precise definition of sentiments is difficult, but, broadly speaking, sentiments appear to be innate human tendencies or instincts tied to the biological structure of the human animal. Pareto held that there were several of these innate human sentiments; that the number of such instincts was nevertheless finite; that any human population would contain the full contingent of sentiments, but that these sentiments are unevenly distributed so that any particular individual would be characterized by a preponderance of a few of them. This was the foundation of individual personality. Pareto did not deny that man is at times capable of complete rationality, but he felt that instances of such self-control were rare in everyday life. Man was much more frequently propelled to action by his sentiments, impulses, "instincts."

Pareto undertook an elaborate analysis of man's written output in order to get at the substance of these sentiments. His analysis convinced him that there were certain themes that persist at the core of all cultures regardless of the overlay of detail which may disguise the similarities. These recurring themes he called the *residues*. The residues seemed to him to be the best available empirical indicators to the nature of the sentiments. The residues[6] were

1. *The residue of sex:* Pareto argued that his content analysis showed a recurring interest in all matters sexual. Often, this concern is elaborately disguised, for example, a concern with morality, celibacy, or asceticism.

2. *The residue of personal integrity:* the recurring need to maintain personal equilibrium or ego stability in the face of disorienting pressures from one's environment. Certain affinities seem to exist between Pareto's description and present social psychological views about cognitive dissonance or balance theory.

3. *The residue of sociability:* the need to relate to small groups of meaningful others. Pareto saw as part of this drive the impulse to

expect uniform conduct within the group and to exert pressure to bring this about. This residue fused gregariousness with the conformity theme.

4. *The activity residue:* the need to express or project one's personality or self in some form of activity.

5. *The residue of the persistence of aggregates:* the tendency to invest certain experiences or dimensions of one's environment with personal, emotional significance and then to insist that these things remain unchanged. This was a conservative drive.

6. *The residue of combination:* the drive to relate things to one another, to think about disparate elements in such a way as to see some pattern in them. Involved in this were the needs to synthesize and generalize. It was from this impulse that the possibility of innovative thought arose.

Each of these themes was elaborately subdivided and classified in Pareto's work. Residues indicated the content of the sentiments or drives. This fundamentally non-rational core of motivational energy, not purposiveness or a problem-solving ability, is innate to man.

Although Pareto's exploration of human nature's essential emotionality is particularly elaborate, this image of man was as pervasive in early sociology as the rational model. Comte, for example, argued that in man "the intellectual faculty, if protracted beyond a certain degree, occasions a fatigue which becomes insupportable. Man is by nature incapable of perseverance in thought; by nature he prefers variety in intellectual experience rather than concentration." [7] He dismissed the eighteenth century model as "a chimeral notion of unlimited (human) perfectability." [8] Instead human nature was basically emotional: man was characterized by "the preponderance of the affective (or emotional) over the intellectual faculties, which though less remarkable in man than *in other animals* yet fixes the first essential idea of his true nature." [9] Among these emotions were a spontaneous sociability, the quest for diversion through a variety of experiences, and what may be termed pure egoism—a strong drive to put one's own pleasure and advantage before all other considerations. Even Durkheim, who as we shall see below developed a rather different conception of human nature, was attracted to this last notion, and argued that an insatiable drive for personal gratification is inherent to man. The last quotation from Comte reveals a characteristic common to this perspective: the wish to show the similarities between basic human nature and that of other animals, in contrast to the rationalists' tendency to stress man's uniqueness.

Sumner too described human psychology in terms of recurring needs or drives: self-interest, pleasure seeking, hunger, sex, vanity, and fear. Even Cooley qualified his views on cognitive man, which have already been discussed, by talking of a need for general emotional support, affection, and nurturance that is basic to human nature. Thus decades before the insights and discoveries of Freud reached sociology in the twentieth century, sociology had a school of thought which conceived of man in terms of basic emotional drives such as egoism, the need for others, the sexual impulse, and so on—an alternative to the cognitive being that others were describing.

Other Views of the Controversy

To Simmel man was both cognitive and emotional, and the difference of opinion just discussed was a moot one. This viewpoint emerged from his now famous distinction between *contents* and *forms*. Forms were the recurring patterns of association between individuals, such as power or conflict relationships. Forms were social phenomena. Contents were the whole array of motivational factors which propelled individuals to act. Some of these were broadly rational, in the sense of consisting of calculated interests and purposes. Others were emotional—drives, impulses, inclinations, psychic states, and so on. None of the contents were social products. They were part of the individual's psyche, and presumably rooted in his innate, biologically determined needs, drives, and capabilities. Simmel's point about human nature was that the sociologist did not need to concern himself with elaborately delineating it. His concern was with social things, specifically with social forms. Anything not of the forms could be assumed to be derived from man, and classifiable as contents. This was admittedly a large, complex array of factors. But the sociologist could legitimately assume them to exist, forming the substructure of social life but not actually social forms. He must concentrate on mapping social forms.

The most militantly sociological viewpoint is Durkheim's. As has already been pointed out, Durkheim sided somewhat with the "sentiment" school by ascribing an innate drive for self-gratification to human nature. Apart from this, however, he really did not seem to believe in the concept of innate human traits. "Individual natures are merely indeterminate material."[10] Men possessed certain physiologically determined reflexes and sensations, and such physically determined needs as the need to sleep when physically exhausted. The potential for consciousness resided in these reflexes and sensations. but consciousness itself, the precondition for rationality, was not innate to man. Durkheim also hinted that certain faculties or talents which equip a man for one type of work over another might be inherited, but he did not press the implications of this any further.

Those were the only traits that Durkheim seemed to view as innate human nature. It was a far cry from eighteenth-century rational man or the nineteenth-century problem solver. It was even far removed from the elaborately instinctual creature described by Pareto. Durkheim's position was that almost anything one might think of as characteristic of man was in fact acquired by him from society; hence the apparent congeniality of this viewpoint with professional sociology's claims to importance. However, this stress on the supremacy of social factors seems alien to Western assumptions, even now after more than a century of propagating the "sociological imagination." Stress on social factors was even more alien in Durkheim's time, and this probably accounts for his defensiveness and the isolation of his proposition in early sociology.

Man and Society

How did these various images of human nature affect early sociology's image of its subject matter? Did these traits imply anything about the form and operation of society, or culture, or association? What were the consequences of life in the group for such elemental human characteristics? This section explores these questions.

A simple classificatory principle is adopted for organizing the various answers given by sociologists to the question "What is the relationship between man and society?" Some sociologists seemed to answer that man was dominant over society. Others asserted the man was wholly subordinated by society. And a third category traced the interdependence between man and society. Early sociologists fell into this system as follows:

Dominance	Subordination	Interdependence
Spencer	Comte	Marx
Pareto	Durkheim	Sumner
Ward		Weber
		Simmel
		Mead
		Cooley

A preliminary word of warning: this categorization is simplistic. None of the early sociologists gave an unqualified answer to the hypothetical question raised above. All made concessions to other views. All subscribed in varying degrees to the view of some interdependence between the two clusters of variables. The above classification is made in terms of their primary emphases, and in the interest of organizing a heterogeneous set of opinions. In the descriptions that follow, some of the major concessions made by different sociologists will be incorporated.

Man Dominates Society

Spencer held that genetically determined, innate variations in human nature profoundly affect the structure of the societies which the various types of men organize.

> Societies are aggregates of men . . . be it rudimentary or be it advanced every society displays phenomena that are directly ascribable to the character of its units . . . . physical traits such as degrees of strength, activity, endurance affect the growth and structure of the society . . . . Emotional traits aid or hinder or modify the activities of the society and its developments. Always too (man's) degree of intelligence and 'the tendencies of thought peculiar to him become co-operating causes of social quiescence or social change. [11]

The aggregate of individuals comprising the group was for Spencer a powerful factor in societal processes. Human nature determined social structure.

In qualifying this position slightly, Spencer allocated a degree of autonomy to societal development. He viewed society as another material thing, subject to the general laws of evolution. Intrinsic to it were mechanical pressures for elaboration of structure, and for the fuller utilization of energy. Society was also in relationship with a physical environment which produced certain accommodations in society's organization. Moreover, social arrangements were part of man's environment and hence a factor in his own adaptive development. The flows of influence, however, were in no way equal. Society was built upon human nature, its form rested on a moment-to-moment basis largely determined by that nature, and the modifications it might produce in man were imperceptible except over very long periods of time.

Since human nature evolved, society was also evolving. It was increasingly more moral, more shaped by intelligence, more capable of providing elaborately for the needs of its members. Cross-cultural variation and the major patterns in history were to be understood in these terms. Even some of the more microscopic internal dynamics of a society were shaped by evolving human nature, for Spencer felt that the maturational process of the child (its gradual development from infant to adult) replicated the evolutionary process from primitiveness to the level of civilization achieved by his racial or national group. Likewise there seemed to be a variation of this type between the classes. Much of the ongoing tensions of life could be visualized in these terms.

Pareto also put human nature at the center of his attempt to explain society. Pareto viewed society as a complex system of ongoing behavioral sequences. Although there are many analytic elements in this system, essentially the loci of most of these elements were in individual human beings who initiated the behavioral sequences. To understand society, one had to start with those human beings and their temperaments. It was true that in a scientific laboratory or in a court of law man could exercise the control over sentiment necessary for completely rational behavior. But these were atypical instances of human behavior. The vast mass of everyday occurrences which made most of the texture of social life, as well as the majority of dramatic, far-reaching events such as those in political life, sprang directly from the impulses which were human nature. Impulsive, irrational natural man created society.

Sentiments prompted most of the groupings and parties into which society could be subdivided. They motivated the intellectual products of which man was often so proud. They might even determine what observers claimed to be "national character." For though the sentiments were universal, different populations might be characterized by a preponderance of individuals with a particular personality (configuration of sentiments). In contrast, society did little to alter or curb the sentiments, except for momentarily distracting men from their normal behaviors with religions and other ideologies. Human nature was irrational, and society is eternally and profoundly the same.

In contrast, Ward, who assumed the same direct translation of human traits into social organization, argued that society is rational. Man was the organism with intellect. All societies showed him at work using this faculty in the struggle to survive. The historical record was a record of progress in the application of rationality to the adaptive need, and the pace of such progress had quickened in recent history. Men were now on the verge of removing the obstacles to the development of rationality in their societies, drawing on an ever-widening pool of ability. The consequence was not only social betterment in material things, but individual fulfillment, since it was the human potential to be rational.

Society Dominates Man

Comte believed in progress. He accepted the eighteenth-century interpretation of history that argued for a continuous and ever-quickening pace of social improvement stemming from cultural progress, especially in the areas of knowledge and morality. Yet he believed that men were basically emotional creatures physiologically. How was cultural progress possible in aggregates of such beings?

The human group, Comte argued, was more than an aggregate of individual human organisms, though that, admittedly, was its minimal definition. Human groups were societies, emergent new realities, operating under their own laws and progressing through their own distinctive processes. Man was held in associations by "spontaneous sociability" and by need. Alone he was too puny a creature to survive. In relationship with others, though, social dynamics created and sustained a collective intellect which made possible mastery of the environment. Moreover, such mastery required complex cooperative efforts. To encourage such efforts, society generated morality: the ability to put collective interests before personal ones. Intellect and morality, the crucial variables in social progress, were social products, the outcome of collective processes rather than the reflection of innate human traits. Moreover, since human nature was deficient in both intellect and altruism, the collectivity had to impose these qualities on man, requiring him to be what it was most painful for him to be.

> The chief moderators of human life are intellect and morality. In both of these the human individual is weak. Intellect and morality must arise elsewhere than in intrinsic human nature, even though they must relate to that nature. Intellect is the property of society, especially of government, and morality the output of the family. Man's quandry is that his needs and his instincts are in tension; [there is] a confrontation between instincts and needs. [12]

The relationship between man and society was therefore a tense one, although the tension could be decreased somewhat by allowing some outlets for basic human impulses. Survival was possible and progress assured only if human nature's basic emotionality and egoism were suppressed. The fact of progress was evidence that human nature had been subordinated to societal properties. This was both a fact and a desirable goal. Although neither the processes by which intellect and morality were actually created out of the collectivity nor those by which human nature was held in abeyance were very clear in Comte's work, this was obviously a very different position from that of Spencer or Pareto.

Durkheim, however, was the most radical in asserting the complete domination of man by social forces. One element of this thesis came from his belief that very little was innate to human nature. Another theme was one that has already been seen in Comte's writings, the militant assertion that societal factors were an emergent new reality, with only the most indirect connections to the aggregate of individuals out of which they emerge.

> Social facts do not differ from [individual] facts in [quantity] only: they have a different substratum . . . . The mentality of groups is not the same as that of individuals, it has its own laws.[13]

Culture (or collective representations), which was the concern of sociology, had its own internal dynamics, and to seek an understanding of this phenomenon in the nature of the organisms comprising the group was futile.

Durkheim made only a few concessions on this point. He admitted first of all that some of the functions of society related to organic needs, for example the needs for sustenance and rest. Second, since social facts worked through men, they depended in part on men not resisting them. Durkheim acknowledged the possibility that human nature might resist social pressures, but he felt that such resistance was both rare and futile.

> The individual feels himself in the presence of a force superior to him . . . . he (is) aware of his state of natural dependence and inferiority, since the superiority of society to him is not simply physical but intellectual and moral.[14]

Third, Durkheim acknowledged that at least part of the cause of social deviance and disorganization was the nature of the individuals making up the society. The one drive he was prepared to acknowledge as given in human nature was the insatiable drive for self-gratification. In his discussion of anomie in *Suicide* he argued that this *malaise* of society was in part explained by the escape of the drive for gratification from social control, and its introjection into the fabric of social life. But even here the ultimate explanation did not rest with the successful resistance to social control by human nature, but rather with society and the weakening (for reasons internal to it) of its control over the organisms of which it was comprised.

In contrast with the small input from human nature to the social process, Durkheim held that society made a massive, almost total input into individual nature. In the first place the organic needs and drives of man actually retreated before the thrust of societal factors. In particular, social factors regulated man's innate insatiability.

Man's goals are set, fixed by society. His passions are limited. Since the individual has no way of limiting then this must be done by some force exterior to him—social and moral forces. [15]

Only society could replace innate egoism with disinterestedness, self-forgetfulness, and sacrifice.

Apart from this conquest of organic nature, society also created most of what one might think was unique to personality. Man received all his ideas and concepts from the group, so that without the group man would be incapable of thinking. From the group, man obtained all the goals and purposes that were his motives for action. From the group, man learned his "basic" emotions, such as religiosity and parental feeling. From the group, personality itself emerged, since personality was "each individual having a sphere of action which is peculiar to him," [16] that is, having a distinctive constellation of roles. Man therefore was a social product; society was not a product of human nature. This is the explicit statement of social dominance, and a complete contrast with views such as Spencer's.

A question that was raised in the description of Comte was what mechanism or processes explain this penetration of the individual by society. This question received more attention from Durkheim. He gave two answers to it. Most of the time his emphasis was on social control, on society working on man from without.

Normative conduct and thought are not only external to the individual but are, moreover, endowed with coercive power by virtue of which they impose themselves upon him, independent of his individual will. [17]

The image is of an organism with pressures working on its boundaries. Society shaped the individual either through direct pressures for conformity coming from the group, or by patterns of formal and explicit sanctions which compelled him to follow social directives whatever his real wishes.

Yet given the view of society's permeation of the individual psyche, this is clearly not enough. Nor does it explain why norms persist. If a norm were external to all group members, and resisted by them all, it would soon stop acting as a constraint on their behavior. Cultural factors have to be accepted and defended either by a majority or a powerful minority if they are to persist over time and operate as constraints on particular recalcitrant individuals. There had to be a place in this perspective for some process by which society is taken into the individual. This was Durkheim's second tactic for explaining society's permeation of human nature. He explored the functions of education and touched on the operation of internalized societal norms. But education for him functioned solely as an extension of social control. Socialization was the internalization of social controls:

> Education is the influence exercised by adult generations on those . . . . not yet ready for social life. Its object is to arouse and develop in the child a certain number of physical, intellectual and moral states which are demanded of him by both the political society as a whole and the special milieu for which he is specifically destined. [18]

There was no place in this for the liberal image of education as a process which develops and liberates the individual, giving him some measure of autonomy from society. The consequence of socialization, for Durkheim, was to create two levels of consciousness in the individual; the personal and the social. The two consciences remained discrete and separate (Durkheim's term for it was "distinct"), and the private self remains in permanent subordination to the social, aware of its "dependence and inferiority" to a force physically, intellectually, and morally its superior. The possibility of fusion into personality, some sort of reciprocal exchange, or at least feedback from the personal to the social self is not considered. It is a bleak and conservative image of the human condition.

Man and Society in Interdependence

The majority of the group under consideration, however, argue for some degree of reciprocity in the relationship between human nature and society. This position breaks down into two general perspectives. The first is that on the short term, and in most empirical situations that one may choose to analyze, social influences are the determining ones. Social processes, however, occur on a foundation of human needs, drives, and traits, and while these human characteristics may over long periods be subordinated to society, they can and do reassert themselves on occasion. This perspective is represented by both Sumner and Marx, and may be viewed as a modification of the social determinism viewpoint just described. The other perspective emphasized an ongoing exchange between man and society, and is further away from the deterministic viewpoint. It is represented by Simmel, Weber, and most emphatically by the symbolic interactionists, Mead and Cooley.

Sumner argued that the six basic human drives—egoism, pleasure seeking, hunger, sex, vanity, and fear—gave rise to behavioral sequences which become institutionalized as the norms of the group. Most behavior that the observer might see was shaped by this normative system. However, norms were derived ultimately from basic human needs or drives, and these were never wholly in abeyance. Norms did change, sometimes under their own internal dynamics, but at other times because they were no longer able to meet the needs which created them, or because better modes of satisfying these needs had been found. Society was an interplay between the needs of the species and the emergent properties of group life. Yet society was a new reality, an entity in its own right. The sociologist studied society, knowing that species characteristics were part of the background to society.

To Marx, the foundations of society were shaped by human nature: man was a producer, and society was always moved primarily by the mode of production, that is by the dynamics emanating from the organization of men around the activities of production. Yet in the detailed historical situations which he chose to analyze, Marx seemed to reverse this relationship: men as we know them became the product not of innate faculties but of social organization. One reason for this lay with his conceptualization of the productive activity or economic institution. This was not a vague notion of men working for material resources, as it was for some other sociologists. Rather it was a carefully elaborated complex of processes, involving many alternative ways of working for survival, multiple relationships to the world of work, and several ways of relating to the means of production. In terms of men's experiences of the economy, there were several modes of production.

Marx also believed that despite the diffuse and innate productive capacity in man, personality in its more complex and variable form developed out of specific experiences that the individual had of his material world. The core of this experience was economic experience. Some of the most crucial differences between the experience of some and that of others sprang from different relationships to the means of production, such as land, capital, physical plant and so on. This was the basis of class distinctions, which Marx saw as the fundamental organizational principle in society. The primary distinction here was between the owners of the means of production, and the non-owners who were dependent on them, and consequently exploited by them. But this was not the only distinction. Within the class of owners, for example, one had to distinguish the big land-owning magnates from the small peasant landholder, or from the urban financier, or from the small-scale entrepreneur. Each of these had different experiences of the economic world. Class distinctions were therefore important not only because they indicated differing overt interests in the economy, but because they pointed to different configurations of personality. The classes consisted of different types of men: different in outlook, abilities, sentiments, beliefs, and so on. From the sociological viewpoint this was one of the truly germane insights of Marx's class concept. Sociologists have been tracing through its ramifications ever since. In terms of the question at issue here, it was an argument for the dominance of societal processes in most situations.

In contrast to Durkheim, however, Marx believed it was not possible to subordinate human nature beyond a certain point. One such breaking point occurred when class-based exploitation deprived groups of men of the minimal requirements for organic survival. Another resulted from those consequences of economic organization which sought to cut man off from his basic drives and capacities as producer. Both conditions were insupportable. They resulted in intense social conflict, and in the eventual destruction of the system of social relations which had created them. Marx argued that modern capitalist society attempted both kinds of tyranny over human nature. He saw in the misery of the urban working classes a situation which denied men the most elementary material necessities. He saw the work situation of modern industry blocking man's basic creative impulses and requiring of him that he merely pour his energy, upon demand, into the mechanical processes of manufacturing. This was the source of that kind of psychic malaise which Marx termed alienation. The end result of this intolerable situation would be the assertion, at least temporarily, of human nature over the social system, and the destruction of a particular form of economic organization. Again one has here a view of society, or rather of history, as an interplay between human characteristics and societal processes.

In contrast to this perspective is the position which argues for a constant dynamic exchange between man and society. Of these, Weber's paradigm is perhaps the least elaborate. At the center of his paradigm is the human being, by nature a purposive actor. As a substratum to this actor are the "mechanical" and "instinctive" processes of the organism. Radiating out from the actor in the other direction was the cultural context, the goals, norms, meanings, and interpretations which were his because of his membership in a particular group. Culture was the sociologist's concern, and since both the traits of the organism, and the purposiveness of the human actor were common to the species man, it must be culture that accounted for most of the variation in human behavior. The three dimensions—organism, actor, interpretation—fused in the ongoing phenomenon of action. Weber does not generalize about how the fusion occurred, but he is certain that the social scientist is interested in understanding the complex, ongoing process of the action of individuals, and that his analysis must stay close to that phenomenon.

Simmel explored somewhat more elaborately the way in which man and society related when he discussed the relationship between societal forms and individual contents. Individual drives and interests—the contents—brought men into interaction. Unlike Weber, Simmel did not treat these drives and interests as social, but as given in the individual. Individual psychological factors therefore lay at the basis of social life. But interaction produced structures or social forms which then became independent shaping agents in social life. Forms were the structures for action which the group created, structures which the individual carried with him in his consciousness, and which translated into activity. The two were in constant interdependence. An illustration used by Simmel may make the relationship between form and content clearer. Suppose that one observes a friendly act by one person to another. It may be possible to explain a great deal of that observation in motivational terms: one individual may be said to love the other, and this affection or content prompted the action. But individual-based explanations cannot explain why the love was expressed in that particular way rather than in some other way. This is what the concept of form will do. Social forms are the reason why human emotions, motivations and so on do not express themselves randomly, but occur in a patterned way. Whatever the array of contents in any group they are limited for means of expression; they express themselves through the forms or structures of social life. This was something like Sumner's model, except that Simmel felt that the exchange between individual needs and social organization was not occasional, but constant. Neither factor could long exist without the other.

The most elaborate discussion of the reciprocal relationship between individual and society is to be found in the writings of Mead and Cooley. They conceptualized man as a being possessed of intellect which was used constantly in the service of adaptation and survival. Specifically this required anticipatory mental activity *vis à vis* the environment. Society, as experienced by man, was that aspect of the environment which was made up on the relational activities of other individuals, particularly of communicative behavior. The link between individual and society was *the self*, a complex concept incorporating the following elements.

(a) *Minded behavior*—the anticipatory, adaptive intellectual processes already described.

(b) *Self-awareness*—an ability unique to man, crucial to the relationship between intellect and social environment. It was the ability to see oneself objectively, in contrast with experiencing oneself subjectively. Self-awareness was the human individual's curious reaction to his own behavior which involved sensing the responses of others to that behavior, of seeing himself as they saw him. This ability was essentially social in origin. Man, in isolation, had no way of seeing himself. His perception of self always rested on the guess he made about how he appeared to others. Hence Cooley's famous term, *"the looking-glass self"*: self-knowledge developed in terms of the information that filtered back to us from other's judgments of us. "The social self," says Cooley, "involves an imaginative activity by the individual whereby he guesses as to how he, as an acting individual, appears to others. In imagination we perceive in another's mind some thought of our own appearance, manner, aims, deeds, character, etc. and we behaviorally react to that perception."[19] Self-awareness implied that part of the individual's linkage to his social environment occurs in the form of mental interaction, social yet private, in which the individual alternated between his own plans and his guesses to the responses to these of others. His overt behavior is guided by this form of interaction.

(c) *The generalized other*—This was Mead's concept, and one which put a nucleus of stability into this model of constant "empathizing." Man did not just react to himself on a moment-to-moment basis in terms of his guesses about the attitudes of particular others. True, this was always going on. But also, over time, man gradually evolved an elaborate but fairly stable set of attitudes about himself, and about any action that he might take. This was the generalized other, a generalization about the attitude of society towards oneself, and towards various behaviors that one may undertake, developed slowly out of one's continuing experience of the responses of others. The generalized other was society within man, internalized social direction and control. Its existence provided man with a constant source of reference, a mechanism which stabilized, patterned, and integrated his behavior, directing his choices between alternate modes of behavior even in the absence of others, sometimes even in opposition to the reaction of present, particular others.

(d) *"I" and "me"*—Man was not, however, wholly controlled by others, immediate or generalized. Mead and Cooley preserve the notion of man's partial autonomy from social control with their distinction between "I" and "me." The "me" was the generalized other, a stable, ongoing process of social control. The "I" was the individual's assertion of will, a reaction against social control. The "I" was an impulse prompted by ego, by the desire for gratification or the need for survival, despite the restrictions imposed by the "me." The

"I" was a product of the "me" in the sense that it was a reaction to
it. It was a fleeting experience, and unpredictable, in contrast to the
stability of "me." It was a source of friction in society, and yet the
point from which creativity and innovation entered the social process.
Above all it allowed Mead to avoid the wholly deterministic implications of much sociological theory, and to preserve a notion of free
will.

Symbolic interactionism provides the most elaborate and subtle exploration of the relationship of individual to society produced in this
earlier period. It has been pervasively influential on modern sociology.
In common with Weber it emphasized those elements of society which
entered into man's consciousness, and avoided what interested Marx,
the structures of social relationships, like the economic system, which
affected man, whatever his level of cognitive awareness of them. The
elaborateness of this model is extended further by Mead's and Cooley's
description of the processes by which the self evolved. Three broad
themes are discernible in this description. Two are Mead's, one is
Cooley's.

(a) *Language*—Since self-awareness required interpretation of
the behavior of others, and minded behavior similarly involved orientation to behavioral cues, the individual's effectiveness in his social
environment depended on his mastery of the symbolic significance
of the behavior of others. Primarily, though by no means solely, this
meant that he must be able to interpret what they said—their verbal
behavior. Self or the behavioral processes described above grew in
direct relationship to the new group member's acquisition of the
language of the group.

(b) *Early socialization*—If society is our unit of analysis, most new
members are the infants born into it. Self or the link between individual and the group arose gradually in the child, paralleling his
physical maturation. Mead distinguished between three separate
phases of this process:

1. *The Preparatory Stage:* a period in which the child engaged in
    meaningless imitation of others, aping the behavior of those
    around him without any understanding of what they were doing.
    A good example of this is the young child "reading" a news-
    paper upside-down, as his father reads the paper. This imita-
    tion implied that the child was on the verge of putting himself
    in the position of others, that is, of getting outside of the total
    subjective experience of himself.
2. *The Play Stage:* the child actually began to act out, in play, the
    part of particular others—mother, teacher, storekeeper, fire-

man, and so on. What is of central importance in such play is that the child began to act back towards itself from the perspective of others, as "mother" to itself and so on. This was the beginning of self-awareness, but so far the "others" were still discrete personalities.

3. *The Game Stage:* this completed the development of self. The analogy is the child engaged in complex team games. He had now to take a number of positions towards himself simultaneously in order to decide on his next move: the perspective of each of the positions in the opposing team, of the umpires, of his own side, of the onlookers and so on. He had to visualize the intentions and expectations of groups of others, rather than of particular others. The child resolved this problem of creating a composite role out of the concrete roles of particular others. This was the process by which a generalized other developed.

(c) *Functions of the primary group*—The third detail in the acquisition of a social self was stressed by Cooley. His argument was that the small, informal, and intimate groups which surrounded the individual—family, friends, work groups—were the major formative influences in the development of a self-image, and in the internalization of social values. This was so not only because of their proximity, but because of their emotional relevance to the individual. Cooley believed in man's basic needs for emotional support, as well as in his cognitive, future-oriented faculties. Primary groups were the source of such emotional nurturance, hence their role as principal agents in the socialization of the child. The views of such groups were particularly salient to the individual's development of a self.

By exploring the many facets in socialization, and linking this whole process to the development of self, symbolic interactionism sketched out the details of the relationship between man and society. These details have survived as an important part of sociology's belief system.

Individual and Society

The question of the individual involved the conception of discrete units of the human species, each to some extent unique and self-directing, and the role that sociology was prepared to assign one or a few such units as determining factors in social life. Views on the relationship of man to society give some hint as to the position of early sociologists on this other question, but there was no one-to-one relationship between the two sets of answers. It should be noted again that sociology confronted this issue in a cultural climate which emphasized the autonomous status of human individuals. Yet sociological opinions on the question ranged across the continuum of possible answers. On the one hand there were opinions like Durkheim's:

> Thanks to the almost unanimous and generally ancient predominance of collective states, they are so far too resistant to be off-set by an individual innovation. How could an individual be strong enough to mould society in his image?[20]

At the other extreme Weber warned against any reification of social life:

> Action . . . . exists only as the behavior of one or more individual human beings . . . . in sociological work collectivities must be treated as solely the resultants and modes of organization of the particular acts of individual persons . . . . for sociological purposes there is no such thing as a collective personality which "acts."[21]

The confrontation between the two perspectives is very clear.

Thus one important variable affecting a sociologist's position on this question was the extent to which he saw society as something with properties and processes wholly intrinsic in it. This is the position which Weber disparagingly called "reification," and which those who do not intend as much criticism label the belief in the "emergent properties" of group life. A strong believer in such a characteristic of society would find it difficult to conceive of individual men being able to radically alter the complex, tradition-founded, self-maintaining system they saw society to be. Hence both Comte and Durkheim refused to consider that individuals could positively affect social life. They do however allow the individual a negative role: deviance, or nonconformity, while social in its genesis, manifests itself as the resistance of particular individuals to societal codes. Deviance is egoistic rebellion by individuals.

Marx, in the mature phase of his theory, took a similar position on the question of the individual's ability to influence society. Marx viewed economy and class much as Durkheim and Comte saw society. They were real, natural forces which worked absolutely on the individual while evolving in terms of their own mechanisms. Marx was, however, moved by a feeling that the relationship, while unavoidable, was tragic. This contrasts with Durkheim and Comte who see the relationship as unavoidable and good. These differing perspectives probably explain their differing positions on deviance. Marx saw deviance in most cases simply as a question of definition, with those in power making the definition. However, true immorality was another manifestation of society's influence on the individual, the most tragic instance of the individual's helplessness in the face of social forces.

But the belief in society as an emergent reality was only one variable shaping a man's position on the role of the individual. Equally important were assumptions about human nature. An assertion that particular individuals might shape social events rested on some belief in personality as a variable and in the capacity of the individual for will or purposive action. When these factors were subsumed under racial, national, or even simple species categories, the possibility of an individualistic interpretation of societal events became remote. This is the case with Spencer:

> The individual is embedded in the social organism . . . . moulded by its influences . . . and cannot so emancipate himself as to see things about him in their real relations.[22]

An interesting contrast with Spencer is Pareto. Pareto, like Spencer, felt that inherited traits in the human population fundamentally affected the form of society. Further, he had a thesis of emerging properties from human association which are properly social characteristics. Yet his views on innate human nature allowed for basic personality variation. Consequently Pareto's theories gave the individual, particularly the political leader, a role in the shaping of events.

For those who saw man as purposive and self-directing—Weber, Mead, Cooley—the problem was not so much one of allowing the individual a degree of autonomy, but of deciding what the full implications of that autonomy were for society and for sociology. To what extent could an individual change society? And what did this imply for the sociologist's methods of inquiry? The problems are both conceptual and methodological: one must decide how voluntaristic a model of society to develop, as well as whether to place the acting individual at the center of one's attempt to study society.

Consensus seemed possible on the methodological question. Weber, Mead, and Cooley saw the individual as the empirical starting point of their investigation of society. The preceding quotation from Weber illustrates this stance well. On the theoretical problem of the relationship between these autonomous units and social or cultural structures, the consensus of the group breaks down. The symbolic interactionists seem content to rest the issue of autonomy in the residual category of the "I," and then to concentrate their investigations on the question of how much of the behavior of apparently autonomous individuals is in fact influenced, though not necessarily determined, by society. Weber is more difficult to pin down this way.

Weber certainly gave a more explicit emphasis to "great men" as agents of fundamental social change than did any other sociologist of this period. Great men in the form of prophets and revolutionary leaders were essential to his formulation of social change. Yet Weber's concern was with culture. He treated culture as a group product and as part of the environment of any particular individual. The relationship of voluntarism to cultural determinism is never formally described in his theory. From specific studies one gets some insight into his general position on this. From these studies it appears that Weber never moved from his position that it was the individual who actually interpreted his situation to himself. Culture manifested itself in such individual based interpretive processes. For purposes of convenience the sociologist might speak of culture as a collective reality, but he must never forget the place of the individual in the cultural process. The individual introduced elements of uncertainty, fluidity, variation, and change into the cultural construct. One could never wholly predict an individual's response to the constellations of meaning existing in a group. Always the individual took meanings from his environment and personalized them in terms of his interests, experiences, psychic tensions, and so forth. Only in this form did they then influence his behavior. For much of the time culture might manifest itself very similarly in the behavior of large numbers of individuals, but this behavior was never exactly the same. Similarity in behavior should not move one to posit a deterministic relationship from culture to individual action—this would require identical behavior. The individual was the active agent, determining the form of his relationship to any particular cultural factor. The individual stabilized or changed such cultural constellations. Of all the men considered, Weber is the most voluntaristic. One tends to overlook this because Weber on the whole avoids generalization. The thrust is implicit rather than explicit in his work.

The most explicit exploration of the conceptual problem of relating individual to group was Simmel's. Simmel argued that the controversy over which was real—society or individual—and which was more important in a system of explanation was essentially futile. Everything depended on what one wanted to investigate—what the research question was. The perspective of the investigator was the determining factor, not the greater or lesser importance of individual or society. Individuals and society were equally "real" and equally "constructed." An investigator was rather like a critic looking at a picture. Sometimes a critic stood up close to study the techniques of the brush work, while at other times he stood back to see the overall design. Western culture predisposed one to study the brush strokes in the social process: its individual components. However, sociologists tended to be preoccupied with an overview of the more general pattern. But some questions of sociological import might be better understood by closeup analysis, using the individual as the major conceptual variable.

Simmel went on to explore what the term "individual" meant. An individual was a particular and relatively stable organization of impulses, drives, interests and so on. This was what was meant by "personality." In terms of the day-to-day juxtaposition of personality and group processes, there seemed to be no doubt that the two conflicted, and that the group brought about a diminution in individuality. At one level, group life created forms which channeled personality's motivational drives and limited it's means of expression. In social relationships *tact* was of important instrumental value. Tact required the individual to blur the sharp, distinct edges of personality in the interests of maintaining a smooth flow of interpersonal contact. It was a self-regulating function by which the individual suppressed his most unique characteristics for the sake of blending in easily with the group. Tact softened the outlines of personality.

Yet what gave personality its distinctive and fairly stable organization? Involvement in the social process apparently did this also. Belonging to certain groups meant that one also became aware of where one did *not* belong. (The personality of the aristocrat, for example, developed out of such dynamics.) Belonging to many groups, in a total constellation rather different from that of other people, made one aware of one's distinctness. Awareness of self as an individual was a product of participation in society. The more complex that participation, the more in one's daily routine one in fact repressed personality in the interests of smooth functioning in a variety of groups, the greater one's feeling of uniqueness, and of individualization. To some extent social processes also offset the effects of tact upon personality. There were self-regulating processes of social distance, recognizing the private and distinctive sanctum of individualism into which one ought not to trespass. These processes could be labelled *discretion*. If tact required the individual to break down some of the parameters of his distinctiveness, discretion on the part of the group reinforced other boundaries around the individual, by preserving certain of his rights to privacy. Simmel's apparent compromise between the individualistic and social deterministic perspectives in fact illustrates his use of a dialectic form of analysis. True to his education in the Hegelian perspective, he sought constantly to show how the answer to a sociological problem often fused apparently contradictory elements, and could be understood only in such terms.

Summary and Conclusions

This chapter has explored some of the issues centering on one of sociology's most important "boundary" problems: the relationship of individual human beings to those social phenomena which the sociologist views as his particular subject matter. Three general areas have been explored: (1) the assumptions early sociologists made about non-socialized human nature, (2) the ways in which they conceptualized relationship between human beings and social forces; and (3) the attempts to fit the individual into sociology's explanatory systems. Table 3 summarizes the various viewpoints held by the earlier sociologists on these questions.

What are the connections between this material and that given in the preceding chapter? Perhaps most striking is the fact that sociologists who attempted a comprehensive analysis of all social events (the macro-social perspective) did not always have common assumptions about the nature of man and his relationship to social processes. Comte, Spencer, Marx, and Pareto all shared the macro-social perspective. As we have seen in this chapter, their views on human nature and on the man-society relationship span an entire range of alternatives. The theoretical orientations to macro-societal analysis consequently vary enormously, from Pareto's image of a social system founded on human irrationality, through Marx's perspective on society as a product of man's purposive, economic nature, to Comte's insistence that society is rational and that it forces impulsive, emotional man to live up to its own standards.

A pattern exists, however, among those who take a narrower perspective on the details of interaction (the micro-social approach). These theorists, men like Simmel, Mead, and Cooley, tended to agree that man is at least partly rational, that his nature is tied into constant reciprocal relationships with societal processes, and that personality variation is of some importance in sociological explanation. (Although he has not been discussed in this chapter, Tönnies also falls into this group.) The shift from a broad synthesizing view of society to a narrower analytic concern with interaction led, at least in this earlier period, to a greater evaluation of the role played by human individuals in shaping the social process. Once stated, this seems to be a fairly

TABLE 3: Views of Man and Society

I. An Area of Agreement

Society is not simply the study of human individuals, yet its subject matter is related to the traits of human individuals—Comte, Spencer, Marx; Ward, Sumner, Durkheim, Weber, Simmel, Pareto, Mead, Cooley

II. Human Nature

1. Human nature varies along racial lines, these variations being based on genetic/physiological differences—Spencer	Human nature to the extent that it has a genetic/physiological basis is everywhere the same—Comte, Marx; Ward, Sumner, Durkheim, Weber, Simmel, Pareto; Mead, Cooley		Man has no "nature"; he is a social product—Durkheim This is a fact of real importance to sociology.
2. Man is by nature cognitive and purposive—Ward, Marx, Weber, Mead, Cooley This is a fact of real importance to sociology	Man is by nature emotional, impulsive non-rational—Pareto, Comte, Sumner This is a fact of real importance to sociology	Primitive races are emotional and impulsive; developed races are cognitive, rational—Spencer This is a fact of real importance to sociology	Man is both cognitive and emotional by nature—Simmel This fact is of no great importance to sociology

III. Man and Society

1. Man is (re) created by society—Comte, Durkheim	Man's basic nature is an influence on society, but society is of greater importance in (re) shaping man's nature—Marx, Sumner	Man's basic nature and society are engaged in constant reciprocal cross-influencing—Simmel, Weber, Mead, Cooley	Basic human nature is the major shaping influence on society—Spencer, Pareto, Ward.
2. Society's relationship to man is therefore one of social control; social scientists should see social control as a major process for analysis; both the exercise of group sanctions and socialization are forms of social control—Comte, Durkheim, Marx		Society enhances, elaborates human personality, primarily through socialization—Mead, Cooley	Society therefore evolves—Spencer; is non-rational—Pareto; is rational—Ward

IV. Sociology and Individual Personality

1. Variations in human personality are important sociohistorical influences, and therefore important to sociological explanation—Weber	Variations in human personality are of some importance in society, and therefore of some importance in sociological explanation—Pareto, Simmel, Mead, Cooley		Variations in human personality are of no importance in society, and therefore of no importance in sociological explanation—Comte, Spencer, Marx, Sumner, Durkheim

obvious relationship. However, if not stated, it might be overlooked. And the student should keep in mind that the relationship may be the other way around: a belief in the importance and rationality of individuals may come first and so propel some sociologists to choose interaction, the arena of individual behavior, as the subject matter of sociology.

An interesting fact brought to light during the course of this chapter is the profound difference that exists between Durkheim and Weber. In chapter 5 they seemed to share common ground in their wish to direct sociology to the study of cultural phenomena. Although care was taken to point out the difference between them on this point, the differences become much clearer as we see how they rest on sharply different assumptions about man in society. To Durkheim man brings nothing to society except an egoistic, craving drive. He is made by society, molded and controlled by it. Personality is not an independent variable in sociological analysis. But to Weber man is, in a broad sense, rational: a thinking, planning, purposive being. Society is processed through him. Personality must therefore be considered by any sociologist as he develops his explanation of social events. Durkheim emphasized society's control over man; Weber focused on man's interpretations and re-creations of sociocultural phenomena. And so, to Durkheim, sociology studies culture as a system of constraints. To Weber, sociology studies culture as a system of meaning, perspectives, and interpretations. Probably the most significant division in earlier sociology—the definition of the sociological perspective—rests on these alternative perspectives.

It is also interesting to trace the connections between the discussion in this chapter and the background characteristics described in earlier chapters. This is somewhat easier if we realize that there were really two arguments going on under the more general heading of "man and society." First, was man rational or emotional by nature? Second, did he influence society in any major way or was he determined by social forces? The first argument relates fairly directly to the philosophical differences described in chapter 4. The second theme relates in a more diffuse way to some of the political and social events described in both chapters 3 and 4.

Those who saw man as emotional or at least as nonrational were positivists: Comte, Durkheim, Pareto. The connection between positivism and a view of man as impulsive or irrational may not be immediately apparent. Indeed it might be argued that an outlook which made scientific procedure an ideology would probably view man as rational by nature. But this overlooks some of the more subtle characteristics of nineteenth-century positivism. In the first place, positivism makes a radical distinction between man in his role of scientist, and men as objects for scientific investigation. The former is separated from the latter; the scientist is the white-coated observer, recording his observations without bias, and interpreting them in the interests of science, with no fear that he is part of what he has been studying, while man, the object of scientific interest, is generally moved by impulse, passion, prejudice, and self-interest. Pareto said this clearly when he admitted that human beings are occasionally capable of rationality, *especially in the role of scientist,* but that in almost all other situations man is profoundly irrational. Positivism, as the ideology of science, proposes a social division between scientist and other men, along classic "us" and "them" lines, with the superior qualities vested in the scientific stratum. Comte tried to make this distinction the basis for a new social utopia in his book, the *Positive Polity.*

Positivism goes on to argue that ordinary men, as objects for scientific study, are like any other objects in the material world. They possess no special characteristics which make them less amenable to the procedures of scientific investigation. Moreover, as we saw in earlier chapters, the nineteenth-century scientific community was deeply influenced by the breakthrough in biology embodied in Darwin's work. They thought in terms of animal species, constraining environmental factors, and the statistical calculation of biological traits which clustered around a mean or average. Man as object, then, was an animal species, like any other species. Like other species he was propelled by impulses and drives rooted in his bio-physical nature. To see him as rational would be to see him as different and separate from other biological types, and so the analytic procedures developed to study other species would be inapplicable to a study of man.

To the positivist, man the object lived in a universe which was determined by the operation of eternal natural laws. Man did not have freedom; he was constrained by his environment. Even the scientist was not a free entity. Science was a collective enterprise which had evolved in social organization. The scientist's superiority rested on the fact that he was part of a scientific community, constrained by its norms and expectations. The special status accorded by positivists to the scientist was not status given to special men, but to special roles within a special institution.

It is easy to see how a positivist might move from the view of man's essential nonrationality in the first argument listed above, to a view about society's deterministic role in the second argument. Even Pareto, who saw man's irrationality as a factor determining social structure, did not believe that man was a free agent. Societal influences might not be the most important determinants of his actions, but human behavior *was* determined by biophysical impulses over which the individual had little control. An outlook based on positivism led one first to a stress on man's basic impulsiveness, and then had a spillover effect in that it encouraged the belief that human behavior was determined by the environment, including the social environment, of the species man.

In contrast, those who stressed man's natural purposiveness and rationality often have philosophic roots either in idealism (like Weber, Tönnies and Marx) or in pragmatism. Since both of these schools stressed man's unique endowment of mind, the connection between the philosophic heritage and the sociological position is obvious enough to require no further elaboration. A few points, however, should be noted. First, a belief in human purpose and rationality has a carryover effect to the second argument listed above in the same way that positivism does. A view of man as rational predisposes one to the belief that he actively relates to his social environment rather than being passively determined by it. Second, Marx had formally rejected idealism, although in fact he was never able to shake himself entirely free from this heritage. This situation may in part explain many of the difficulties in his answers to the problem of man in society: his rejection of general human rationality coupled with his acceptance of a narrower economic purposiveness in man; his ambivalence about the nature of man's relationship to social forces, as both active agent and determined product; his views about man's potential for free thought and his actual enslavement by false consciousness. Finally it should be realized that in the elaborate statements of Mead and Cooley we have not just the carryover from a philosophical outlook to social science, but a development, on the basis of philosophic predispositions, of complex social theory, in response to a problem posed by the latter field.

In considering the second theme in this argument, that of man's relationship to society, the best link to the earlier chapters is to their various descriptions of ideology. The belief in an autonomous individual who shapes history and society is the basic assumption of liberalism, while the belief in an omnipotent sociocultural system underwrites conservatism. But the relationship is more complex than this, for liberalism was the ideology of the middle class, a stratum whom we have already seen as supportive of scientism, or of positivism. In contrast conservatism's main appeal was to the elitist groups who survived in industrial society but whose heyday was in an earlier feudal period; and idealism originates in the religious world view of that period. So those who were attracted to a belief in individualism were at the same time being urged to view man as emotional and irrational, while those who saw man as determined by social forces were also closer to a philosophical system which stressed human rationality. In either situation the beliefs appeared paradoxical. Indeed, they were more than this. For, as we have argued, positivism encouraged the belief in social determinism; idealism was conducive to a belief in human purposiveness. In each situation then, the beliefs were contradictory. This tension probably explains the difficulties that earlier sociologists had with the various questions implicit in the problem of man and society. In a sense they were middle class men being forced to choose between the assumptions of liberalism and those of positivism. Whatever choice they made forced them into a liaison with some aspect of a feudal world view which created further tension for them. This tension helps to explain the odd combinations that earlier sociologists produced as they wrestled with the problem area described in this chapter. It also helps us understand the appeal of a compromise position, such as that represented by Weber or Simmel, in which a partly rational being stands in a relationship of interdependence with social forces; and it helps to explain the impact of a philosophy of compromise—pragmatism—on sociology's effort to develop consensus on the question of man in society.

Finally, it should be noted that out of this discussion emerged several of the rallying points for contemporary sociological discussion: the competing accusations of reductionism and reification; the knotty problems of individual will and emergent group properties; the alternative pressures to macro- and micro-analyses of social life; the importance of social psychology as a core sub-area in the wider field. In terms of this discussion, one also comes to understand the emphasis placed by sociologists on the processes of socialization and social control. These are the processes which provide us with links between individual human beings and society.

NOTES

1. For a description of these ideas, see chapter 4.

2. Herbert Spencer, *Principles of Sociology* (New York: Appleton, 1890), p. 308. Italics added.

3. Ibid., pp. 53-54.

4. Auguste Comte, *The Positive Philosophy* (London: Chapman, 1853), p. 88.

5. Max Weber, *The Methodology of the Social Sciences*, trans. Edward Shils (New York: Free Press, 1949), p. 165.

6. Pareto's actual sequence of residues is I. Combinations; II. Persistance of Aggregates; III. Activity; IV. Sociability; V. Individual Integrity; VI. Sex.

7. Comte, *Positive Philosophy*, volume I, 128.

8. Ibid., p. 88.

9. Ibid., p. 128.

10. Emile Durkheim, *The Rules of Sociological Method*, trans. Sarah Solavy and John Mueller, ed. George Catlin (Glencoe, Ill.: Free Press, 1950), p. 106.

11. Spencer, *Principles of Sociology*, pp. 8-9.

12. Comte, *Positive Philosophy*, volume I, p. 132.

13. Durkheim, *The Rules*, pp. xlvii-xlix. Italics added.

14. Ibid. pp. 121-24.

15. Emile Durkheim, *Suicide*, trans. John Spaulding and George Simpson (Glencoe, Ill.: The Free Press, 1951), pp. 247-48.

16. Emile Durkheim, *The Division of Labor in Society*, trans. ed. (Glencoe, Ill.: The Free Press, 1964), p. 131

17. Durkheim, *The Rules*, p. 2.

18. Emile Durkheim, *Education and Sociology* (Glencoe, Illinois: Free Press, 1956) p. 71.

19. Charles H. Cooley, *Human Nature and the Social Order* (New York: Scribner, 1922), p. 183.

20. Durkheim, *Suicide*, p. 142.

21. Max Weber, *The Theory of Social and Economic Organization*, trans. Talcott Parsons (Glencoe, Ill.: Free Press, 1947), pp. 89-90.

22. Herbert Spencer, *The Study of Sociology* (Ann Arbor: University of Michigan Press, 1961), p. 158.

7

Culture and Society

Man in society participates in a world of shared ideas. This is an assumption common to the group of sociologists being studied. There are variations in how much attention they pay to it; differences of opinion as to the origins of these ideas; sharp arguments about the consequences of this fact for social life. But no one rejects the notion completely. Contemporary sociologists call the ideas common to a society its culture. Earlier sociologists, lacking this consensus on a label, use a variety of terms. They speak of meanings, derivations, collective representations, and so on. But they are all referring to the same general phenomenon. This chapter describes earlier sociological explorations of the culture concept.

In investigating early definitions of sociology, the problem of culture and society is as important as that of man and society. The concept of culture was of major importance to many earlier sociologists, shaping their definitions of sociology's subject matter, their methodology, their theories of order and change. Some of the most important empirical work of this period centered on culture. Although theoretical battles are still waged on precisely how culture influences social behavior, consensus on the need to consider culture is much greater in contemporary sociology than in the earlier period, and a great deal of energy is devoted to exploring its analytic components. The consensus marks the triumph of certain viewpoints over others in the earlier period. The analytic com-

137

ponents of culture were initially formulated in this same period. Familiarity with these writings thus not only gives fuller knowledge of the earlier priod, but also allows better understanding of the contemporary conceptual framework.

These various implications of the culture concept shape the structure of the chapter. The main part of it describes the various earlier views on what culture was. This is the major point of continuity with present-day views on culture's analytic components. It also allows us to describe some of the empirical work done on culture in the earlier period. This main section is preceded by a brief exploration of the intellectual setting in which the earlier descriptions occurred. It is followed by a short section which reviews positions on the origins of culture.

The Background

Three broad currents of thought served to heighten awareness of the cultural variable for nineteenth-century sociologists. The first was philosophic idealism, already discussed in detail in chapter 4. Briefly this perspective emphasized the interpretive role played by the human intellect, or mind. It argued that the world, as we knew it, existed only in human consciousness, and that these states of consciousness or configurations of ideas were the investigator's elemental data in his quest for knowledge. It stressed the variability in states of consciousness and the configurated complexity of ideas. Its counsel was that mind and its products were crucial. Philosophic idealism was strongest in German academic circles. Sociologists reared in this tradition had to confront its major thesis and work out their position towards it. As chapter 4 also pointed out, pragmatism placed similar emphasis on consciousness and interpretation in human activities, affecting the thinking of American social scientists.

The second factor was eighteenth-century Enlightenment thought, whose influence continued well into the nineteenth century. This perspective stressed the importance of certain kinds of ideas, explaining social change very largely in terms of these factors. The important change-producing ideational factors for Enlightenment thinkers are the products of man's capacity for rationality, particularly his science and philosophy. Human progress, which they saw as the major thrust of societal change in the West, was the consequence of these cultural factors. Not all ideas, however, contributed to progress. Against rational thought, science, and philosophy, Enlightenment thinkers placed factors like religion and tradition. These acted as resistance to progres-

sive change, as barriers to rationality. As such they ought to be
eliminated. To Enlightenment thinkers man's idea world was a thing in
tension: rational components confronted the irrational. Interpreting
history as a record of quickening progress,these writers placed their bets
on the historical triumph of rational ideas.

The third element in the intellectual climate which affected sociological views on culture was political conservatism. Conservatism joined
battle with the philosophy of the Enlightenment. Where Enlightenment thinkers stressed reason and science, conservatives emphasized
tradition and history. Where Enlightenment thinkers outlined the direction in which society ought to move, conservatives labeled this un-
realistic fantasy and stressed what society presently consisted of. To
conservative thinkers culture was an extensive, intricate network of
traditions, gradually and cumulatively established during the historical
existence of the group, an elaborate composition which regulated man's
life chances and his relationships to others. Tinkering with the culture
could only have unforeseen and disastrous consequences for the overall
pattern, and for the group whose complex needs were regulated by this
pattern. Culture determined social life. It was primarily a pattern of
traditions and habits. Its bastions were religion and family life.

Thus from a variety of positions sociologists heard a single theme:
ideas were important, by they world views, scientific truths, or traditions. Ideas existed in complex systems or configurations and must be
approached as such. Given their own location in "idea" circles it is
little wonder that from some position or another they felt themselves
compelled to deal with the phenomenon of culture. It is indeed rather
remarkable that some of them could still choose to deemphasize the
implications of culture for social life.

Comte: Science and Morality

A very clear and direct link exists between some of these background
factors and Comte's definition of culture. In particular he addressed
himself to the confrontation between conservative and Enlightenment
thought. As the discussion of man and society showed, Comte felt that
man was subordinate to society because of his need to survive in his
environment and his incapacity to do this alone. Society alone, never
the individual man, could systematically and substantially apply intelligence to the problems of survival. At the core of social life, in
Comte's eyes, were the process and products of intelligence operating
in response to the problems posed by the environment to human sur-

vival. This cluster of factors he called *"intellect."* In many ways what he meant by intellect approximates what one today calls culture.

Comte did not define intellect simply as rational thought. Instead he divided it into two components. The first is *knowledge,* which relates directly to the problem-solving process of group life, and involves some element of rationality. Knowledge refers to the facts or beliefs that a group has about its environment, the techniques it evolves *vis à vis* that environment, its technology, science, and so on. A cumulative pool of resources, knowledge makes it possible to develop strategies in the struggle with the environment. The second facet of intellect is what Comte called *morality.* Morality refers to the ethical codes a group evolves which act as a constraint on the egoism of individual group members. These codes make those individuals capable of placing group concerns first, and thus facilitate the social organization and cooperative activity necessary to the group's struggle with its environment. Intellect is therefore both an effort at rational problem solving and a system of shared ethical orientations, a definition very close to the modern concept of "culture."

Human progress involves steady ameliorative developments on both fronts—knowledge and morality. Comte interpreted history as a record of human progress marked by three broad cultural stages. In the first stage, both knowledge and ethics were religious in orientation; in the second period, the orientation became philosophical; the third period, only recently emerged, had started when knowledge and morality began being shaped by a scientific outlook. For the duration of each phase, and for most of history, there was congruence between the kind of knowledge and the kind of morality prevalent in society. Only in periods of transition, as with the contemporary shift to scientific knowledge, did tensions exist in the cultural realm. Comte's response to the argument between Enlightenment and conservative writers was that both rationality and ethics are essential to culture, both work together in the interests of human survival, and there is no innate conflict between them. The two groups were generalizing from an observation of tension in their own time to some eternal tension between reason and tradition-based morality. But this tension was only a temporary condition resulting from a situation of cultural transition.

Comte's attempt to resolve the conflict between conservative and Enlightenment thought seemed to lead him, implicitly, to a third component of "intellect;" a general *outlook or world view* which, whether religious, philosophical, or scientific, shapes both knowledge and morality. This introduces an element of variation and relativity to Comte's image of culture. Similar elements would loom large in later explorations of the culture concept. It is, however, only latent in

Comte's approach. His formal treatment of knowledge and morality implies that culture (intellect), to an increasing extent with the passage of time, is an accurate translation of obvious societal needs and environmental circumstances.

Marx and Pareto: Ideology or "False Consciousness"

Marx also related directly to the perspectives described above as background factors. His response to the arguments about what aspect of culture was more important was to interpret them as meaningless squabbling on a moot point, for culture was not particularly important in human history. The important variable was experience, particularly economic experience. Ideas were always a mere reflection of the relationships, interests, and behaviors which were founded on the economic institution. They never seriously altered that institution. It was not that men in society did not share, to some extent, in a body of common ideas. This was indeed so, except during moments of revolutionary confrontation. But these ideas were an unimportant factor in the historical process, deserving no elaborate analytic investigation.

Yet it is possible to abstract from Marx's writings his own conception of culture. This is because, conscious of defying prevailing beliefs on the importance of culture, he devoted considerable energy to his attack on that position. Marx did not wholly ignore culture, though he advocated that analysts of society do so. He conceived of culture as something more than an aggregate of discrete, isolated ideas. It was a system or configuration of beliefs, values, and general orientations. Each historical period has its own characteristic cultural configuration. Religion, in its broadest sense, was Marx's image of culture, and he believed that each age will have its own characteristic religion.

The crucial point that he made about such idea configurations, however, is that they reflect the interests and experiences of whatever class is, in that period, dominant in the society. To the extent that men who are not members of that class share in the prevailing culture, they are distracted from an accurate assessment of the society's economic and power relationships in terms of their own interests and experiences. They are allowing their exploiters to define their situation for them. They cannot avoid being further exploited by this arrangement. Culture then is not irrelevant to Marx's schema. It plays a role in history, though never the determining role. It is an instrument of social control, functioning to reinforce patterns of power and privilege generated by the economy. Although some of this function results mechanically from institutional arrangements, the power structure is also capable of using culture deliberately in the interests of social control.

Given these themes of the unreality of shared ideas, their failure to mesh with the "facts" and their deliberate use in a system of exploitation, the appropriate label for the phenomenon is not culture, which has a neutral connotation on all these dimensions, but *ideology*. To the extent that exploited men accept the power structure's ideology they are in a state of *false consciousness*. Yet, for Marx, ideology's hold on exploited groups is always tenuous, requiring constant effort by the power structure. Ideas are generated by experience, and the experience of exploitation is a constant counterpoise to ideology's effectiveness.

The same theme of nonreality and of essential irrelevance runs through Pareto's treatment of culture. As the last chapter described, Pareto argued that man's actions are usually prompted by innate sentiments or impulses, and he proceeded to enumerate six such clusters of sentiments which he claimed characterized the human animal. But he had hunted for the sentiments by analyzing man's written statements. Even after discovering the themes that recurred in these statements —his indicators to the sentiments—he still felt confronted by the written statements themselves. These indicated that man was a prolific verbalizer, constantly spinning off ideas, weaving these into patterns, and defending the elaborate ideational edifices against subsequent criticism. These edifices of ideas Pareto called *derivations*.

Derivations were triggered by the underlying sentiments: by man's desire to explain himself, give reasons for his behavior, appear consistent and logical. They related to the sentiments of integrity, activity, and combination. Man's sentiments prompted his action, which was therefore essentially impulsive and irrational. Yet man also had a need to appear rational, to make sense of his behavior to himself and others. This need was the source of his whole vast culture, which was little else than rationalization after the fact.

Ideology had important psychological effects. It justified prior action, reinforced particular behavioral sequences, and even eventually acted as a trigger for behavioral sequences in those already so predisposed. Historically there had been an infinite variety of such idea systems. The operation of any of the sentiments, specific interests, and random situational factors might shape the format of an ideology. Moreover, although each sought a logical format, all ideologies were essentially illogical. They rested on unquestioned assumptions. Their links with the empirical world were tenuous. Their format was shaped by impulses and situational factors rather than by logical standards. From the logical standpoint all ideologies were unalloyed nonsense. Pareto undertook an extensive analysis of belief systems and showed over and over again their underlying illogical nature.

Derivations then are false consciousness in Pareto's eyes. They serve to mask man's awareness of the true reasons for his own behavior and that of others. They appear to make sense of reality, but they are illogical delusions without any firm base in reality. They make neat little meaningful packages of man's world and actions, but do not have much basis in what we are actually doing.

In treating culture as an instrument of self-deception, Marx and Pareto appear to be taking a very similar position against those who argued for the worth and importance of societal belief systems. But from another perspective Pareto was, deliberately, arguing against Marx. Marx derived ideology from broad institutional arrangements, and argued that changes in such arrangements will free man from ideology. Pareto traced ideology back to human nature, thus denying that man will ever be free of false consciousness.

Durkheim and Sumner: Norms

Comte and Marx were influenced by eighteenth-century perspectives on culture. Later sociologists were frequently affected by the ideas of Comte and Marx. In particular they became involved with Marx's thesis on culture, directing their arguments against his. Pareto's attempt at modifying Marx's thesis has already been described. Other sociologists took a different tact. They held that culture was an independent and important variable in social life. In developing this argument, they described the ramifications of culture in a variety of ways. These descriptions added new dimensions to the field's conception of culture, and often survive today as conventionally accepted analytic subcategories of the culture construct.

One such perspective was an emphasis on culture as a system of rules for behavior, or, in contemporary terminology, as a system of *norms*. Norms are socially accepted answers to questions about how one ought to act in all the various and particular situations of daily life; they are procedural directives which cause men in a society to follow certain paths and to overlook others which may strike the observer as equally feasible. This conception of culture lies at the core of Durkheim's treatment of the term.

Durkheim argued that a society's norms were shaped by characteristics of the group itself: size, spatial density, degree of homogeneity, intensity of interaction, and the demands placed on it by its physical environment. Interaction occurring under these variable conditions spontaneously created distinctive systems of norms. These norms were significant for all group members, since they all experienced the various group-level characteristics. True, a large heterogeneous population would contain subcultures (enclaves of norms which related only to the experiences of certain groups). The ethical codes of professional groups in modern society were examples of this. But even in such societies there would be some common culture, meaningful to all because it derived from a common experience of the society's general characteristics. And the less heterogeneous the society the greater would be this area of common culture in relationship to subcultural enclaves. Durkheim here rejected Marx's view that cultural phenomena relate genuinely only to the experience of an elite, and were elsewhere deliberately imposed, by an exercise of power, on the consciousness of subordinate groups. A hierarchical model of power relationships was as peripheral to Durkheim's sociology as it was central to Marx's.

One can abstract from Durkheim's various writings several other characteristics of normative systems. Such systems develop slowly, over generations. A society at any one point in time lives within a system of cultural traditions which it has, in large measure, inherited from the past. Norms will vary in degree of explicitness: some are formally stated as laws, others are only inarticulately felt, like customs. Norms also vary in their form of appeal. Some are adopted purely for convenience. They rest on the society's rational conception of what is expedient. Contract laws are a good example. Others draw on deep emotional currents in the population, being sacred rather than expedient. Taboos against murder or incest are of this type. Still other norms elaborately specify the details of an action sequence. and seem mainly directed to heightening group consciousness of its common identity. Such are a society's rituals. Norms are always associated with *sanctions*—procedures for ensuring conformity to the behavioral rule. Sanctioning agents may be specially appointed, such as the judiciary, or may be the whole group. Norms link together into systems of procedures centering on some important aspect of cooperative life. These systems are *institutions*. Durkheim believed that sociology's purpose is to study institutions.

Durkheim's concept of culture includes elements other than norms. In his analysis of suicide he pointed out that society regulates the goals or aspirations of the individual. Culture therefore includes ultimate *values* as well as procedural norms. In his discussion of religion he traced both the *beliefs* and the *conceptual apparatus* of a culture back to the experience of social process. Durkheim's image of culture is one of the broadest of this period. But he saw the normative system as the crucial dimension of culture, the one which most clearly demonstrates the separate reality of society and its dominance over individual behavior. This aspect of culture was most significant for him.

Sumner explored the concept of social norm even more formally and elaborately than Durkheim. His views have become a classic component of the sociological belief system. Sumner set forth his typology of norms in his book *Folkways*, the avowed purpose of which was to study the sociological importance of "usages, manners, customs, mores and morals."

One of the most fundamental of all elements of the social process as Sumner saw it is the tendency of individuals to repeat actions which have been successful in satisfying recurring needs. These repetitions then continue, because they become habits. When the needs are group needs, the habits become habits of the group. Basically all norms are social or group habits.

Group habits originate in the minds and actions of the stronger group members, and then spread through the group by imitation. In any society man gradually builds up, by a process of trial and error, a repertoire of procedures which experience has shown to be conducive to satisfying recurring needs. These Sumner called folkways, habits accepted without self-conscious soul-searching. Over time folkways acquire the power of tradition.

Men, however, tend to intellectualize their habits. They reflect about them, justify them in terms of their contribution to the group's welfare, press them in the direction of greater explicitness and consistency. When habits move to this level of formal recognition, when they take on the attributes of being the "truth" or the "only right way," they have become a particular type of norm: the type Sumner called *mores*. Mores are institutionalized norms, consciously upheld by the authority of the society. Mores, habitual procedures garbed in philosophical and ethical generalizations, wield enormous importance in group life. They guide our thoughts and actions from childhood. They are entrenched in the emotions of group members who will fight bitterly for their preservation.

Social *institutions* are simply arrangements of these folkways and mores. Clusters of folkways and mores develop around dominant group interests, sometimes gradually and in an unplanned way as with family relations, sometimes deliberately and abruptly as with many complex organizations in modern society. Finally *laws* emerge as conscious attempts to regulate areas of conduct on the lines laid down by mores and folkways. Two powerful influences on American sociology, Durkheimian positivism and social Darwinism, thus gave the professional paradigm an emphasis on socially shared ideas which concentrated on the rules of procedures for behavior built into the assumptions of the group.

Weber: Values and World View

This section describes in some detail Weber's research on the culture of modern industrial society.[1]   Two reasons prompt this description. Weber's work in this area is one of the most important substantive bequests from this period to modern sociology, a rich lode of ideas which is still being mined in research and theory. As such it compares with Marx's work on class, or Durkheim's on social deviance. Second, Weber believed that the sociologist should analyze historically real and distinctive situations. More than for any other sociologist in this group his general concepts and assumptions become apparent to us chiefly through analysis of his situation-specific work. His views on culture are therefore transmitted to us chiefly through his work on the culture of specific societies.

Weber's research on culture was prompted by his absorption with Marx's interpretation of history, and may be viewed as an attempt to modify, or even to negate, this interpretation.[2] Marx was preoccupied with Western capitalism. Weber directed his attention to the same phenomenon. There were broad similarities in the way each man conceptualized modern capitalism. They both saw it as a ramifying set of self-maintaining relationships, focused on economic activity, dominating all of modern society, and providing the infrastructure within which modern man shaped his life. The two men differed, however, on the question of how this pattern of social arrangements developed in the first place.

To Marx, capitalism had developed out of the tensions and conflicts of prior economic arrangements. Its origins lay in the economic relationships of feudalism: its material conditions, its class confrontations, and the dialectic processes for change which were immanent in such tension. Weber admitted that material and economic factors contributed to the development of capitalism, but argued that an explanation which incorporates only such variables is inadequate to explain the relatively sudden emergence in history of such a pattern of relationships. Weber's hesitation stemmed from his belief, described in the last chapter, that man is purposive; that his actions are always motivated; and that he must have goals towards which he directs his behavior. Any adequate explanation of momentous social change must deal with the question of what suddenly drives men to orient differently to action, so that new relationships replace those of the prior system. What are the new motives, goals, perceptions, and where do they come from? Based on this argument, Weber's research on the culture of modern capitalist society has three broad thrusts: describing the distinctive motivations of capitalist man; uncovering the historical sources of such a motivational pattern; and demonstrating that without this variable it is impossible to develop a complete explanation of capitalism. With the last theme Weber most directly confronted Marx, though all three efforts make important inroads into that position. This section will focus on the first and third themes in an attempt to understand Weber's conception of culture. The second theme will be explored in the next section.

Weber's research on these questions was presented in a number of books. The most famous is *The Protestant Ethic and the Spirit of Capitalism*, the original essay, in which he analyzed modern capitalist culture and investigated its origins. This book, however, is only a preliminary exploration of the counter-Marxist argument. In a series of other books he then investigated the culture of classical China, Hindu India, and ancient Judaism. His intention was to do similar work on Islam and on primitive Christianity, but he died before the research was completed. Throughout this massive undertaking his purpose remained constant: to show that cultural factors were essential to an explanation of a capitalist economic order. But an additional outcome of this later work was that Weber's description of capitalism's cultural configuration became much more elaborate.

In *The Protestant Ethic and the Spirit of Capitalism* Weber argued that men who involve themselves most fully in the economic activities of industrialized, capitalist Europe are committed to two basic goals: a desire to amass money and a passion for hard work. Nor are these needs purely egoistic. Capitalist man does not pursue money simply out of greed and a desire to purchase luxury. He does not work hard simply as a means to acquire the wealth for this ultimate goal of self-indulgence. Rather he believes that he is ethically bound to pursue profit and to work. Whatever his personal inclinations, he feels he must do these things if he is to be easy in his own conscience and judged a good man in the eyes of his community. The man who does not work, even if wealthy, is suspect. The man who is both idle and poor is almost certainly immoral. Men driven to action by such beliefs form the dynamic core of the capitalist economy even in its fully entrenched phase. Weber felt that the historical emergence of a sizeable group of men moved by such motives was essential to the early development of capitalism.

The beliefs in profit and hard work have further ramifications. Capitalist man places no quantitative limits on the pursuit of wealth. There is no point beyond which he has "too much," ceasing to be within the group of those judged good. Yearning for wealth in capitalist society is a yearning for unlimited wealth. Yet success along these lines is only morally correct if the wealth is obtained through systematic, lifelong, hard work, and work which within the manifest pattern of laws and mores is technically honest. The speculator, the one-time gambler, the underworld maneuverer, even if realizing fabulous wealth, is not acceptable in capitalist society. But within these constraints for systematic, long-term, honest work, the member of that society may choose any kind of work he feels like, and, so long as he obtains wealth thereby, he is a good man. No single career—manual or white collar work, or speculation in some particular commodity like land or finance—alone can earn a man the applause of his group. Weber's position is that this particular configuration of beliefs and values is a unique phenomenon in man's history, and that it is essential to the possibility of a capitalist social order.

Weber supported this position by his study of India and China. He argued that many of the material conditions deemed by Marxists and others to be essential to the development of capitalism were present in both these civilizations. These were not "primitive" societies which could be categorized as not yet evolved to the point where capitalism was feasible. Societies typed as primitive were small social groups with simple social organization and a moment-to-moment tenuousness in their very ability to survive, due either to the hostility of their physical environment, or to the aggressiveness of their members and their foes. India and China were not like this. They were societies with vast populations and huge urban centers. They had evolved complex systems of organization, particularly obvious in their rational bureaucratic structures. They had experienced long periods of peace and internal stability. They were skilled in many of the economic activities that go along with capitalism, such as extensive trading systems and complex financial manipulation. They possessed large reserves of precious metals which formed a basis for amassing capital. The Chinese were at least as technologically inventive as Europe, the Indians at least as skilled craftsmen. China possessed a class system which was formally open, and which in fact permitted considerable individual mobility. And India, while lacking this, had powerful organizations of merchants and manufacturers capable of pushing for the advancement of their economic constituencies.

The reason why this aggregate of variables conducive to capitalism did not crystallize into a social system similar to that of the Western industrial order could be traced back ultimately to the cultural systems of these two societies, and particularly to the beliefs and values of their dominant classes. In India this was particularly clear. Here the society was dominated by a priestly caste absorbed with ritual and with a mystical contemplation of other-worldly forces. Men believed themselves and the possibilities of their life totally structured and dominated by fate, by the eternal order of things. One worked in the traditional occupation to which one's birth committed one, or one ceased to work at all and sought instead the contemplative religious life. Wealth had no virtue; ascetic monastic poverty instead was an ideal. And ordinary men led lives dominated by superstition, by ritual, and a magical world view. India was, in Weber's term, an enchanted garden.

In China the situation was somewhat more complex. The ruling classes honored wealth, and replaced mysticism with a practical and rational orientation to the world of everyday things. But this class felt no proselytzing zeal. It took no responsibility for persuading ordinary men to its own practical and rational perspective. The Chinese masses were like the Indian population, firmly wedded to superstition, ritual, and magic. In terms of beliefs China was far more radically stratified than either Europe or India where dominant and subordinate classes shared, to some degree, in a common belief system. Moreover the Chinese elite was characterized by a pronounced sense that the givens of life ought to be accepted and honored. They felt this not because they believed like the Indian that fate was omnipotent, but because they valued harmony, balance, and an absence of conflict, and because they believed that what was was good. So they honored authority and tradition, and where the Indian aspired to ascetic monasticism, and Western man to specialized economic competency, the Chinese elite sought to be men of broad humanistic education and of a balanced cultivation of aesthetic skills.

Culture then was the catalyst. Alone it could not produce capitalism. The material factors had to be present. But the beliefs of men were necessary conditions if these material variables were to mesh into a capitalist order. If the beliefs were not conducive, some other system of social relations was possible, despite the propitious material factors. Culture was critical in two ways. First it had direct implications for human motivation in the economic area. Men who thought as the Indians and Chinese did could not be attracted to the frenetic life of the marketplace, as the Western bourgeoisie was. Second, the beliefs that characterized the Indian or Chinese ruling classes meant that they committed themselves to the maintenance of institutional arrangements which were barriers to a capitalistic economy, institutional arrangements which were allowed to disintegrate in the West because men were not moved to support them enthusiastically. India's embeddedness in as rigid and closed a stratification system as caste was one example. The Chinese absorption in the affairs of the kinship group, and their support for a religiously-based political system were other illustrations of this. The end product of the varying belief systems were social systems which were unique and completely distinct from each other; systems in which economic activity had varying degrees of social importance; systems of which capitalism was only one historical type. Weber rested his descriptions of the ethics of different societies on an impressive foundation of painstaking scholarly research.

In the course of this research, Weber's description of Western man's belief system became much more elaborate than the initial description of a work and profit orientation had been. In contrast to Indians, Westerners and Chinese were oriented to the material everyday world around them. In contrast to both Indians and Chinese, Westerners believed that they should actively engage themselves in that world rather than passively contemplating it, or openly remaining aloof from it. They felt that they could affect and must change that world, rather than submit fatalistically to it or attempt to live in harmony with it. Westerners were "disenchanted": they had no patience with magic, tradition, or ritual, but aspired instead to be practical, rational, and matter of fact. They valued change, where others honored tradition. They were individualistic, impatient of the duties and responsibilities of kinship, community, or class. The compulsion to work and to amass wealth became the irresistible forces that they were because they rested on this restless, aggressive, hard-headed individualism.

Weber's view of the strategic elements of culture differs then from Durkheim's emphasis on normative constraints, although it does not exclude these factors. Weber emphasized the goals to which men aspire, the criteria they use to differentiate the ethically valuable from what is ethically useless or harmful. These aspects of a society's idea world we today call values. Work and profit were values in Western society, according to Weber. He did not only focus on discrete values, however. As he probed most deeply into the cultures of different civilizations he increasingly emphasized the relationships between values, and the linkages of these to constellations of beliefs and assumptions. Culture becomes a complex configuration of values and beliefs which profoundly affect man's personality and behavior. Today this configuration is labeled frame of reference or world view.

Mead: Symbols and Meanings

A different slant on the concept of socially shared ideas is found in Mead's work. Mead's perspective on culture stems from his belief that man is in constant interaction with his social environment of other acting men, and that interaction is a process of communication.

Communication begins with an exchange of *gestures:* sounds, signs or other sensory stimuli. All animals use gestures—the dog growls in anger, the hen clucks in anxiety, the man clenches and raises his fist. Yet all animals, except man, respond to gestures instinctively. The growling of the dog triggers a similar series of behaviors in other dogs. The chickens instinctively move towards the clucking hen. But Mead believed that man *interprets* the gestures of others. He ducks from the clenched fist, not "instinctively," but because he thinks "he is going to hit me." An act of interpretation, or a layer of *meaning,* is inserted in human interaction between the gesture of one individual and the response of another. By the same token a gesture need have no fixed, unalterable, "natural" meaning. The clenched fist might imply solidarity, or greeting. Human culture is variable, not universal. Mead felt that man, of all the animals, has the least elaborate instinctive apparatus, and the most complex ability for interpretation and imputing meaning. Gestures in human communication are meaningful or *significant symbols.* Mead's view of culture concentrates on this notion of significance or meaning, the adjunct to behavior in human societies, and an essential ingredient for such behavior.

If communication involves the use of significant symbols, effective communication depends on the probability that all the individuals in interaction interpret symbols similarly. Cooperative action of any type, and even competition, is possible only if the actors share in a common pool of significant symbols. Without it communication is impossible, and therefore social interaction cannot occur.

> The organized community is an area of common consensus; it rests on a system of universally significant symbols which enable the largest conceivable number of human individuals to enter into some sort of social relations with each other, a relation arising in the general human social process of communication.[3]

Although Mead acknowledged the normative and value components of culture, he emphasized the cultural component of a symbolic network with common or shared cultural significance. In this system language plays a very important part, and it is to this that Mead gave most attention. But if one generalizes about the concept of a shared symbolic network, one can extend it to many more factors. In modern society, for example, there are common forms of music, drama, and other expressive arts; the flag; the fir trees, eggs, and other paraphernalia that signify feast days; the shorthand communication of advertising, and so on. In Mead's eyes man's ability to adapt to and shape his immediate social environment depended on the extent to which he shared in this common meaning structure.

The Origins of Culture

Where does culture come from, be it knowledge, norms, ideology, values, or symbolic structures? The question has two dimensions: the general one which asks why societies have a cultural environment at all; and the more specialized one which asks for an explanation of a particular society's distinctive culture, that is, which asks for the reasons for cultural variation. Competing answers to these questions were developed by the earlier sociologists.

A Product of Human Nature

Several sociologists believed that culture, however they described it, had its source in the particular physiological structure of the human organism: his brain (Mead); his impulses for rationalization (Pareto); adaptive experimentation for the satisfaction of elemental needs (Sumner). Since these were characteristics of the species man, culture was a phenomenon common to all societies. Each man, in part, worked out his own cultural perspective. More important, individual men were born into ongoing cultural systems and were influenced by them. Culture as a general concept then had some explanatory value for the sociologist. But the particular variations and manifestations which it took, according to historians and ethnographers, needed no special investigation. The sociologist was concerned with uncovering general features of all societies. That they all had ideologies, or normative systems, or symbolic networks was a fact of general import. That these phenomena varied in content from one particular society to another was not significant. It could be put down to random, fortuitous circumstances.

A Product of Social Relations

Another perspective on the questions about culture's origins stressed that culture, as a general phenomenon, was a social product, reflecting traits found in societies, rather than those of the human organism. Given this fact one could argue that a core of cultural similarity could be found in all societies, or in all similarly structured societies. Beyond this point, cultural variation could be viewed by the sociologist as fortuitous, although if pressed he could always explain the particular idea or belief in terms of particular characteristics of the society in which it occurred.

One answer of this type was Cooley's. His position is that the child everywhere receives his earliest socialization in a particular type of social group, the primary group; specifically he develops within the confines of a family. Here he experiences an elemental cluster of emotions and attitudes: love, kindness, respect, authority, suspicion of the outsider, and so on. The values of all societies are attempts to generalize, justify, and guarantee in the wider world of adults this basic core of experience. The ability of any individual to understand such values, at a level deeper than that of pure cognition, rests on its mesh with his own experience of family relations. His adherence to and support for such values will be constantly reinforced by continuing significant relationships in a number of primary groups. Since primary association and the family institution are common to all societies, at the deepest level one can discover certain fundamental values which are universal, and at this level all men can communicate. Cultural variations that occur above this level are more superficial than the nucleus of value universality.

Comte was another sociologist who felt that culture is a social product, since man is too small in intellect and too deficient in altruism to be capable of generating knowledge and morality. How exactly society creates culture he did not specify, but one can detect a partial overlap with Cooley. Morality or values, Comte stated, is the product of the family. He went on to add that knowledge is created by government. He handled the question of cultural variation by means of a law of progressive social development. All societies are subject to the law of developmental change. Each society is at a certain level or stage of development, and true to the law will pass through the later stages of such change. Cultural variation reflects the different levels of development simultaneously observable in the world. Two societies at a similar stage of development will be culturally very alike. The variations that one may observe even among such societies are superficial outcroppings on a solid rock of cultural similarity.

The most elaborate, and in some ways most mysterious argument along these lines is Durkheim's. He did not feel that one facet of social organization generates culture, as Cooley did. Rather it appeared to him that all the distinctive organizational traits of a group contribute to that group's system of norms, values and beliefs. Moreover, Durkheim's description of the process by which these norms and beliefs emerge differs markedly from that of Cooley Cooley pointed to the individual's immediate and personally significant experiences of interaction with others. From these experiences values are generalized, and from the overlap in individuals' immediate personal experiences, and their similar efforts to generalize about these, a common or shared culture arises. Durkheim, in contrast, did not feel that an individual's experiences of society are mediated through the everyday experiences of primary relations. Rather members of society immediately confront, or more accurately, they have forced upon their consciousness, the awesome and massive dynamics of social organization or society. They cannot precisely articulate this but they nevertheless feel it. This kind of awareness gives cultural norms and values their abstractness and their almost holy aura. If man simply generalized from his practical and personal experiences he would seldom or never raise them to such levels of abstractness and sanctity. But one finds that these traits are universal to culture. The reason must lie in man's ability to sense society as a very general, very potent "thing."

Even though abstractness and reverence pervade all cultural systems, the substance or content of different cultural systems may still vary because the traits of different societies or organized groups vary. One significant trait, for example, is the level of homogeneity or heterogeneity in the group, particularly that resulting from its division of labor. Members of a homogeneous society will have many more direct sensations of the society as a total, massive force, than will those of a highly complex differentiated system. Their norms will carry much of an aura of sanctity; violations of these norms will summon forth the outrage that results when something holy has been desecrated. Simply organized societies, in other words, are far more dominated by repressive, punishment oriented, normative systems—by systems of taboos. In complex society, individuals "sense" the society to be a unity of different, interdependent parts. That becomes their image of reality. Their norms are in many instances directed towards regulating this interdependence, restoring it to its state of well being, and are less marked by overt emotionality. Durkheim referred to the experience of homogeneous society as *mechanical solidarity,* and to that of heterogeneous society as *organic solidarity.* The former has legal (and normative) systems which are *repressive;* the latter has a *restitutive* legal/normative system. The developmental thesis which Comte put forward finds an echo in Durkheim's writings. Durkheim also felt that one can account for much cultural variation by seeing different societies as ranging on a continuum from "primitive" to "advanced." Primitive societies are homogeneous; advanced societies are highly differentiated. Their cultural systems vary accordingly, though the pure type "simple" or "advanced," completely mechanical or completely organic, does not exist in the empirical world. Any empirically observable social system will be some blend of mechanical and organic factors.[4]

Other characteristics of the group will similarly shape its culture: the "social density" or intensity of interaction in a group, its particular economic organization, and so on. One must also allow for some traditional continuities in studying culture; a sort of collective memory. But "survivals" do not simply survive forever. They are either reinforced by contemporary events and structural arrangements or they are replaced by new conceptions born of more recent experience.

A final aspect of Durkheim's perspective is that he gave religious organization an important role in his exploration of the emergence of culture. The group's experience of itself as a unity—mechanical solidarity—is, as has already been said, an awe-inspiring sensation. All groups seek to verbalize and capture this sensation. Their religious beliefs and religious practices are precisely such attempts to re-create and sustain this experience of society. This explains the universality and special status of religion in all societies. Religion, born of man's inchoate sense of awe in the presence of society, then serves to rekindle that sense of awe. It is true that in highly differentiated societies religion recedes in importance. But Durkheim seemed to feel that no society is ever so complex as not to experience itself as a solidary unit, or to maintain beliefs and practices which heighten such experience. Those beliefs and practices, even if manifestly the product of the state, are the society's religion.

Durkheim thus explained the organization and content of a society's belief system in terms of the structure of interaction in that society. He explained the stability of a belief system by means of the individual's awe and reverence for it, awe and reverence derived from the individual's ability to "sense" the power of society. The religious institutions of a society have special status in the list of social institutions, for they embody man's ability to express this sense of a pervasively powerful environment, and his own humility in the face of that experience.

Developments from Doctrine

Weber placed even greater emphasis than Durkheim did on the link between the religious institutions of a society and its more general cultural system. Characteristically, his thesis develops out of explorations of particular cultural patterns. The best known of these is his investigation of the origins of capitalism's ethos. By means both of statistical data and of a parallelism of ideas, he demonstrated that the sources of this ethos very probably lie in certain forms of ascetic Protestantism, of which the best known to us today is Calvinism. His argument along these lines is as follows. First, one can demonstrate statistically that such Protestants, even in nineteenth-century Europe, were far more attracted to technical and business careers than were Catholics. Second, if one scrutinized the doctrine of ascetic Protestantism, one could show quite satisfactorily that is was very likely to lead to a motivational system like that associated with capitalistic endeavor.

Calvinists believed in an inscrutable, omnipotent God, who had made the world and put man in it to work for the extension of His glory. They believed that man was a duality of flesh and spirit, the former an ephemeral thing of sin, the latter an enduring phenomenon which had a probability of grace and salvation. To this probability, to the question of the ultimate fate of the individual's immortal spirit, Calvinists directed their most distinctive doctrinal tenet: the doctrine of *predestination*. Predestination argued that God had, from the beginning, willed some individual souls to eternal salvation, others to eternal damnation. The reasons for this were inaccessible, and nothing one could do could affect the original decree. It was a bleak, austere faith.

Since God was beyond man's comprehension, and since His intention in creating man was to have an agent in the material world who would actively extend His glory, Calvinists were oriented away from mysticism and ritual observance, and towards an active perspective in the material everyday world and a proselytizing zeal for increasing the ranks of believers. Since God had made the world it was presumably planned and orderly. Discovering this order gave man some insight into God's nature, and gave man the potential for control of the world. in the service of God. The duality of flesh and spirit, and the disparate values of the two aspects of personality drove believers to asceticism, a fundamental suspicion of anything which might be judged as an indulgence of the flesh.

Above all the doctrine of predestination was tremendously anxiety provoking. Predestination argued that man could neither influence nor know his spiritual fate. Weber felt that while the first tenet (inability to influence) survived, the second (inability to know) gradually yielded to the anxiety of the average believer. Men came to feel that they could detect the signs of a man's salvation or damnation. A man whose soul was in a state of grace would live a godly, righteous life. He would be devoted to God, rigorously ascetic, hard working in the practical material world in which God bid man to serve Him. Such a man could convince himself and others that he was, probably, one of the saved. But what if man, through his hard work, grew rich? The money could not be used for personal enjoyment, for indulgence. It must be saved, accumulated, ploughed back into the work arena, there to create still further riches. The consequences of this last development were twofold. First it resulted in that amassing of capital out of which Western industrialism developed. Second, and more important, it meant that wealth in an expanding, less intimate religious community became itself an index of salvation: a sign that one worked hard, was ascetic, and so on. Wealth, hard work, and economic practicality evolved slowly out of Calvinism. Weber traces this gradual development in the writings of Calvinists. The original Calvinist "saints" were not capitalists, of course. It took a long time for the capitalist spirit to emerge from the community of Calvinist believers. Eventually however, it assumed explicit, autonomous, and self-sustaining cultural status.

A diffuse, all-enveloping system of values and beliefs, therefore, emerges from close contact between individuals and a systematic, explicit body of doctrine. Up to the time in which Weber wrote it seemed to him that the most likely source of such a body of doctrine was the religion of the particular society. He traced the ethos of classical China back to Confucian precepts about the essential harmony of the universe, and of all its component units. He linked the economic ethos of Hindu India to its religious beliefs in the transmigration of souls, the hierarchy into which these souls were born, and the belief that spiritual mobility from one life to another was determined by the extent to which one dutifully conformed with the demands of status in any particular life. The links between explicit religious doctrine and a more general orientation to life were sometimes quite direct—as for example the Calvinists' explicit requirements for asceticism. Often, however, attitudes evolved "unpredictably," as a result of the interplay between the formal doctrine and the needs and anxieties of innumerable individual psyches. The capitalist concern with profit was one example of a distinctive cultural factor gradually emerging out of generations of individual stress and accomodation.

The Role of Charismatic Leaders

The problem of cultural development can be pushed further, in two different ways. First, why do these culturally important systems of doctrine appear, and in one particular form rather than another? Weber's explanation is only partly sociological. Doctrinal systems, he stated, are the creation of particular men, of historically important individuals who are genuinely creative in the formulation of new belief systems. To Weber, Calvin was an important influence in the structuring of the doctrine which would later bear his name. It is true that there are periods in the historical life of a society which demand new doctrine, because the older systems of thought for whatever reasons lose legitimacy. It is also true that certain cultures may be more conducive to the frequent emergence of new belief systems: Weber argued that ancient Judaism, by giving both honor and antonomy to those who assumed the role of prophet, had built-in mechanisms for frequent doctrinal renovation and innovation. But an important part of the explanation for the particular belief system being investigated is the individual who promulgated it, and his capacity for creative, independent action.

The second question is why these new belief systems get accepted and spread. Again Weber based part of his explanation on personality: some individuals manage to popularize their ideas because of the power and "magic" of their personalities. They are *charismatic*—the word was introduced to sociology by Weber. Another part of the answer has to do, as we have already described, with the receptivity of the society to new ideas, either generally, or at particular moments in its history. A third cluster of explanatory variables is the organization of disciples and apostles with which a charismatic leader surrounds himself. There seems to be a certain inconsistency here in Weber's argument. Unlike any of the other sociologists whom we have so far reviewed, Weber is concerned with the emergence of *specific* cultural systems. He links them to religious doctrines in an effort to make clear both their particular patterning, and the general, universal processes that enter into the shaping of culture. But in terms of the last two questions raised—the content and spread of the doctrinal systems which give rise to distinctive cultural patterns—he pointed merely to the general, universal processes, leaving the question of the doctrine's particular content to the dynamics of charismatic personality.

The Work of a Ruling Class

Unexpectedly perhaps, Marx gave a more elaborate answer than Weber did to the questions of doctrine's particular content and its spread. To Marx, a particular belief system will initially prove attractive to that group in society who see some relationship between the beliefs and their own material interests, needs, and experiences. The belief system may actually be distilled out of those interests, needs, and experiences by the group, in some sort of collective effort. Or it may be created by a small number of intellectuals, who, of all the groups in society, have the ability to identify with the perspective of other social groups. The belief system will spread beyond its particular interest group as that group acquires power in the society, for power gives it access to the channels of communication and persuasion. In this later stage the belief system functions not merely as a legitimizing morality for its original interest group, but as an instrument for social control of other groups or classes. Therefore, a definite "career" pattern can be drawn for any belief system. During a particular class's heyday of power, its own interest-based beliefs will define the morality of the society; and given the allegiance of all the idea-creating, idea-transmitting social agents, that belief system will be the belief system of the bulk of the population. But as the logic of the relational patterns produce new, ambitious social groups, these groups will produce counter-ideology: ideology which reflects not only their own interests but also their rejection of the prevailing belief system. As the new groups organize and increase their power, the society polarizes into ideological camps. Some of the intellectuals and other idea-processing agents defect to the antiestablishment class. Inevitably the two camps move into open conflict. The outcome determines the new power structure and the new society-wide belief system. The cycle starts once more. Marx does not distinguish, as Weber does, between a circumscribed doctrinal system and a diffuse system of beliefs and orientations. But although it is usual to regard Weber and Marx as holding alternative positions on culture, on this issue of the mechanics of cultural evolution the two perspectives seem to be complementary. Together their explanation is far richer than the mechanistic and mystical thesis put forward by Durkheim.

Summary, Discussion, Conclusions

Starting with the belief that man is distinguished from other animal species by the elaborateness of his thinking, early sociologists went on to explore the implications of this for human society. They described the idea components of social life as knowledge, morality, ideology, norms, values, frames of reference, and systems of symbolic meaning. They sought the origins of these cultural components in the human organism, in the social group, in categories of special interests, and in other systems of ideas. One feature of this discussion has emerged in bits and pieces; this is the considerable interest with religion which runs through much of their writings. Comte, Durkheim, Weber, and Marx all dealt at length with the positive or negative implications of religious life for the well being of society. The nine-

TABLE 4 : Views of Culture

Theorist	His label for culture	Characteristics of culture stressed or implied	Culture's origins	Culture's functions
1. Comte	"Intellect"	1. technological knowledge 2. Morality or altruism 3. Implicit—"world view"	Society as a developing phenomenon	1. Societal development 2. Control of individual egoism
2. Durkheim	"Collective representations"	1. Norms with sanctions 2. Institutions, laws 3. Implicit—values, world views	Social structure; religion of special importance	Social control, integration
3. Sumner	"Folkways and mores"	1. Norms 2. Institutions, laws	Human adaptive behavior, and imitation	Social adaptation
4. Weber	"Meanings" "Culture"	1. Values 2. World views	Doctrinal innovators, status/power groups	Human motivation
5. Cooley	"Meanings" "Values"	1. Language 2. Values	Social experience especially in primary groups	Human communication
6. Mead	"Significant symbols"	Specifically language	Human physiological abilities	Communication for adaptive behavior
7. Pareto	"Derivations"	Ideological belief systems of intense "religious" fervour	Human needs for rationalization; elites may be first proponents	*Ex post facto* justification; social mobilization
8. Marx	"False consciousness"	Ideological belief systems often intense "religious" fervour	Ruling class interests	Control of subordinate classes

teenth century saw the last major confrontation in intellectual circles between religious and secular perspectives, a confrontation ending largely in the victory of the latter. Table 4 summarizes the major points raised in this chapter.

Nowhere is the link between early sociology and the wider social and philosophical community more obvious than in this early absorption with the question of culture. We have described some of these general themes in the early part of this chapter. Some of the men in this group extended these themes in almost pure form into sociology. Weber's approach clearly reflects his socialization in idealism; Durkheim and Sumner both picked up the dominant themes of conservative thought. As such these systems are transmitted to us in later sociology, even though we are no longer immediately linked to the philosophical systems in which they originated.

Other sociologists made more obvious attempts to carve out for sociology some new position *vis à vis* these various traditions. Comte, for example, sought to reconcile radical and conservative positions in a new compromise. Pareto sought to dismiss all these positions by arguing for the irrationality and irrelevance of almost all types of socially shared ideas. Marx too attempted to argue away the social importance of cultural variables.

It is also interesting to see how the positions taken in this chapter relate to views about sociology's subject matter described in chapter 5. The central question is how important a place culture should have in a system of sociological explanation. Weber and Durkheim, who differed in so many ways, shared common ground on this issue. They were as close as one can get, in this group, to a position of cultural determinism. Culture, however they defined it, was the major explanatory variable for both of them in their definitions of sociology. Comte too came close to this position. Others flatly rejected this thesis, and argued that sociology's subject matter deals only peripherally with cultural variables. Pareto and Marx were of this persuasion. Still others preferred to focus on the constant associational relationships of social life, though they were prepared to build a cultural component into this conception of sociology's subject matter. Mead, Cooley, and Simmel took this position. Finally the Darwinists subordinated the role of culture to that of the massive, universal evolutionary process. Spencer largely excluded cultural variables from what he defined as sociology's primary concern; Sumner, while paying far more attention to societal belief systems, saw them as created by adaptive needs and surviving or changing in the service of such needs. Although the last position has receded in contemporary sociology, the three other judgments of culture's functional importance are still influential.

The links between this chapter's material and that of the preceding chapter about man and society are more complex. The evolutionary thinkers, Spencer and Sumner, fitted culture into their belief in man as an adaptive, evolving species. Pareto had so little faith in the human potential for sustained systematic thought that he almost wholly discounted the importance of culture in man's social life. But those who saw man as a cognitive, purposive being, shaping at least in part the processes of his life in society, very naturally assumed that man's idea products were essential to understanding social life—the ideas of Weber, Mead, and Cooley all illustrate this viewpoint to different degrees. Yet there were others far less optimistic about human nature, men who viewed man as a creature of egoistic impulse, who still placed great faith on cultural variables. To Comte and Durkheim culture was the mysterious product of social organization, acting as a force for coercion and control of that egoistic human nature, a force which alone made possible social order and social progress. So it was that men who evaluated human nature so differently came to curiously similar conclusions about the importance of the collective ideas of the human group. But those who were optimistic about man's potential rationality saw culture as something creatively acted out in day-to-day living; those who, pessimistically, viewed man as a creature of unregulated impulse make culture the omnipotent force to which men bowed or paid the consequences. Only Marx saw culture not simply as societal control over all human nature, but as control over subordinate classes of men by those more powerful, a product of human nature and economic realities which made stratification and exploitation an almost unavoidable fact of history.

Yet most of these men, as was said much earlier in the text, were scholars concerned with the technical details of theory, and were self-defined sociologists concerned with making clear the dimensions of the new field. So while the basic assumptions on which they approached this question differed widely, most of them went on to work through in careful detail the technical ramifications and implications of their concept of culture. At this level they infused new elements into the sociological belief system: concepts such as those of folkways, symbolic systems, and false consciousness.

While one can find almost all of the earlier positions on culture still in evidence, there seems to be no doubt that the bias in favor of an emphasis on culture has survived as the dominant one. And this gives us and the earlier sociologists a common problem. How does one go about the empirical, scientific study of such elusive variables as socially shared ideas? This question is one of those taken up in the next chapter.

NOTES

1. Many of the ideas in this description of Weber are drawn from Talcott Parsons' monumental study of earlier sociological theory in *The Structure of Social Action* (Glencoe, Illinois: Free Press, 1937).

2. There has been some debate on whether Weber's work in this area is a qualification of the Marxist thesis, as I think he intended it; or whether it is a rejection of that thesis since logically it denies Marx's fundamental hypothesis that economic relations alone determine historical change and societal dynamics.

3. George Herbert Mead, *Mind, Self and Society* (Chicago: University of Chicago Press, 1934), p. 158.

4. Emile Durkheim, *The Division of Labor in Society*, trans. ed. (Glencoe, Ill.: Free Press, 1964).

8

Methods for Sociology

Two elemental questions are contained in the early attempts to delineate sociology as an academic field. First, *what* did it purport to study? Second, *how* did it intend to go about its work of investigation? The first question, about sociology's subject matter, was discussed in chapter 5. The second question concerns sociology's methods. Explorations of this issue will be described here.

At one level, of course, the question of sociology's subject matter and that of its methods cannot be separated from each other. This was already evident in chapter 5 which, as part of the discussion of sociology's subject matter, described a general consensus that sociology was scientific, and explored broad research orientations to social facts, social action, social systems, and so on. It will become even more clear in this chapter, as one observes how the varying beliefs about what sociology should study guided the development of research techniques.

Two sources of information exist which can tell us what early sociologists believed on the question of methods. There are the formal methodological statements which many of them made, self-consciously addressing themselves to the problem of sociological research, and there is the research which they actually did. Both sources are used in this chapter. The former indicates aspirations which they had for their field. The latter shows the practical accommodations which they developed under pressures of limited technology, a complex subject matter, and their own beliefs about the purpose of sociology. Some of these accommodations became later norms of sociological research.

This chapter is organized around three broad issues; (1) the debate on the scientific status of sociology; (2) the major research techniques used in this period; and (3) a summary and discussion which, more extensively than the preceding chapters, traces some of the continuities and discontinuities between present and past research strategy.

Sociology as Science

It is both conventional and, strictly speaking, a mistake to view the methodological discussion of this period as an argument between those who felt that social phenomena could be studied scientifically and those who rejected this notion. The former perspective, based in philosophical positivism, is supposedly represented by men like Comte, Spencer, Durkheim, and Pareto. The latter position, rooted in philosophical idealism, is presumably that of Simmel, Tönnies, and Weber. Since Durkheim's *Rules of Sociological Method* and Weber's *Methodology of the Social Sciences* are the most extensive methodological publications of this period, Durkheim and Weber have been treated as the major representatives of the two viewpoints.

It is true that Durkheim and Weber had different standpoints. It is also true that each man without directly mentioning the other did address himself to the general position represented by that other. But the chief problem with the conventional groupings of "positivists" and "idealists" on this question is that it simplifies Weber's thesis, and exaggerates the division between him and Durkheim. It similarly distorts Simmel's viewpoint. Only Tönnies can be viewed strictly as an idealist, ignoring, though not explicitly rejecting, the use of scientific technique in the study of society. For him sociology was simply the study of man's social nature, with the aim of understanding him intuitively and intellectually. There is no mention of science in that definition. Moreover his first rule of procedure was

> *Nosce te ipsum* (know yourself): if you want to understand others look into your own heart. Everyone of us has manifold relationships, direct or indirect, with other people. Thus the question arises, how do I know other people?[1]

The brilliant and germane insights of *Gemeinschaft und Gesellschaft* were then created by applying the capacities of intellect for reasoning, and for logical and imaginative thought, to that nexus of personal experience and knowledge; there is no further formal attention to methods. It is indeed far removed from the requirements for empirical science.

Tönnies' proposal that one search one's own heart for sociological truths was, however, unparalleled in the methodological discussion of this period. Elsewhere there was consensus that sociology was empirical, that it was oriented to a realm of material observations, and that sociological investigation began with sensory data. Simmel stated that

> sociology as a *special science* . . . need [s] a concept of society which subjects *socio-historical data* to a new mode of co-ordination and abstraction.[2]

Weber was even more explicit on this point.[3] The methodological argument of this period was not about whether sociology could be scientific. The major founders of the discipline agreed on this point. No explicit idealist-derived alternative to that position was developed. The argument that occurred was about positivism, about the extent to which the research techniques and goals of natural science exclusively defined what scientific procedure was. This worried Weber in particular, and also Simmel. Even within the group of professed positivists unanimity on the implications of this question was not complete. Much of this section will describe the argument about a positivistic sociology. But first we will look at something which the conventional approach tends to overlook: the important common ground that existed because of the general agreement that sociology must be an empirical science.

Points of Agreement

If sociology was to measure up to its claims of being scientific, its investigations must begin with and constantly be tested against the rigors of empirical observation. There was consensus on this point. Its best known advocate was Durkheim:

> All that is given, all that is subject to observation has thereby the character of a thing. To treat phenomena as things is to treat them as data, and constitute the point of departure of science . . . . social phenomena are things . . . . they are the unique data of a sociologist.[4]

But the precept was scattered throughout the writings of the period, in the writings not only of Pareto, but also of men like Weber and Simmel.[5] The names they gave to the empirical basis of their investigation varied, but the term on which they seemed to be most in agreement was "*social facts*." Only Weber seemed to shy away from the phrase, referring instead to "concrete events." Durkheim, as chapter 5 showed, put "social facts" at the center of sociology's definition of its subject matter.

However, several points of view on the definition of social facts can be found. Pareto spoke of men's "theories," Weber of conduct (including thought and attitudes), Durkheim of constraints, and so on. Another important type of variation reflects the alternative pressures of positivistic and idealistic assumptions. Some writers deify "the facts," insisting that they can and must have sovereignty in the investigatory process:

> Principles depend on facts, not facts on principles. They are governed by facts . . . . accepted hypothetically only so long as they are in agrement with the facts; and rejected as soon as they are in disagreement.[6]

This was Pareto's statement. It closely reflected Durkheim's position. Others, however, stressed that the observer to a considerable extent shaped what he perceived as "facts," and that interpretation (Weber), or perspective (Simmel), or theory (Comte) must be recognized as elemental to the process of inquiry.

Sensory data was an important, or maybe *the* important starting point for sociological investigation. The field needed procedures for handling data. At the level of general directives there is considerable agreement. One begins with careful, *disciplined observation:* Comte treated this as one of the three major procedures of sociology; Spencer devoted a full volume[7] to exploring the problems besetting such observation and the controls over it which the sociologist must exercise; Weber painstakingly analyzed past documents and biographies; Pareto exhaustively searched the written output of various societies; in America, Cooley carefully recorded the early development of his own children—and so on. In the course of these investigations and discussions, it also became clearer where sociologists would seek their facts. Direct observation of behavior was, of course, one source. But it did not seem to rank as more important than secondary sources, particularly from ethnography, history, and official records.

> The sociologist must take as the object of this research groups of facts . . . and adhere strictly to them. Such . . . subjects as history, ethnography and statistics are indispensable[8]

Data collected this way must be analyzed in terms of sociological concerns and purposes. Such concerns and purposes centered around the need to *abstract and generalize* about society. As Durkheim puts it:

> Sociology raises other problems than history or ethnography. It does not seek to know past forms of civilization with the sole end of knowing them and reconstructing them. But rather, like every positive science, it has as its objective . . . . to show us essential and permanent aspect [s] of humanity.[9]

And Weber agrees:

> The science of sociology seeks to formulate type concepts and generalized uniformities of empirical process. This distinguishes it from history which is oriented to . . . individual actions, structures and personalities . . . . As in the case of every generalizing science, the abstract character of the concepts of sociology is responsible for the fact that, compared with actual historical reality, they are relatively lacking in fullness of concrete content. To compensate for this disadvantage, sociological analysis can offer a greater precision of concepts.[10]

It has often been asserted that Weber rejected the generalizing role of sociology. However, the preceding statement shows that, at least in his later phase, he viewed sociology as a generalizing science. His hesitations were about how far one could press a generalization, what the functions of generalization were, and what it was that one generalized about. These points will be reviewed later in this chapter.

As part of this process of manipulating data, there was a need to classify it under general rubrics. *Taxonomy* played a crucial part in the early work of sociological investigation. Meaningful categories were developed and data sorted into numerous classificatory systems. Mention has already been made of Weber's four categories of action: rational, value oriented, traditional, and emotional. Later chapters will consider the typologies created by Comte and Spencer for studying societies; Durkheim's analysis of types of social order; Cooley's classification of groups and Tönnies' of relationships; Weber's categories of social power, and so on.

Another scientific approach to data was *experimentation*. Sociologists of this period felt that the pure laboratory type of experiment was almost impossible for sociology, but that various types of "indirect" experiments were possible. Comte stated this well:

> It might be supposed that . . . experiment must be wholly inapplicable in Social Science; but we shall find that the science is not entirely deprived of this resource . . . . We must remember that there are two kinds of experiment—the direct and indirect: and that it is not necessary to the philosophical character of this method that the circumstances . . . be . . . artificially instituted.
>   . . . Experimentation takes place whenever the regular course of the phenomenon is interfered with in any determinate manner. The spon-

taneous nature of the alteration has no effect on the scientific value of the case . . . . It is in this sense that experiment is possible in sociology.[11]

Indirect experiments as practiced in this period comprised various kinds of controlled observation of judiciously selected cases. Comte suggested careful analyses of social instabilities or "pathologies" in order to isolate the variables producing order and disorder. Durkheim seemed to follow this suggestion in his study of suicide, but in his work on religion he turned to another tactic for experimenting (he explicitly referred to it as experiment), one already suggested in *Suicide*. This consisted of carefully testing a series of alternative hypotheses against the data of a microscopically analyzed case study. For Weber experimentation was possible by

comparing the largest possible number of historical or contemporary processes which, while otherwise similar, differ in the one decisive point of their relationship to a particular factor the role of which is being investigated.[12]

This was the model he followed in his comparative work on religion and economic ethics. As was discussed in chapter 7, Weber compared the civilizations of China and India to that of preindustrial Europe. He demonstrated many socioeconomic similarities. He then explored the variations in religious ethics in the three societies, and the structural consequences of this. He used this point of variation to explain the emergence of capitalism in Europe, and the absence of such a phenomenon in China and India. This whole process was for him a form of "natural" experiment. Indeed the urge to approximate an experimental situation in sociology seemed to lie behind the absorption with comparative sociology, a cluster of research techniques which will be described shortly.

Another mode of handling data seems to have been suggested by the unique characteristics of sociological data itself. The field was concerned, in one way or another, with the behavior of human individuals. The fact had to be confronted that even when one isolated some general kind of behavior for study, there appeared to be infinite variation in its actual manifestations given the role played by individual will, experience, personality, and so forth. How could one make any firm statements about behavior? To one degree or another most sociologists seemed to accept the function of *statistical statements* about social behavior. Simmel put it as follows:

What we are suggesting, in brief, is that similar elements be singled out of the complex phenomena so as to secure a cross-section, whereby dissimilar elements reciprocally paralyze each other.[13]

Pareto was much more specific on the element of quantification involved:

> To that end it often helps to consider not the individual phenomenon actually observed, but average situations where the effect of certain laws are attenuated and those of others are emphasized . . . . No one can tell whether John Doe will live or die next year; but we can tell, approximately, how many people out of a hundred-thousand John Doe's age will die.[14]

Of all the members of the group under consideration, Durkheim most wholeheartedly and thoroughly utilized statistics in sociological investigation. His conceptualization of this means of investigation is elaborate enough to be treated in a separate section of this chapter.

The only sociologist who adamantly rejected any resort to statistical concepts was Comte, who roundly condemned any suggestion that the field use "the pretended theory of chances" (or probability). His reasons are rather obscure. Partly they rest on his hostility to any form of reductionism in the study of society: statistical statements did derive ultimately from the behavior of individuals, and Comte refused to acknowledge that society could be analyzed or explained at any level in terms of individuals. Partly it seemed to be professional pique and a feeling of rivalry with the theories of contemporaries like Quételet. In contrast, Weber did not wholly reject orientations derived from social statistics—he suggested caution in this approach. He was afraid that the sociologist might be carried away by the impressiveness of quantified data, and might as a result forget the true purposes of sociological investigation. As Weber defined these, sociology studied meaning or culture as it shaped and manifested itself in the behavior of real, concrete individuals. Statistics were only justified when they served these ends. The only statistical rates which were useful to sociologists were those that implied something about meaningful or motivated behavior:

> Statistical uniformities constitute understandable types of action . . . and thus constitute "sociological generalizations" only when they can be regarded as manifestations of the understandable subjective meaning of a course of action . . . . There are statistics of processes devoid of meaning such as death rates . . . the amount of rainfall [etc.]. But only when the phenomenon is meaningful is it convenient to speak of sociological statistics. Examples are such cases as crime rates, occupational distributions, price statistics [etc.].[15]

All of these activities—observation, generalization, classification, experimentation, and the use of statistical analysis—had a common goal.

Sociology was a science which would offer *explanations* of the phenomenon which it studied, in terms of the variables which produced or caused it. This contrasts with such alternative goals as description and the recording of events, which many saw to be the role of history. But at this point, we come very close to a point of fundamental confrontation in the field. Only at a very general level did any common definition of "explanation" exist. Precisely what one meant by the term was a bone of contention among sociologists. The question is better treated as part of the next section, which describes the confrontation that occurred on the scientific status of the profession.

The Debate on Positivism

The positivists in sociology were moved by a deep admiration for the success achieved by the physical and natural sciences. They were convinced that following the procedural guidelines of those sciences in the study of social phenomena would lead sociology to similar success. They therefore sought to model sociology as closely as possible to natural science, pursuing the same goals, struggling to approximate its means or techniques as closely as possible. To a positivist the word "science" meant the procedures for investigation best represented by fields like physics, chemistry, and biology. Pareto and Durkheim were the most articulate proponents of a positivistic sociology, but similar statements were made by Comte, Spencer, and many of the Americans.

The most thoughtful questioning of this viewpoint came from Weber. His position has remained a major rallying point for critics of positivistic sociology, and will accordingly be described in some detail. "Science" for Weber meant a general style or mode of inquiry, oriented to empirical observations, struggling for precise, disciplined study of these observations, subject to verification, and so on. The methods of the natural sciences seemed to him only one possible manifestation of this form of inquiry, a manifestation worked out in response to the specific requirements of studying material objects. Sociologists should face the fact that what they wished to study was qualitatively different from the objects which concerned natural science. They should confront their own distinctive subject matter as open-mindedly as early natural scientists had puzzled over theirs. This would lead them to develop research procedures which were scientific in general intention, but particularly suited to investigating sociology's own subject matter.

What distinguished sociology's material from that of the natural sciences was the phenomenon of mind. Man not only engaged in overt activity; he also thought. Moreover, thought had vital consequences for behavior. The world of interpretation and meaning which it produced gave content to the motivations which propelled man to act, and shaped the decisions by which he chose one sequence of behavior over another. Mind and behavior were so interconnected that one could not hope to study one without the other. From that perspective natural science could be viewed as dealing with a one-dimensional realm: the manifest movements, changes, variations, and structures of material objects. Sociology's subject matter was two-dimensional. Not only was there the manifest behavior of man, patterned, changing, variable, and so on, there was also the world of consciousness, interpretation, and decision making. Natural science had never had to deal with such a phenomenon, and had no guidelines to offer for studying either consciousness or its relationship to behavior.

Thus, sociology was more than natural science. In a quest for causal explanations it could go beyond the correlational uniformities which were the "laws" of natural science. Sociology could also probe the interpretive and motivational core of the individuals whose behavior was the actual link between two clusters of variables. Sociology could say more about how and why A led to B than natural science could say about its cluster of variables. One example is the observable relationship between religious affiliation and economic behavior. In Europe one could show that Protestants were more attracted to business than Catholics, no matter what statistical controls one exercised. One could stop the investigation at this point, talk of a "lawlike relationship," and hypothesize why this might be. All sorts of reasons might suggest themselves. One might talk for example of the varying intensities in communal relationships in Protestant and Catholic groups (as Durkheim did in studying suicides). But the sociologist could go further in his investigation. He could study the consciousness of the Protestant, his values, beliefs, suppositions, and so on. By contrasting it with the consciousness of the Catholic, he would not only know that religion and economics were related to each other, he would understand, in specific detail, how and why they were related.

This enrichment of explanation, however, came at a price, at least from the standpoint of the positivist. It involves a return to the problem of generalization raised in the preceding section. Weber held that there were limits to the extent of generalization one could make about mind, if one were to maximize its explanatory value.

One explained behavior in terms of complexes of beliefs and assumptions. At one level a belief pattern was really unique to the individual who held it. At another level one could distill the essence of the beliefs of many similar individuals, generalizing about their "culture." But beyond this one could not go. One could not generalize about the culture of individuals who were dissimilar in situation, even when they behaved similarly. One could not assume any cultural similarity, for example, between Catholic, Hindu, and Confucianist just because none of them seemed attracted to capitalist industrial activity. One had to know each cultural configuration in its historical uniqueness if one wished to explain behavior by means of mind.

When Weber spoke of sociology as a generalizing science, he meant that sociology could generalize about the approximately similar beliefs of individuals who were similarly situated in a historically real society. Sociologists could overlook the multitudes of individual variations in beliefs that existed even among such "like" individuals. However, sociologists could not generalize across cultures to universal contents of meaning. The results would only describe trivia. Since behavior was so closely linked to mind, this meant that there were few if any universally applicable explanations of behavior in society. In contrast natural science could make universal generalizations about cells or atoms or whatever other objects concerned it. In this sense sociology was less than the physical and natural sciences.

This conclusion was intolerable to positivistic sociologists. The trait of natural science which they most admired, the one that most clearly conveyed a sense of its power, was the ability to make statements which were universal in their application. This ability meant that the scientist could not only explain something with which he was familiar, he could also anticipate the nature of what was yet unknown. Particularly he could predict to the future—"prevision" it, as Spencer put it. That was power indeed. It gave him control, sometimes over the future event itself, and always over his own response to it.

> Science, in furnishing us the law of variations through which moral health has already passed, permits us to anticipate those coming into being . . . . we shall be able to foresee them and forseeing them, will them before hand. [16]

This was Durkheim's aspiration. To deny sociology the right of generalizing across cultures was to seriously curtail any predictive powers in the field. To positivists this permanently relegated sociology to a second class status.

The positivists' response to the position which Weber represented took many forms. The most straightforward was a flat assertion that there were important characteristics common to all cultures. Durkheim illustrated this:

Since all religions can be compared to each other, and since all are species of the same class, there are necessarily many elements which are common to all . . . . At the foundation of all systems of beliefs and of all cults there ought necessarily to be a certain number of fundamental representations of cultures and of ritual attitudes which in spite of the diversity of forms which they have taken have the same objective significance and fulfill the same functions everywhere.[17]

Faced on occasion with a "diversity of forms" so great as to confound the attempt to find "elements in common," one solution was to assert that the variations were lawlike, reflecting stages in the development of culture. Durkheim and Comte both used this device.

A second and more telling attack was to deny the importance of interpretive processes in the shaping of social phenomena. Pareto, for example, argued that interpretative schema or derivations were epiphenomenal to behavior, that man was propelled by a finite set of instincts rooted in his biological nature, and that consequently one could make generalized statements about his behavior in society. Comte and Durkheim stated first that men do not really know why they behave in particular ways. For example:

The reasons with which the faithful justify their religious practices . . . generally are erroneous; but the true reasons do not cease to exist and it is the duty of science to discover them.[18]

Second, man is subordinated to the pressures of societal forces which emerge out of the general phenomenon of human association, and consequently have certain generalizable features:

Social facts . . . . far from being a product of the will . . . . determine it from without; they are like molds in which our actions are inevitably shaped.[19]

A third approach was to study dimensions of mind other than its intrinsic content—the dimension which Weber emphasized. Durkheim for example focused more on the structure or organization of culture: its complexity, its consistency, its integration, its level of development, and so on. Mead studied the process of consciousness, rather than its content. The implication was that these aspects were generalizable and had explanatory value sufficient to compensate for the variations in cultural content which, since ungeneralizable, would have to be omitted from a scientific explanation of social behavior.

These different standpoints led to a now famous exchange on the place of scientific laws in sociological analysis. The exchange is the more significant because there appears to have been no fundamental difference of opinion about what was meant by the phrase "scientific laws," at least in the later group of sociologists who participated in the exchange. Laws were empirical generalizations about the relationships between certain specified categories of things, generalizations which on the basis of much observation were held to be universal in their application. In fact, these generalizations had such status that one could deduce from them the state of specific things which one had not directly investigated, because they belonged to that more general category of things about which one had a scientific "law."[20]

The discussion of the role of laws in sociology is thus clearly an extension of the more general concern with the function of generalizations. Laws, however, are a special class of generalizations. Mere generalizations are arrived at inductively as the last stage in a process of empirical investigation. Laws are the product of a logical exercise *vis à vis* such generalizations, in which further abstraction has occurred, and relationships with what is already known to be lawlike have been mapped. The result is a general principle which can be used for deduction at the start of a process of empirical investigation, since the principle is held to be universal and without exception:

> Laws . . . never suffer any genuine exception. To speak of a uniformity which is not uniform is to say a thing which has no meaning. What is commonly called an exception to a law is really the superimpositions of the effect of another law upon its own normal effects.[21]

To the positivistic sociologist the discovery of the laws of social life was the goal behind the application of the "logico-experimental" method to social data. Such laws would give sociology equal status with any other science. It would also open up a range of research alternatives for the field: to explain the particular observation by subsuming it under the law; to approximate a true experimental format with hypotheses formally stated and arrived at deductively from law; to build scientific theory, or systems of such laws with wide explanatory value. Nor did the positivist doubt that such laws operated in social life and that they were discovered by the scientist. The task might be somewhat more complex for sociologists because of the difficulty in approximating a true experimental design and because of the complex overlapping of several laws in any sequence of behavior which one observed, but such laws could be isolated. Quantification and statistical investigation would assist in the investigation. Indeed, the earlier positivists, Comte and Spencer, claimed to have found such laws, laws of social development.

Weber denied neither the possibility that such laws existed nor that they had a place of sociological investigation. But he criticized the proposal of positivistic sociologists that the discovery of such laws constituted the ultimate goal of sociological investigation. How was it that positivists were proposing to use such laws? Positivists said the laws were to explain social life, but in practice this meant the explanation of particular slices of social life, particular and real configurations of events. Positivists hoped to explain individual sociohistorical phenomena by means of general, abstract laws. Weber felt such explanations were unnecessarily impoverished. They ignored that dimension of explanation which was sociology's peculiar resource: explanation in terms of the actors' motivations, interpretations, purposes, etc. This was the link between the operation of general principles and the specific features which they manifested in the individual case under consideration. Mind was as much a "cause" of the detailed behaviors being observed as were the mechanical effects of sociological laws. As mind worked in a particular sociohistorical event, it had to be described in its essence and uniqueness. The content of mind reflected the content of the culture in which the thinking individual was located. A particular cultural configuration resulted from a unique constellation of past historical events and had to be so explained. Laws were not useless in sociology; they were in fact very important in the preliminary stages of investigating a social event. Using them one could discover the "givens" in the situation, the things that mechanically and deterministically had to be. One then moved beyond this stage of an exploration of what was distinctive about the particular event, to explanations of this in terms of the actors' world view, and to explanation of the world view by means of a causal chain of historical events. [22]

Weber illustrated this in terms of economic behavior, but an illustration from modern experience may make his point clearer. Suppose one wished to explain a recent sequence of urban riots. Sociologists have developed several general principles which help one to get to the variables which go into such uprisings: anomalies in the system; the development of particular beliefs; a precipitating factor; and so on. These would allow the investigator to isolate many of the general factors at work. But in explaining the particular riots, Weber would have argued, one would have to go further and specify the content of the beliefs, the interpretations of the anomalies, the reason why a particular event acted as a precipitant. One cannot assume that the mechanical working through of laws explains everything about the particular actions of cognitive beings. One would also have to say why the interpretations and beliefs had the content they did, in terms of the prior real historical experiences and beliefs of the particular group that rioted. Only then, Weber felt, would one have "explained" the event fully. It is difficult to evaluate the absolute merits of these two viewpoints (the positivists and Weber), except with the eclecticism of Simmel, who felt that the choice between the two approaches would have to be shaped, in each instance, by the purpose at hand.[23]

A final point in the discussion has to do with the different kinds of "explanations" to which the two viewpoints aspired. Since much of this has already been covered it will only be briefly described. Positivists believed that the explanations offered by sociologists should resemble the kinds of explanations offered by physical and natural scientists. That is, sociologists should seek to develop general theories out of systems of laws, and particular events should then be explained in terms of these theories.

Weber's notion is more complex because of his belief that more than one level of variables was operating in any event. Empirical generalizations should blend with descriptions of the particular culture, and with historical analyses of the development of that culture. At the core of his explanatory system was the analysis of the cultural or meaning structure of social actors. Only when this was done was there the possibility of adequate sociological explanation. Moreover, culture could not be described and explained by means of generalizations: it had to be *understood*. The analyst had to get inside the perspective enough to feel or understand it. This aspect of Weber's explanatory system had received much attention. It would not do, however, to believe that he had a wholly subjective approach to explanation. In the first place, he felt that as a scientist one had to offer proofs as to the validity of the perspective one ascribed to the actors. Actual statements by members of the group, for example, should be offered. Second, the "understanding" type of explanation had to be linked to empirical observations and precise historical explanation. This latter gives one a causally adequate explanation of the events themselves. One had above all to offer concrete empirical evidence that the situation one was explaining had either occurred or was likely to occur as one described it.[24] Weber too wished to be scientific. His image of science, however, differed from that of the positivists.

Research Strategies

Five general tactics are described here. In one way or another all have been significant in the later research activities of sociologists. They are: (1) *Verstehen*, and (2) the ideal type, both developed most fully by

Weber; (3) statistical analyses, and (4) functional analysis, both strategies of positivism; and (5) the Comparative Method, which in its pure form was an adjunct of positivism. The Comparative Method, capitalized, should not be confused with the cross-cultural researches of Weber. That comparative procedure will also be discussed in this chapter.

Verstehen

Although the term *verstehen* is associated with Weber, the general idea which it suggests as an investigatory procedure can be found, with varying degrees of explicitness, in the work of all those who attempted to study mind as a variable of consequence for sociological analysis. One perceives it at work in Simmel's description of actors' orientations to each other; in Tönnies' exploration of the variations in consciousness of self and other in communal and urban relationships; in Mead's analysis of the psychic maturation of the child; and in Cooley's practice of "sympathetic understanding." But the term *verstehen* has reached contemporary sociology from Weber's writings, and this description concentrates on his particular treatment of this research procedure.

Verstehen was the strategy suggested by Weber for probing the dimension of meaning which was so crucial to him in understanding and explaining social behavior. Essentially it involved a form of mental investigation and experiment in order to arrive at knowledge and understanding of the significance that an observed behavioral sequence had for the actor or actors involved in it. Several stages were involved in the process. One started with detailed observational data about long or complex behavioral sequences in which the particular act or acts which one wished to understand were embedded.[25] One then attempted to match the observations against one's general model of rational (or pragmatic) behavior.[26] If there was no mesh between the two sets of things one considered the specific ways in which the observations differed from the process of rational action, and by this means one managed to relate the behaviors to one of the other categories of action—ideological, traditional, emotional. Classification of social action was, however, not enough for a field which attempted the interpretive understanding of human behavior. From this basis in observation and classification one must proceed to an effort at imaginative recreation of the subjective activity that lay behind the observed behavior. That was *verstehen*.

Two alternative processes were involved. If the behavior was rational, one could cognitively go through the various stages in the subjective processes, intellectually grasping the elements involved and investigating further its goals, perception of means, and so on. If the behavior was of some other type, one attempted through empathy and sympathetic imagination to participate in the actor's meaning framework. Either way one was engaging in a form of mental role-playing in order to arrive at an understanding of the actor's consciousness as he acted. Success meant that one could explain the actor's behavior in terms of its significance to the actor. Such penetration into the subject's mind and ideas often gave one an insight into the broader context of meaning in which he moved, allowing one to understand the significance of other observations not previously linked to the original activity, allowing one even to predict other possible behaviors not yet observed but plausible within the context of motivation and meanings. *Verstehen* produces not only understanding of an immediate behavioral sequence; it can lead to insights into the wider culture in which the behavior is located.

Weber did not assume that an exercise in *verstehen* would always end in success. He felt one always could understand rational behavior, but emotional or ideological behavior were only accessible to empathetic understanding to the extent that one was familiar oneself with the particular kind of emotional experience involved, and traditional behavior was accessible to the extent that the values involved stood in some personally comprehensible relationship to one's own values. The researcher could not understand subjective states wholly alien to his personal experience. Weber felt that he himself could not understand behaviors marked by excessive zeal and fanaticism. If the subjects described their subjective processes one must record this as data, even if the attempt at *verstehen* failed. If the subjects could not describe their state of consciousness, and the experience was alien to the observer—as was the case with many mystical experiences—mind could not fit anywhere into the pattern of explanation. Further difficulties arose because the motives involved in action were often mixed and contradictory, but this problem, in theory at least, was not an unsurmountable one for the *verstehen* method.

As a scientist, the sociologist who employed *verstehen* as an investigating procedure had certain responsibilities. First, his insight into the significance of the action had to be organized and described as clearly as possible. Second, he had to verify the accuracy of his description of the actor's meaning structure. The best way to do this was to relate the description to concrete observations or data. Weber did not elaborate on this, but the dictum seems to have more than one implication. Clearly there should be a precise fit between the description of mind and the details of the original observation of overt activity. But given

Weber's reference to "psychological experimentations" in this context, it seems that an effort should also be made to obtain further data about the subject's ideas, motives, etc. This might involve his response to direct questioning or to various forms of psychological testing (such as the modern Rorschach tests). Such procedures were very minimally developed in Weber's day and he saw little hope of such verification. Other means include statistical descriptions of mass behavior (including attitudes and thought) or careful comparative work. Only if none of these techniques were appropriate ought one to resort to "the dangerous and uncertain procedure of the 'imaginary experiment' which consists in thinking away certain elements of a chain of motivation and working out the course of action which would then probably ensue, thus arriving at a causal judgement."[27] Given Weber's caution in suggesting it, it is curious that this last is often the image one has of *verstehen's* verificational procedures.

A final cautionary note which Weber made in the use of *verstehen* was that it could only be employed to explore the consciousness of an individual or group of individuals. One must not attempt to pursue the illusion of a "collective conscience" such as that of a political party or a nation. Such entities did not experience consciousness. Only individuals did, though one could generalize about the average or typical beliefs of a group of individuals. A country's constitution, for example, could not be treated as an empirical observation of the society's thought processes. It could, however, be used to investigate the ideas and beliefs of the men who had drawn it up, and of the generations of individuals who had believed in and been guided by it. To Durkheim, in contrast, such a document would be a "social fact" and an excellent indicator of the collective consciousness of that emergent reality, society.

Ideal Types

As with *verstehen,* the ideal type is generally associated with Weber because he gave the most elaborate and explicit exploration of this research procedure in his *Methodology of the Social Sciences.* Also like *verstehen,* this procedure was more generally used in early sociology than this conventional association implies. Indeed, all the Germans in the group—Marx, Simmel, Tönnies, and Weber—used it. As Weber pointed out, most historical research which went beyond the mere chronicling of events involved some more or less explicit attempt at ideal typing. The method would present itself naturally to men trained in a history-oriented philosophical tradition and concerned with the analysis of what they called "sociohistorical" events.

In the case of the ideal type, however, there was more than mere repetition of an approach among the various sociologists who employed it. It is evident that there was actual interplay between the various articulations of the concept, and that Weber's work climaxed several earlier conceptualizations. He explicitly referred to Marx's use of ideal types,[28] and a good case has been made for his actual familiarity with Simmel's concept of "pure forms" at the time that he was formulating his own programmatic statement of the concept.[29] This is not to say that he simply restated the ideas of others—far from it. What he did was to make more explicit a notion which others had approached more tentatively, and to draw out its implications as a methodological device for sociological investigation.

Ideal types are mental constructs. They are created by abstracting from sociohistorical reality a few of its traits, and then emphasizing these traits and their relationships in order to arrive at a simple, logically consistent model of the phenomenon under investigation. One might, for example, be investigating "Gothic architecture" or "capitalist economy" or "modernizing society." In each case one would have to make clear what one meant by the term by describing its essential characteristics and relationships. What one has is a model or "pure form" of the phenomenon. Nowhere in the empirical world will one observe so pristine a manifestation of it. It is a "utopia,"[30] not in the sense of "good" or "perfect," but in the sense of theoretically simplified to the point of conceptual "perfection."

An ideal type is based in empirical observation. One cannot create it out of fantasy, or out of one's personal values about how a thing ought to be. It involves

> the synthesis of a great many diffuse, discrete, more or less present and occasionally absent concrete individual phenomena which are arranged into a unified construct.[31]

Yet an ideal type is not just a description of reality, an averaging of its various traits. It is a creation of the researcher. His interests, his research problem, his intellect determines what general features will be incorporated into the model, and what of the many other characteristics of the real situation will be excluded. Even when two men investigate the same general phenomenon, for example the "capitalist economy," their ideal types may differ markedly because of variations in their problem and interests. If each type has some basis in concrete events, and is useful in research, each is equally "correct." The researcher creates the type too by relating its features in terms of consistency, plausibility, and logic. In its purity and relative simplicity an ideal type is far removed from the real world. It is a theoretical construct.

Given Weber's emphases many of his ideal types are constellations of ideas and beliefs: the four kinds of action, for example, or the "spirit of capitalism." But this is not a necessary restriction. Ideal types may deal with forms of relationship. Weber analyzed power and bureaucratic relationships in this way. He saw Marx's analyses of economic and class relationships as admirably pure types. Simmel utilized the technique primarily for analyzing forms of social relationships.

The purpose of creating an ideal type is to compare it to empirical events. There has been some argument on this in the literature so we quote Weber, in full.

> The ideal type has only one function in an empírical investigation. Its function is the comparison with empirical reality in order to establish its divergences and similarities, to describe them with the most unambiguously intelligible concepts, and to understand or explain them causally.[32]

This comparison has several functions in research. It may serve as an initial orienting principle which directs one to particular aspects of the empirical event. It can serve as a structure for describing the event, in terms of its similarities and dissimilarities to the model. It can help to develop hypotheses requiring further investigation as to why these similarities and dissimilarities exist; that is, hypotheses about the distinct, individual character of the empirical event. Finally it is a means of arriving at explanations of the event in terms of both the causal sequences of events and the subjective activity of the participants. Suppose, for example, that one is analyzing the conditions of victory and defeat in a military campaign. One might begin by creating an ideal type in which both sides have maximum possibilities for success. Each has an ideal commander-in-chief who knows the total fighting resources of each side and all the possibilities contingent on these, and who has a concrete, unambiguous goal of annihilating the other. Each commander will act completely logically. Against this one analyzes the actual military campaign under consideration. The type points one to the critical variables for investigation, it gives one a format for describing the actual event, it allows one to discover the reasons why the events developed as they did in terms of resources, events, and psychic states of the participants.[33]

The dangers in using ideal types all stem from forgetting that the type is theory and beginning to view it as fact. One may then force historical data to conform with the type, begin to believe that the type reflects the true essence of history or mysterious dynamics lying behind history. Weber pointed out that these abuses had developed in Marxist theory. And indeed, the same mutation has occurred with some of Weber's own types, such as those of power and bureaucracy.

Although the general description of the ideal type procedure is clear enough, some of the practical stages involved in developing an ideal type are not made clear in the various writings on them. For example, are there any exact procedures for moving from those "concrete individual phenomena" to the theoretical dimensions of the type? How does one determine what specific features are essential to it? Admittedly a combination of observation, interest, and logic govern this, but what combination? In practice both Weber and Simmel made these various decisions almost intuitively, and both defend this general tactic in terms of the relative immaturity of the field. Simmel's statement is particularly terse:

> Scientific practice, especially when it works in new areas, cannot do without a certain measure of groundwork which is intuitional. Only later are students able to become fully conscious of the motives and norms of this primary stage and to elucidate it conceptually. Certainly scientific labor must never be satisfied solely by such vague intuitive procedures. However one would condemn science to sterility if before assuming new tasks one must make a completely formulated methodology the condition of taking the first step.[34]

Statistical Analysis

Although several sociologists agreed that statistical analysis would be useful in sociological research, only Durkheim fully explored its implications. He did this both in his methodological writings and in practical research. His ideas are based on the work of social statisticians like Quetelet, whom he discussed in *Suicide.*

The logical beginning of Durkheim's approach is in his exploration of the phenomenon of *rates.* A rate is a numerical datum. It is based on the calculation, for a particular population, of the frequency of occurrence of some form of behavior, in proportion to fixed numerical units of the population. In speaking of violent crime in a society, for example, one may describe it as occurring at the rate of 14.8 incidents per 100,000 of the population, in a particular year; or, as in Durkheim's own research, one may speak of a suicide rate of 23.7 per 1,000,000 of the population, in France in 1857. Durkheim found his rates in official publications and records. Sociologists have not yet found a way to obtain data on this massive a scale by direct observation. They still must use official sources.

The fascinating characteristic of such rates, to Durkheim, was their stability over time. Only minor variations are observable from year to year in a rate like the suicide rate. Often if one averages these out over a five- or ten-year period, one finds almost identical rates from period to period. When changes are observable, they are not erratic fluctuations but trendlike steady increases or decreases. The rate for one society, however, tells one nothing about that of another society. Each society will have its own distinctive yet stable rate. Nor does the stability hold over very long periods in time. Between one major epoch and another in a society's history one may observe marked differences in its various social rates. Durkheim's position on this is that the structural differences between one major historical phase and another in the society really mean that one is again dealing with two societies. And the fact remains that within a particular historical phase of a society, there will be a stable predictable rate for many forms of behavior. How could this be if these behaviors were wholly determined by individual will? There must be characteristics of the society which distinguish it from other societies, which endure over decades, and which work on the population so as to produce its particular rates of crime, suicide, marriage, and so on. Regardless of how one explains an isolated instance of such behavior, the rate itself is a social product, a social reality. It is a social fact, an index to the nature of the society.

The next step is to explain selected social rates, like the rate of suicide. This not only satisfies immediate curiosity, but it leads to a discovery of patterns of social relationship which are the structure of the society; that is, it is a means to the long-range goal of discovering social laws. One arrives at an explanation of a social rate by correlational analysis, or what Durkheim called *concomitant variation*.[35] Essentially this involves demonstrating parallelism in the variations that occur in two series of social statistics—parallelism between two rates. For example, one shows that the suicide rate varies with religious affiliation, and that this relationship holds year by year, region by region, regardless of sex and age, and regardless of whether the various affiliations are in minority or majority status. If one has demonstrated that the relationship exists, one is then on the path to isolating a cause of suicide.

There are two strategies for seeking such relationships. One would be to consider current hypotheses about the phenomenon being investigated, such as popular explanations of suicide in terms of mental breakdown, alcoholism, and climatic variation. A second, more sociological approach, would involve investigating the possibility of relationships with other social facts: level of education, income, religious affiliation, marital status, and so on. Durkheim demonstrated to his satis-

faction that there was no substance in the popular, "non-social" explanations, and illustrated many marked relationships between the
suicide rate and other social facts. He demonstrated these by table
after table of figures, to an extent unequalled in this period of sociological investigation.

Demonstrating a series of correlations, however, does not explain
the phenomenon under investigation. One has to seek the relationship between these empirical indicators and major structural characteristics of the society. Various problems present themselves in this task.
First, one might discover that the suicide rate correlates with several
social indicators. One has to abstract the more general societal characteristics one is seeking from these social indicators. Another part of
the problem will be that the various events summarized in a rate like
the suicide rate may be of widely different types: there may be several
classes of suicide, in terms of their antecedent conditions, yet they are
fused in a single rate. Another problem could be that the social indicator correlates with the rate because a third unknown factor simultaneously affects both of the observable variables. There may also be an
intervening factor, produced by one of the observables, and in turn
producing the second.

Obviously, a tremendous interpretive task is involved in developing
explanations out of statistical correlations. Durkheim performed what
has remained a classic in such interpretation. He developed definitive
categories of suicide and explanations in terms of social solidarity in a
way which is more craft than science. In interpreting the suicide rate
and its correlates, he fused a concern for the data with a commitment to
strictly social levels of explanation, and handled this with a combination
of logical and intuitive thought. Wherever possible he tested a conclusion with further quantitative data. In contrast to Simmel and Weber, who accepted the interpretive role, Durkheim regretted it. He wished
that there were more "mechanical" means of deriving explanation from
observation, but did not know what these might be.

One obvious criticism of this research strategy is that it has to rely
on official records, which though they may be accurate enough on one
variable, may be deceptive on the picture they give of others. Durkheim was aware of some of the arbitrariness of such statistics for he
discusses the unreliability of officially recorded reasons for suicide.
But he does not explore the arbitrary nature involved in actually count-
ing events—the fact that privileged groups may appear to have low
rates of suicide or crime only because their influence with officials
is sufficient to keep such events in their groups "off the record," or
that an increase in a rate may only reflect an improvement in recording

procedures. He could not have been completely unaware of these possibilities, but he still believed that the massiveness of such data indicated something about the actual pattern of events in the society. And as he pointed out, such data, whatever its inadequacies, was "harder" than most other sociological data (for example, anecdotal ethnographic information).

One final point on Durkheim's technique should be noted. He made, in passing, a curious distinction between "social rates" like the suicide rate and "demographic rates" like that of mortality.[37] Clearly both have social antecedents which explain their patterning. The difference seems to be in the volitional and selective nature of events which make up the former, and the biologically determined and universalistic nature of the events making up the latter. Yet having implicitly defined social rates in terms of a component of will or choice, he went on to argue the reverse: social rates are socially determined. Thus he left unanswered one question which Weber did not feel could be left unanswered. How did the structural causes affect individual experience, so that the individual chose to commit suicide? Nothing more obviously shows the difference between the two approaches. To Durkheim the explanation was complete when one could trace the observations back to universal aspects of the social structure. To Weber the explanation would only have been complete if the two statistical observations could have been linked together by some interpretive understanding of the outlook of the individuals who willed their own death.

Functional Analysis

As has been apparent in much of this text, one of the basic tensions in early sociology was between those who argued for the purposiveness of individual behavior, and those who stressed that since social forces had deterministic qualities, society was a reality deserving the particular attention of the sociologist. To the former, any sociological explanation of an observation must incorporate some consideration of the individual's decisional processes: *verstehen* was their attempt to do this. To the latter any sociological explanation of an observation must incorporate some consideration of its implications for society: functional analysis was the procedure developed to do this. Comte, Spencer, Durkheim, and Pareto all adopted some version of this procedure.

Functional analysis requires of the researcher that he explain or analyze his observations of recurring social phenomena in terms of the consequences these phenomena have for the wider social system of which it is a part. For example, one explains a society's religious rituals not in terms of the religious history of the group, but more generally in terms of the implications of ritual for social cohesion in the society. Both Comte and Spencer naturally oriented themselves in this way to their observations of social processes because of their commitment to organismic thinking. Their attempts to conceptualize society as a unit invariably resulted in the conclusion that society resembled a living biological organism. This meant that it had a number of different internal parts, that these parts were dynamically related to each other, each making a distinctive and essential contribution to the life of the total unit. Given such assumptions, recurring social processes, or institutions, appeared to be the components of the social organism. One could describe each part in terms of its peculiar characteristics or "structure," but this was rather like dissecting a biological organism and studying its organs separately. One might understand the anatomy of the creature, but one gained little knowledge of its life processes. One had to know how the separate components operated in the living organism: one had to study its "functions" in the life process of that organism. This imagery and procedure is more explicit in Spencer, but the same general principle is to be found in Comte's insistence that sociological analysis must always relate the component part to the wider civilization.

One additional trait of this analytic procedure emerged in the writings of Comte and Spencer. Just as the functioning of some part of a biological organism might either contribute to or detract from the health of that organism, so the observed social process could be either healthful or "pathological" for society. The analyst must determine this. Functional analysis, from its outset, involved more than a description of the consequences of something for the wider social entity—it also involved an assessment of those contributions in terms of their "good" or "bad" qualities. A healthy social system for Spencer was one that, given its level of evolutionary development, was maximally adapted to environmental demands. For Comte, a healthy social system was in a state of orderly progressive development. On the whole, though, functional analysis emerged more in Comte's and Spencer's practice of sociology than in their methodological statements. This left several points of ambiguity unconfronted.

Durkheim's links to organismic thinking are less explicit, and his discussion of functional analysis is more formal. He defined function as a relationship between a set of dynamic processes and the needs of the wider social system. He distinguished between relationships which contribute positively to society, those that detract from effective social life, and those that contribute nothing ("survivals"). As with Comte, Durkheim's criterion for determining an observation's functional status was its contribution to social order. In indicating the procedure involved in this approach, he stressed that one is investigating the relationship between observed processes and societal needs, these being clearly distinguished from the needs of individuals.

> The function of a social fact . . . consists of the production of socially useful effects. To be sure it may . . . happen to serve the individual. But this happy result is not its immediate cause. *The function of a social fact is to be sought in its relation to some social end.*[38]

Durkheim also took up a question which Comte and Spencer left unresolved: Does the usefulness of a process explain why it exists? Durkheim distinguished between ultimate and immediate causation. The ultimate causes of a social fact cannot reside in the fact that it is useful. Such usefulness can, however, partly explain why it continues to exist, for a society would not long survive if the majority of processes occurring within it were not useful to it. The origins of a social fact, however, lay in the basic characteristics of the society: size, density of interaction, forms and intensity of relationship, links to other societies, and so on. The continuation of a social fact was in large measure dependent upon the persistence of these factors which produced it. Scientific explanation of a social phenomenon thus depended on the investigation of these basic societal traits, and the laws which governed them. Functional analysis contributed something to the explanation, but only a relatively modest amount.

For example, religious beliefs in a community functioned to heighten group solidarity. The quest for group solidarity did not, however, give the beliefs their substance or sanctity. The substance of beliefs reflected the actual social relations of the society: totemism, for example, was shaped out of particular family- and clan-related social relationships. The sanctity of the beliefs reflected the sense of awe which society itself produced in the individual. Solidarity produced by a body of religious beliefs, however, sustained both awe and social relationships, and thus the functions of a phenomenon fed into the broader explanation of the phenomenon in an ongoing social system.

Pareto's development of the analytic procedures of this approach is more elaborate, and is shaped by an analogy not to organismic entities but rather to mechanically operating systems. Durkheim had occasionally substituted the word "utility" for the word "function." Pareto chose to speak of utility.[39]

The choice of a standard for assessing utility was strictly up to the researcher. He might be interested in social stability, in which case he analyzed a social system in terms of the processes producing stability. But he might have some other goal, for example prosperity, happiness, or conflict. In each case, if his goal was explicit, he could investigate the conditions of the social system that produced it. The norm for assessing function was selected by the researcher. He could if he wished select some goal to which the members of the society aspired, or he could choose something which interested him personally. The researcher also determined the object which was to be treated as the "wider system," in relationship to which the utility of a process was to be assessed. It could be individual, community, nation, human race, and so on. One then investigated the case at hand for processes which contributed to the chosen state (utilities), and those which detracted from that state (detriments). Both utility and detriment were relative. Some processes made greater or lesser contributions to, or greater or lesser detractions from the selected goal. The measurement of utility was a scientific goal for the sociologist. The sociologist also had to determine if the utility was direct or indirect, immediate or long term. Careful investigation along such lines led one to an assessment of net "utility," or the extent to which the society was actually approximating the selected goal, and of "maximum utility," the conditions with maximized a society's chances for arriving at the selected goal or condition. On the question of explanation Pareto seems to reverse the position represented by Durkheim, Comte, and Spencer. Pareto agreed with Durkheim that one could not explain the existence of some behavioral regularity by showing it to be functional, but he argued that one could explain conditions in the wider social system (its prosperity, stability, conflict, etc.) by functional analysis. Functional analysis was a way to arrive at scientific explanation.

Functional analysis, therefore, was practiced throughout the nineteenth century, gaining in procedural precision as the century progressed. What were the purposes of such a procedure, apart from the question of explanation on which we have already touched? Several benefits of functional analysis emerge in the discussion of it. It assists in the classification of social processes and in the development of generalizations about types of processes common to all societies. In examining an empirical case, functional analysis led to "a satisfactory understanding" of it. In the light of Pareto's "maximum utility" concept, and the goal, common to this group of early sociologists, of generalizing about society, functional analysis was also important in the development of general models of societal organization. Above all, functional analysis served to keep the belief in society as an emergent reality alive and influential in empirical investigation.

One constant question raised about functional analysis is whether its assumptions are teleological. That is, does the usefulness of a process imply purposiveness in the actors making up the group (in that they create or sustain those social institutions)? In this period, given the perspective of the men who developed the tactic, the question is beside the point. All of those stressing functional analysis (Comte, Spencer, Durkheim, Pareto) denied purpose or will any place in their definition of sociology's subject matter. They were not concerned with it. They were interested in the organization and dynamics of an emergent, material, social system. Functional analysis addressed itself to that interest. It determined what the interplay was between society and the relational processes occurring within it. Whether or not those processes were designed or not did not enter the picture, as Durkheim said. Or, as Pareto looked at it, it was up to the researcher to decide whether or not this further question would be investigated, but it was not essential to the framework. A greater inconsistency, given the perspective, was that this technique left a tremendous interpretive role to the researcher, and no sure way of verifying his conclusions. This was a limitation to those who aspired to strict inductionism, "mechanical" means of determining causation, and clear methods of verification. It was Pareto's hope that measurement and a close relationship to empirical observation would do this eventually, and that only the "immaturity" of the field curbed functional analysis from being strictly positivistic.

The "Comparative Method"

In its capitalized version, the Comparative Method[40] was a procedure used by Comte and Spencer. If their functionalism derived from their organicism, their mode of comparative research was shaped by their even more profound faith in a law of progressive societal development. The Comparative Method was a technique to find empirical support for this hypothesized social law. It was also a response to the flood of ethnographic data thrust on them in the nineteenth century by the penetration of Western interests into other parts of the globe.

The Comparative Method began by attempting to organize this ethnographic data. Some aspect of social life was selected and the data intensively reviewed for descriptions of its manifestation in the variety of societies then known to exist throughout the world. For example, political life might be the phenomenon selected. Every available description of political life would then be ordered by the researcher in terms of what logically appeared to be their place on a continuum ranging from most simple to most complex. Sometimes society itself would be the unit of investigation. Then it would be level of "civilization"—involving an amalgam of morality and technological knowledge—that would be rated simple to complex. The early sociologists firmly believed

that the multitudes of cases that this continuum revealed contained all
the various stages of the development of society.

> It exhibits all possible degrees of social evolution to our immediate ob-
> servation. From the wretched inhabitants of Tierra Fuego to the most
> advanced nations of western Europe, there is no social grade which is
> not extant in some points of the globe.[41]

There were, however, problems with applying this kind of data directly to an argument for a law of social development. In the first
place, the most rigorous exercise of logic could not sometimes distinguish which piece of data was more simple than another. Second,
simply ordering a group of descriptions gave no evidence of developmental *change,* for the various cases were existing simultaneously
and spatially separate from each other. To resolve this, those who
used this tactic turned to history, and archeology. Here one got
evidence of actual changes in social structure in individual societies.
The historical-archeological record, however, was also unsatisfactory
in its own way. It was incomplete. There were important gaps in it.
It was detailed only for the last three or four thousand years of human
existence. By juxtaposing the ethnographic and historical series however, the weaknesses of both appeared to be compensated for. Particular sequences of "more" or "less" complex phenomena in the ethnographic data could be established by reference to the actual experiences
of historical societies. An argument for change from one ethnographical-
ly recorded form to another, as the experience of mankind, could also
be supported by pointing to some such transition experienced by a real
society. And the gaps in the historical record could be filled by logically
deducing the missing evidence from the ethnographic series. Together the two series showed all the stages through which mankind's social
organization had, and would move. One could describe the phases in
the law of societal development. Through much of the nineteenth
century the Method was hailed as a triumph of scientific thinking.

This procedure has been vigorously criticized ever since that time.
To men like Weber who deprecated the attempt to arrive at generalizations about all societies the method was a particular abomination. Not
only was it an outstanding effort at such generalization, but it was an
attempt to generalize about history itself, to impose some universal
sequences on the varied histories of actual societies.

To those who were idealist in their philosophical assumptions, the
procedures of functional analysis (discussed in the preceding section)
were logical enough even though they rested on a reification of society.

Moreover, functional analysis was addressed to research questions which did not much interest the idealists. But the Comparative Method brought positivists into the particular territory, history, which idealists had long regarded as their own domain, and the "invasion" was accomplished by what idealists considered to be acts of barbarism against the evidence.

Even those who did not share Weber's assumptions were critical of the comparative method. They pointed out that it was a peculiarly biased procedure, and one marked by extensive circularity in argument. Throughout it was shaped by the assumption which underlay the "law of development (or evolution)" itself: namely that Western European societies were the most developed that had ever existed. This assumption lay behind any continuum carved out of the ethnographic data. Invariably modern Western societies were placed at the pole "most complex." While it is easy to see how this might be done with technology, it is more difficult to see how it could be induced from the evidence of say, religious or family life, not to mention morality or art. In filling out the ethnographic series from history the problem again was that the most elaborate historical record was that of Western societies. So the element of movement came from that source, and an identical direction of change was then imposed on the much sparser data from other societies. In the end the Comparative Method attempted to substantiate the theory of social evolution with research categories and data-handling techniques specifically shaped by the assumptions of that theory.

Although the explicit exponents of the Comparative Method disappeared in the latter part of the nineteenth century, its ghost continued to haunt comparative analysis in sociology. For one thing, Marx and Engels accepted both the theory and the "proofs." It was built into their model of history, and bequeathed to their successors. Spencer's procedure of taking ethnographic facts out of the general context of their culture, and interpreting them in relationship to some general hypothesis is to be found both in Sumner's and Pareto's research. The belief in a continuum of simple/complex or primitive/developed certainly lay behind Durkheim's monumental study of aboriginal religion.

> It is certain that ethnology has frequently brought about the most fruitful revolutions in the different branches of sociology . . . . for the same reason that the discovery of unicellular beings has transformed the current idea of life. Since in these very simple beings life is reduced to its essential forms . . . . In order to discover the laws of the phenomena which he studies the physicist tries to simplify these latter and rid them of sec-

ondary characteristics. For that which concerns institutions, nature spontaneously makes the same sort of simplifications at the beginning of history.[42]

Durkheim's work on the *Elementary Forms of Religious Life*, however, is a good example of the form that comparative sociology would
take from then to the present. In itself it is not explicitly comparing
societies. It is a case study of a single "foreign" culture, painstakingly
recreating the details of its social and religious life from, in this case,
anthropological evidence. Durkheim's purpose, however, was not
merely to recreate the society, but to arrive at some generalization
about social life, or to test some hypotheses about social life. Underlying much of the investigation was an implicit comparison between this
exotic and "simpler" form of society and the familiar "developed"
world of the sociologist's own society.

Another form of comparative research is Weber's investigation of
the economic and religious ethics of some of the major civilizations.
As has already been indicated, this had so little in common with the
Comparative Method that it should not really be included in this section, except that the broader intention of the section was to introduce
the role of comparative research in early sociology. The substance of
Weber's investigation has already been described in chapter 7. The
methodological purpose of this research approach was outlined in
the earlier discussion of sociological experiments: to compare cases
roughly similar except for variation in the one factor under investigation, in an effort to isolate the reasons for that variation. Weber
selected societies of approximately equivalent levels of cultural complexity, societies whose economic ethic varied. He sought, with an
overwhelming demonstration of scholarship, to map similarities and
differences, testing the hypothesis that the variations in economic behavior could ultimately be derived from variations in the religious
ethos of the different societies. In so doing, he illustrated one of the
problems besetting such comparative work. In the case of societies,
one can only find cases of "rough" similarity, and this still leaves
too much dissimilarity to allow one to approximate a convincing experimental test of a hypothesis. At most, one arrives at a plausible
analysis.

Marx has been omitted, for the most part, from the preceding discussion. In terms of his direct methodological contributions, there has
been little to say. By developing substantive concepts about social life
which have fed into the sociological framework, Marx had an important
role in the definition of sociology. In outlining a technical guide to
sociological research which has affected the field, his role is marginal.

The boundary between substantive concepts and research techniques is, of course, highly permeable, and this kind of connection to sociological methods could be made with Marx. But enough has been said elsewhere about Marx's substantive concepts to allow the reader to establish the connections.

Part of the reason for Marx's marginal status is that a discussion of a field's research methods involves a definite act of identification with the discipline. In terms of professional role playing, it is an "introspective" thing to do. Those who engage in such activity formally view themselves as members of the field, and feel themselves responsible for elaborating its technical framework. In this sense Marx was not a sociologist. Another part of the reason may be that later sociologists have tended to concentrate more on Marx's analysis of society than on his analytic procedures. Yet another reason is that Marx's analytic procedures on the whole add little new to the preceding descriptions. Ideologically, Marx was a strict positivist, denying the possibility that mind affects the procedural format of a science of society, and committed to the discovery of general laws which would explain contemporary events and allow prediction. Like Comte or Spencer, Marx felt that he had discovered such laws, and that much of the task left to him was explanation and prediction in terms of them.

However, Marx did present some points of contrast with the positivists. If we use the preceding discussion of the comparative method as a framework, Marx was more concerned with the historical than the ethnographic series. This distinguishes him from most positivists, and gives him a common substantive ground with Weber. As political reformer, Marx drew heavily in his analysis on his own observations of political events like the various political upheavals in France. In this sense he used primary data (observations which he himself had made) more often than most sociologists of the period. The most important difference, however, is his dialectical approach to the analysis of data. This he inherited directly from the German philosophical schools. Positivists stressed the supremacy of immediately observed social facts. Proper respect for these and accurate reference to them would give one knowledge of the world; an ordered, mechanically functioning realm. Marx respected the facts too, but for him they were starting points, indicators of contradictions in the immediate world. Locating these points of tension revealed the dynamic possibilities of change and progress in the world, the embryonic form of the future. It was a different approach to "facts." Instead of treating them as whole and complete, it splintered them into their conflicting possibilities. The tactic was also used by Simmel. In contrast with Simmel, however, Marx's approach has been variously interpreted by sociologists. Some have viewed his use of the dialectic as an analytic procedure, others have taken it to be his assumption of the nature of the real world, which then suggested a path for empirical investigation. On the whole the latter interpretation has prevailed in sociology, the Marxist dialectic affecting the profession's views on the substance of social change and social conflict. Fuller exploration of the concept is therefore reserved for the chapters on these topics.

Summary and Conclusions

Almost all the early sociologists agreed that sociology was an empirically oriented science. Stemming from this general consensus were a series of common conclusions about the goals and research procedures of the field. A fundamental disagreement occurred, though, on how much the fact of human motivation and interpretation created special research problems for sociology, or to what extent sociology could simply take over both the broad aspirations and the specific research procedures of the physical and natural sciences. Durkheim was the chief spokesman for the pro-science or positivistic position, Weber its chief critic. Several specific research procedures were developed in this period: *verstehen*, ideal typing, statistical and functional analysis, as well as several versions of comparative analysis. All this is summarized in table 5.

It is usual in this section of each chapter to link the material of the chapter with that preceding it. This can be done very briefly here, for the links to earlier material have been made throughout the main part of the chapter. Moreover by now the various pieces of these differing "visions" of the sociological enterprise have been explored from so many angles in the last several chapters that it is no longer necessary to make the linkages so explicit. The roots of the differing perspectives described here lie in the philosophical differences described in chapter 4. Some of the other developments described there in terms of statistics and ethnography are also pertinent. Springing from the more basic philosophical differences are the arguments on human purposiveness and on the importance of collective ideas described in chapters 6 and 7, as well as the long argument on the status of society as a "real" and "powerful" thing which has been traced through chapter 4, 5, and 6. Instead of exploring these connections much further, we will look instead in more detail than has been customary in preceding chapters at the connections between this earlier debate on research strategies and the contemporary situation on the same problem.[44] No attempt will be made to review contemporary

TABLE 5: Views on the Methods of Sociology

I. General area of agreement (partial exception, Tönnies)

1. Sociology is *data oriented* to "social facts."
2. Data should be obtained by *controlled observation,* either directly, or indirectly through historical, official, or ethnographic records.
3. Data must be classified by means of *taxonomic systems.*
4. Sociology can approximate an *experimental design,* primarily through some form of comparative case study analysis.
5. *Statistical statements* about human behavior are legitimate tools for sociological investigation (exception—Comte).
6. Sociology's goals are *generalization* from the data and *explanation* of social phenomena.

II. Area of fundamental disagreement

1. (a) The processes of individual consciousness are essential to sociological explanation (Weber, Tönnies, Mead, Cooley)
   (b) The processes of individual consciousness are irrelevant to sociological explanation (Comte, Spencer, Durkheim, Pareto)

2. (a) The processes of individual consciousness cannot be studied wholly by procedures developed in the natural sciences (Weber, Tönnies)
   (b) The processes of individual consciousness can in large measure be studied by procedures developed in the natural sciences (Mead, Cooley)

3. Individual consciousness derives from culture and varies with cultures (Weber)

4. (a) Sociology cannot generalize across cultures (Weber)
   (b) Sociology can so generalize (Comte, Durkheim, Pareto, Cooley, Mead)

5. (a) Sociology therefore cannot have universal laws or make universal predictions (Weber)
   (b) Sociology aspires to both universal law and prediction (Comte, Spencer, Durkheim, Pareto, Cooley, Mead)

6. (a) Ultimate sociological explanation is of individual actions in particular socio-historical contexts (Weber)
   (b) Sociological explanation is of universal social or behavioral phenomena (Comte, Spencer, Durkheim, Pareto, Cooley, Mead)

7. (a) Sociology therefore must devise its own research techniques (Weber)
   (b) Sociology must approximate as closely as possible the techniques of the natural sciences, since its subject matter is not qualitatively different and its goals are identical (Comte, Spencer, Durkheim, Pareto, Cooley, Mead)

III. Particular techniques used in this period

1. *Sympathetic understanding or verstehen* (Weber, Tönnies, Cooley, Mead, Simmel)—see pp. 179-81
2. *Ideal types* (Marx, Simmel, Tönnies, Weber)—see pp. 181-84
3. *Statistical analysis* (especially Durkheim)—see pp. 184-87
4. *Functional analysis* (Comte, Spencer, Durkheim, Pareto)—see pp. 187-91
5. *The "Comparative Method"* (Comte, Spencer, Sumner, Marx, Durkheim)—see pp. 191-96

research procedures systematically. What follows is only an impressionistic sketch of some of its more striking features.

If we focus on the practice of research in contemporary sociology, the form of the present discussion differs quite markedly from that of the earlier period. A great deal of the polarization has disappeared; the area of consensus is far wider. Consensus seems to be built around certain procedures which were not present in the earlier discussion. There has been innovation since the period discussed. Yet the assumptions necessary for such innovation were present in the earlier period. The present consensus represents no clear victory for either the Weberian or the positivistic positions, but an amalgam of concessions to both.

Earlier sociologists had relied heavily on secondary data—data derived from direct observations by someone other than the sociologists. For example, they drew on the reports of ethnographers, on historical writings, on government publications. In contrast modern research is based chiefly on primary data, observations made firsthand by the sociologist. Even when secondary data is analyzed the bulk of this comes from earlier research made by social scientists, especially by other sociologists. Data collected directly by the investigator or by another social scientist shapes most of the research reports published in major professional journals. This means that, despite laments to the contrary, contemporary sociologists have data which is substantially more reliable and more easily matched to sociological interests and concepts than the data used in earlier sociology. There is no inconsistency between this development and the earlier aspirations of sociologists. Rather it reflects what they had wished for: a maturation of the field in both data collection procedures and reserves of collected material. What it does mean, however, is that much present discussion of research procedures concentrates on techniques for primary data collection, in contrast to the topics of the earlier debate.

Certain features of the contemporary perspective mark a victory for positivism. These can be summed up as attempts to limit the amount of pure interpretation by the researcher in the process of inquiry. Contemporary research generally seeks to test specified hypotheses. The process of doing this usually requires the study of large numbers of cases. Every effort is made to obtain quantifiable, measurable data. The analysis of these is supposed to stay close to the "facts," essentially stating the hypotheses, describing the research procedure, cataloguing the data, and drawing modest, immediate conclusions from it. These studies on the whole are oriented to a continuous present; few take a longer time perspective. The goal is empirical generalization about society. The concern with history and long-term change, with descriptions of unique, individual situations, with "understanding"—all goals of the Weberian approach—are much less prevalent. Such activities as the development of ideal types or even functional analysis have been pushed further back from the actual research process than their originators seemed to think was necessary. They are now seen as part of the process of theory construction, and modern sociologists draw a fairly sharp line between the latter and empirical research. This is a very definite point of difference with the earlier practice of inquiry.

Modern sociological research is founded on the interview and questionnaire. Whatever the formal pretensions of the field, most of its primary data consists of the responses made by individuals to questions put to them by the researcher. The implicit assumption of this is that the individual, not some larger social unit, is the object for investigation. Again the trend has been to decrease the numbers of questions which treat this individual as an informant about experiences which he has shared with others, or at least as an informant about his own behavior, and to increase the questions about his attitudes, feelings, opinions, and beliefs. Sociological research is increasingly social psychological in its concerns. The discussion of research techniques focuses on measures for tapping and measuring the individual's ideas and feelings. As certain commentators have put it, "sociology is becoming the study of verbally expressed sentiments and feelings, rather than an analysis of human performance;"[45] or of societal structure.

The interview-questionnaire procedure was not discussed in the earlier period. It has been an innovation since that time. It certainly seems to represent a victory for the Weberian approach over the positivistic. The positivists were adamant that the ideas and beliefs of individuals were not of major consequence to the study of social reality. Weber, although cautious about quantification and statistical averages, did not reject them, and he certainly held that ideas and beliefs were crucial. Yet Weber's victory is not total. His major concern was with essence rather than average. He rejected the effort to make cross-cultural generalizations about beliefs and ideas. He sought to embed configurations of meaning in the historical events which he felt had created them. None of these interests characterize the present use of interview-questionnaire procedures.

The true victory in the present situation is that of the general culture in which sociology developed. The interview-questionnaire procedure reflects both its faith in technological-physical science procedures and its belief in the autonomous individual. Weber had been in tension with the former, Durkheim and others with the latter. Both points of confrontation with dominant cultural beliefs have disappeared. The process seems to have been a gradual evolutionary one.

What is not clear is whether the profession has rationalized this accommodation to the culture. The formal debate still seems to follow the old tracks of the Weber-Durkheim argument. A positivistic application of interview-questionnaire procedure, which is the norm of sociological research today, would have satisfied neither vision of sociology.

NOTES

1. Ferdinand Tönnies, *Community and Society (Gemeinschaft und Gesellschaft)*, trans. Charles P. Loomis (New York: Harper Torchbooks edition, 1963), p. 237.

2. Georg Simmel, "The Problem of Sociology" in *Essays on Sociology*, ed. Kurt Wolff (New York: Harper Torchbooks, 1959), p. 313. Italics added.

3. See for example Max Weber, *The Methodology of the Social Sciences*, trans. Edward Shils (New York: Free Press, 1949), p. 72.

4. Durkheim, *The Rules of Sociological Method*, trans. Sarah Solavy and John Mueller, ed. George Catlin (Glencoe, Ill.: Free Press, 1950), p. 27.

5. See for example Vilfredo Pareto; *The Mind and Society* (New York: Harcourt, 1935), p. 72; Max Weber, *The Theory of Social and Economic Organization*, trans. Talcott Parsons (Glencoe, Ill.: Free Press, 1947), p. 97; Georg Simmel, "The Problem of Sociology," pp. 313, 316.

6. Pareto, *Mind and Society*, p. 27.

7. Herbert Spencer, *The Study of Sociology* (Ann Arbor: University of Michigan Press, 1961).

8. Emile Durkheim, *Suicide*, trans. John Spaulding and George Simpson (Glencoe, Ill.: Free Press, 1951), p. 36.

9. Emile Durkheim, *The Elementary Forms of Religious Life* (New York: Free Press; 1915), p. 13.

10. Weber, *The Theory*, p. 109.

11. Auguste Comte, *The Positive Philosophy* (London: Chapman, 1853), volume II, p. 100.

12. Weber, *The Theory*, p. 97.

13. Simmel, "The Problem of Sociology," p. 322.

14. Pareto, *Mind and Society*, pp. 53-54.

15. Weber, *The Theory*, p. 100.

16. Emile Durkheim, *The Division of Labor in Society*, trans. ed. (Glencoe, Ill.: Free Press, 1964), p. 34.

17. Durkheim, *The Elementary Forms*, p. 17.

18. Ibid., p. 14.

19. Durkheim, *The Rules*, p. 29.

20. See for example Pareto, *Mind and Society*, p. 52; and Weber, *The Theory*, p. 107.

21. Pareto, *Mind and Society*, p. 52.

22. Weber, *Methodology*, pp. 72-80.

23. Simmel, "The Problem of Sociology," p. 321.

24. Weber, *The Theory*, p. 90, 99.

25. This is my extrapolation from the general thrust of Weber's methodology and from the logical implications of the *verstehen* technique. Weber's illustrations of a man shooting, or a man chopping wood (that is of isolated actions) make little sense taken

alone. Without wider knowledge of the events surrounding these acts, one could not decide whether the incident was rationally motivated (a hired guard), traditional (a military salute), ideological (an assassination) or emotional (revenge or rage).

26. This typology is presented in chapter 5.

27. Weber, *The Theory*, p. 97.

28. Weber, *Methodology*, p. 103; see also the discussion in Irving Zeitlin, *Ideology and the Development of Sociological Thought* (Englewood Cliffs, N.J.: Prentice Hall, 1968), pp. 119-22.

29. F.H. Tenbruck "Formal Sociology" in Wolff, *Essays*, pp. 61-99.

30. Weber, *Methodology*, p. 90.

31. Ibid., p. 96.

32. Ibid., p. 43.

33. Ibid., p. 42.

34. Simmel, "The Problem of Sociology," p. 326.

35. Durkheim, *The Rules*, p. 130.

36. Ibid., p. 132.

37. Durkheim, *Suicide*, p. 48.

38. Durkheim, *The Rules*, pp. 110-11.

39. Pareto, *Mind and Society*, pp. 1459-74.

40. This discussion draws on Nisbet, *Social Change and History* (New York: Oxford University Press, 1969), pp. 189-208.

41. Comte, *The Positive Philosophy*, volume II, p. 104.

42. Durkheim, *The Elementary Forms*, pp. 19, 21.

43. This summary is based in part of the article by Julia Brown and Brian Gilmartin, "Sociology Today: Lacunae, Emphases, and Surfeits," *The American Sociologist* 4: 283-91.

44. Ibid., p. 288.

Part Three

Explorations of
Societal Processes

9

Explorations of
Social Order

This section of the book turns from a consideration of methodological questions about the nature of sociology to a review of three substantive problems which absorbed the research and theoretical energies of earlier sociologists. This chapter looks at their work on the question of social order. The following two chapters describe their efforts to conceptualize and explain social conflict and societal change. The issues of order, conflict, and change do not in any sense exhaust the list of substantive questions dealt with by earlier sociologists. They are, however, important issues, and sufficiently general to subsume many aspects of sociological investigation. The intention of this section is not to be comprehensive, but rather to be illustrative.

"The problem of social order" refers to a cluster of more specific curiosities. Why does a group persist over time, particularly that large, complex aggregate called society? What binds individuals together, offsetting trends to disintegration? What facilitates cooperative activity in a complex organizational phenomenon like society? These and similar questions are aspects of the problem of order as raised by sociologists. The question of social order has great theoretical significance in contemporary sociology. In the earlier period, however, as Western society experienced one of its major historical periods of change, social order seemed precarious and the issue was particularly poignant and absorbing. The answers worked out in this period still furnish us with major parts of our answer to the question of social order.

Looking over the materials of this period, one can detect five separate factors to which earlier sociologists pointed in attempting to explain the persistence of social groups. These are:

1. Instincts or biological traits of group members.
2. Cultural consensus, or the fact that group members have certain beliefs, values, and attitudes in common.
3. Affective solidarity, or the existence of emotional ties among group members.
4. Functional interdependence, or the existence of complementary needs and functions either at the individual or at the group level.
5. Formal social control, or the existence in society of structures which formally coordinate activities, implement collective goals, repress individual deviance, and so on.

Of these five answers only the instinct explanation is no longer offered by contemporary sociologists. The others are still dominant themes in the discussion of social order. The rest of this chapter deals, in turn, with the five themes listed above: briefly with the first, more fully with the others.

Individual Human Traits

The view that persisting societal stability could be explained primarily by means of a trait or set of traits common to man as a species had been fairly prevalent in the social philosophy which antedates sociology. The trait most often selected was that of spontaneous, innate sociability, an emotional need to be with others. An echo of this is to be found in Comte's writings. He speaks of man as a gregarious species, and points directly to a spontaneous sociability as one of the few traits conducive to social life which is natural to the human organism. Simmel too leads one to believe that man has an inherent need for "sociation"; so much so that he will at times create special structures which function simply to satisfy that need, such as the social gathering. An emotional drive for human contacts is part of what Simmel sees as the psychological orientation of men to society.

A new twist to this argument is provided by Spencer. Sociability, he felt, is not a trait of primitive man. Rather it evolves as man evolves, and becomes increasingly marked in more civilized man. The trait evolves out of man's relationship to his environment, but then becomes part of his genetically transmitted constitution. Hence Spencer's belief in the inevitability of social progress, and in the decreasing need for humanitarian intervention by the state in the "more civilized" societies: the members of those societies were becoming innately more moral, socially oriented beings.

As was described in chapter 6, Pareto was the sociologist most concerned with exploring basic human nature in this period. Two of the residues of sentiments which he described appear to be conducive to social persistence and order. He spoke of a gregarious impulse in human beings, the need to be with others and to have one's immediate circle of acquaintances conform to some common beliefs and norms. He spoke too of a conservative drive, which prompts men to resist the alteration or disappearance of familar things or procedures. The latter drive, in particular, pushes men out into the wider arena of social life in an attempt to marshall resources against change. But these sentiments, like all others, are unevenly distributed among the members of a population, and among various populations. Certain individuals and cultures are more prone to a stability-order perspective than others. Such individuals, working out their basic drives in a society, are agents in the social system for order.

None of these sociologists, however, felt that an explanation of social order in terms of human nature was wholly sufficient. To some degree, all seemed to agree that the impulses of men translated into social structures or beliefs which were the more immediate mechanisms for social stability. This point is least evident in Spencer's approach, most evident in Comte's. Comte indeed is absolutely insistent that man's sociability is too weak a trait to account for social order. The quest for these emergent social processes for order prompts most of the statements made by these men on the general question of social order. To contemporary sociologists these statements about social processes for group persistence and group stability are the more interesting ones. They are reviewed below.

Consensus and/or Solidarity

Consensus in a group means that it is characterized to some extent by cultural homogeneity: its members have in common certain beliefs, values, norms, world views, and so on. In contrast, if one says that a group is solidary one means, first, that its members are conscious of belonging together, of having a common identity; and second, that they find that awareness emotionally satisfying. A solidary group is one in which emotional links and a sense of oneness tie its members together.

Consensus can operate without group members being aware of the fact. Solidarity always implies that at some level group members are consciously sensitized to the fact of group belongingness, and that they react to that awareness positively and emotionally.

Answers to the question of social persistence and order are, in this earlier period, most frequently phrased in terms of consensus or solidarity. While it is possible to distinguish, analytically, between the two processes, many of the sociologists in this group fuse the two ideas into a single, order-producing concept. It is possible, in fact, to range this group of answers on a continuum, with those who emphasize value consensus at one pole, those who stress solidarity at the other, and the various combinations ranging in between. This is the organizational principle for this section of the chapter.

Consensus

To Mead society was consensus, or, more exactly, society can only exist in so far as consensus exists in the group. Society to him is cooperative activity which rests on communication among group members. Communication, cooperation, society are all impossible if group members do not participate in a common symbolic system. The existence of society, to Mead, implied that some degree of consensus, some area of shared meanings, exists in the group. Institutions, which manifest themselves to the observer as recurring behavioral sequences in society, rest on sets of attitudes toward recurring individual problems shared by all members of the group. Mead was insistent on the importance of consensus, but his exploration of its origins and functions in society is not elaborate. His chief interest and most rewarding insights are into the social-psychological link of individual and society through a system of shared meanings (see chapter 6). His discussion of the functioning of a more large-scale society in terms of these mechanisms is far weaker. Yet it is at this level, beyond the boundaries of the intimate face-to-face grouping, that some of the most interesting aspects of the question of social order rest.

Comte too viewed cultural consensus as a far more important mechanism for social order than the individual's spontaneous sociability. Primarily social order rests on consensus, or as Comte phrased it, *consensus universalis*. Only to the extent that all the institutions of society share a common morality, subscribe to a common body of knowledge, and have a common orientation to the world is order possible. Consensus can be said to operate at two levels. The first level lies in the morality, knowledge and so on of individual group members. This level is fairly obvious. Less obvious is Comte's emphasis that consensus must also operate at the level of organizations and institutions. For example, in a society where certain institutions (education and political life) are religious in orientation, while others (like the economy) are scientific, order is impossible and conflict is always present. Consensus at this second level is not just a similar outlook among individuals, but a similar orientation in the organizational, institutionalized aspects of life, with their consequences for the behavior and the socialization of its members. How such consensus (or lack of it) arises was not elaborately explored by Comte, however. He felt that the laws of social development dictate the degree of social consensus at any one time, and takes the question no further.

The third and by far the most elaborate view of social consensus and social order is Max Weber's. As usual his hesitancy about generalization means that we must develop our answers out of separate and distinctive blocs of his writings. The first of these is his work on religion and economic life, which was already explored in chapter 7. The second is his work on authority and legitimacy.

In studying the works on religion, the first question to raise is "How did Weber conceive of social order?" or "How would he conclude, from observations of behavior, that a degree of social order prevailed in the society under investigation?" Extrapolating from his writings, social order for Weber seems to be indicated by the historical phenomenon of aggregates of individuals acting similarly, and producing by this accumulation of similar action organizations and institutions which are harmoniously interrelated. Social order then is repeating patterns of action. The action orginates with individual actors, but when viewed at the societal level it is apparent in whole institutions of behavior, institutions which frequently reinforce each other. For example, in these books on religion Weber was chiefly concerned with order in the economic arena: recurring, individually-based sequences of economic behavior, which produce distinctive economic systems in different societies. He goes on to show, however, the links between this aspect of life and other institutional areas. The class system, the family, the political institution all work to reinforce and strengthen the particular norms of economic life, and are in turn strengthened by it. This is order at the two levels which Comte discussed. Weber, however, made an attempt to trace the links between them.

A second question is "How does Weber explain social order of this type?" There seems no doubt that Weber saw such order as the product of cultural consensus. Men in a particular society had certain common values, goals, outlooks. This repetitiveness in orientation explained repetitiveness in action at the individual level. As we saw in chapter 7, Weber described many different constellations of values in his cross-cultural studies. Each he saw as historically unique. Yet each produced, within the particular society where it operated, rather similar individuals and thus a type of social order.

The third question is "How do the members of a society come to have this common constellation of values and beliefs?" Weber's answer to this is that, at least up to his own period, the source of these attitudes had been religion. Historically, men had always been closely tied to some sort of religious institution. These institutions had all been characterized by the fact that they were structured around explicitly stated systems of beliefs and ideas; all religions, that is, build on dogma. In relation to such relatively stable bodies of ideas men developed the more generalized values and orientations represented in cases like the *geist* of capitalism, the ethos of Confucian China, and so on. Weber traced not only the logical extensions of religious precepts to other aspects of life, but in even more detail, the way in which the doctrine combined with psychic needs and other conditions of life to create, in a slow, evolutionary process, a distinctive social ethos.

The final question that can be raised is "What happens to consensus and order in modern society, since systematic inculcation of a single system of religious beliefs is no longer the norm?" Weber indicated several possible answers to this. In the first place order and consensus is not a fixed, constant condition of social life in Weber's schema (as it seems to be for Mead). Order is variable and problematical. His framework allows for the possibility of a society with no single explicit doctrine which would have a concomitant reduction of consensus and of stability. Second, in terms of organization rather than of beliefs, he saw modern capitalism as the most rational form of social organization that had ever appeared in man's history. Organizationally it was unusually suited to considered, system-level policy decisions and planned action. Such a system was fully capable of creating the doctrine and culture necessary to its own continuance. One has only to think of the way in which certain modern states develop specific, though secular, doctrine or ideology, to understand this point. A third answer is offered in Weber's exploration of power and authority to which we now turn.

The investigation of religious and economic cultures was primarily oriented to a single class of men: the bourgeoisie of capitalist Europe and groups of similar high status and power in other societies. The kind of social order depicted in such research was that between men of roughly similar status, who with similar motivation and with varying

degrees of success pursued like ends in the marketplace or in those institutions which were of central importance in the particular culture.
But society is stratified, and different strata have such different resources, privileges, and powers that they seem more dissimilar than
similar. How does one explain the persistence and stability of a stratified, differentiated, complex society? What binds the peasant and middle class civil servant together? Marx had a clear answer to this formulation of the social order problem. Between different classes the relationship is never "naturally" orderly. It is more naturally one of tension, resentment, fear, conflict. Order in a stratified society is obtained
only by the imposition of the will of the ruling class on subordinated
groups. It is obtained by the exercise of power; by superior resources
and force. Weber confronted this thesis, and attempted to develop an
alternative explanation of the order which exists between groups with
differing degrees of power.

Weber argued that Marx has too simple a notion of power relations.
While admitting that the power-conflict model does exist sometimes,
as in the relationship between a conqueror and the conquered, he
feels that many power relationships rest on a substratum of consensus, and are therefore indicative of "psychic" order rather than of tension and resentment. In exploring this idea Weber introduced two
words into the specialized sociological vocabulary: *authority* and *legitimacy*. Authority means that a power relationship is embedded in a system of beliefs and sentiments meaningful to both ruler and ruled.
Both parties see themselves as part of a single community with rights
and obligations towards the other. Those ruled do not see conformity as
an unwilling concession to superior force, but as a moral obligation.
Power wielded under such circumstances has an aura of legitimacy
to both those exercising it and those experiencing it. It is authority.

Weber felt that in almost all societies those who exercise power
do so within this context of legitimacy, although admittedly the degree
of legitimacy possessed by any particular regime is variable. But to
some extent the subordinates in a power relationship concur, subjectively, while outwardly complying. Pure power relationships do
exist, but these are costly to those in power and unstable, and are less
frequent than relationships of authority.

Where does legitimacy come from? What brings about concurrence
by the ruled with the power relationship? Weber pointed to several
sources. The quality and personality of the leader may win him such
status. Such is the basis of *charismatic authority:* authority granted
to the leader because of his dynamic, magical, apparently extraordinary qualities. Authority may rest on the traditions of the society—a

convergence between the characteristics of the ruling group and the sacred principles of the society. Such is *traditional authority*. Authority may rest on a system of explicit rules which define and regulate the power relationship, and which is respected by all the parties involved in it. Power derived from a constitution or a legal system is of this type. This is *rational authority*. Whatever its basis—and most actual authority systems draw strength from more than one of these sources—authority is a form of social consensus. It indicates that an area of shared meanings links together the different classes of men and smoothes the relationship between them.

Solidarity

Of the group under review, three sociologists stressed the emotional ties between men rather than their attitudinal similarities: Simmel, Cooley, and Tönnies. They made this point by means of their concepts of sociation, primary groups, and *gemeinschaft,* respectively. There are characteristics common to all three of these concepts, and more particularly to the last two.

Sociation, primary groups, and *gemeinschaft* all are attempts to describe the solidary characteristics of the relationships between individuals, rather than those of a large-scale social system (in contrast with the consensus answers already described). All three men (Simmel, Cooley, and Tönnies) chose interpersonal relationships as their unit of analysis. They viewed solidarity as a characteristic of small groups which experience face-to-face contact. The social bond of solidarity, a prerequisite for social stability, exists at this level of social organization.

Solidarity, as Simmel described it, is an orientation of individuals to each other and to the relationship in process between them Resting on an emotional need for human association, solidarity is a quality which permeates almost all relationships, an orientation which seeks to preserve the relationship for its own intrinsic worth. Relationships are formed for a variety of other reasons; the pursuit of material benefit, for example. They may in fact terminate when they cease to function in the service of such needs. But during their development they produce *sociation,* the sense of solidarity as just described. This gives the relationships dimensions beyond those for which they were initially formed. It may even preserve them beyond the point when the initial reasons for them no longer operate. And many forms of social relationships were created solely in the interests of solidarity: clubs, secret societies, social events, games, and so on.

Cooley stressed the emotionality of the human organism, and the emotional satisfaction experienced by the individual in primary groups.

Primary groups, because of their small size and relative informality and intimacy, are the kind of human associations which allow members free play of their emotions. As such they function as an emotional outlet for individuals. More important, here the individual has his best chances of social and emotional support from others. The primary group is tremendously important to the individual—he identifies with it most strongly, and it is where he has his most meaningful and satisfying experiences. Relationships in such group are strong; processes for restoring harmony after moments of conflict are numerous and effective. Primary groups offer islands of stability and solidarity in complex societies.

Tönnies emphasized identification more than emotional satisfaction. He argued that in some forms of human relationships the individual loses his sense of separate autonomy and feels himself to be merely one component in an essential unity. His identity merges with that of the wider relationship, his needs become submerged in it, his activities are those which pursue group interests. This is *gemeinschaft,* or community. The phrase describes a form of relationship, but includes, as Simmel did, psychic orientations as part of that relationship. Communal relationships can occur anywhere, but are most common in those forms of association which we enter by chance: the family, the kinship group, the neighborhood or community. They are intrinsically pleasurable and rewarding relationships.

A feature common to all three approaches is their correlation of solidarity with some kind of attitudinal consensus. Cooley and Tönnies, concerned with natural groups like the family or neighborhood, implied that those groups in which solidarity is experienced tend to be characterized from the outset by cultural consensus. Simmel pushed this a step further. Sociation, he said, cannot develop between men who are markedly different from each other. Sociation therefore leads individuals to blur their differences by devices like tact, discretion, and so on. Sociation makes men similar and equal for the duration of the relationship; it manufactures a synthetic consensus. The final stage in this thesis is put forward by Cooley and Tönnies. Solidarity creates real consensus, not only in the group in which solidarity is experienced, but also in the wider social system. The experience of solidarity, of unity and meaningfulness in association, invests all the other aspects of such groups with an aura of sanctity or morality. Values in the group and in the society derive their significance, their "value," from meaningful experiences in those solidary groups which are so important to man.

Although all three men were concerned with relationships as elementary analytic units, there is variation in the extent to which they were, on this issue, speaking about all forms of social interaction. Sim-

mel indeed saw sociation as a variable quality in all relationships. Tönnies and Cooley, however, placed the experience of solidarity only in
certain kinds of relationships: primary or communal relationships.
They tended to restrict the possibility of a solidary experience only to
specific kinds of groups. This difference produced differences in the
extent to which the three men could hypothesize about solidarity as an
order-producing mechanism in the larger society. Simmel saw sociation
as a system-wide process for social order. It appears in relationships
everywhere, and although specific relationships are transient, relationship as a phenomenon is the elemental unit in all societies. A sense
of solidarity thus permeates much of social life. In contrast Cooley
could only approach a wider system of social order indirectly, as a
product of the consensus which primary groups generate, and as a
result of the management of individual tensions, a trait which characterizes primary relationships. Cooley was pessimistic about modern societies, which he felt destroy many of the prerequisites of primary association, and thus make order problematic. Tönnies too felt that the
kinds of groups characterized by *gemeinschaft* become less frequent
in modern society, and a form of social order based on solidarity also
becomes rare. His prognosis is less bleak than Cooley's, however, because he felt that *gemeinschaft* does not completely vanish in modern
society, and because he conceived of an alternative type of relationship, also with implications for order, which characterized much of
modern social life. (This is discussed on pp. 220-22).

Fusing Consensus and Solidarity

Simmel, Cooley, and Tönnies all had difficulty making solidarity a
social order process in the wider society. Only Simmel seriously attempted to do this by diffusing the experience throughout the relea-
tional network that he saw society to be. Even so his actors experience
a feeling of oneness with particular, immediate relationships. This
feeling, replicated in all the individual relationships of a society, con-
tributes to social stability. But there is no identification, directly, between individual and society in this thesis. Solidarity remains a property of small groups, not of the social system. Sumner, Marx and
Durkheim seemed to address themselves to the problem of solidarity in
social systems. In their efforts, consensus and solidarity blend into a
single order-producing process.

Sumner was described earlier as one who systematically explored
the concept of social norms in his book *Folkways*. From this concept,
he went on to develop an explanation for social order. Any society, he
argued, will be characterized by a degree of cultural consensus, in the

sense that its members have certain common expectations about behavior. These expectations may operate at the level of habitual, unreflective responses to situations or may be consciously stated, rationalized, justified, and systematized. But in any large complex society all individuals do not share uniformly in this normative system. Some will subscribe to certain aspects of it but not be aware of other aspects which absorb the attention of other groups. This uneven sharing in a culture gives rise to an important organizational principle in social life: the distinction between *in-group* and *out-group*. Society breaks down into groups, each of which adheres to a normative system somewhat at variance from others operating in the society. As an individual crosses these normative lines, meeting members of other groups (outgroups), he becomes sharply aware of how he differs from them and how his own group (in-group) is distinct. The out-group is not only seen as different, it is also judged to be inferior to one's in-group, precisely to the extent that it is seen to be culturally different from the ingroup. The in-group's culture becomes the standard for judging the desirability of others. [1] This is *ethnocentricism*.

Ethnocentrism is a social dynamic which produces both order and conflict in society. Sumner sees the two processes as closely related ones. Society is not a homogeneous unity. It is, instead, made up of a series of self-consciously solidary groups, the members of which are emotionally identified with their group because of their contacts with others whom they perceive as different, unfamiliar, inferior, threatening. A feeling of hostility or tension towards some group creates a sense of solidarity with another. This is an individually-based psychological process in which all members of society engage. The object of solidarity is determined by what object is perceived as threatening. In the complex flux of daily life man's contacts with the unfamiliar are so numerous that he constantly redefines his in-group. It may be his family, his community, his work-group, his profession, his political party, his social class, and so on. On occasion the identification is with the whole society, the nation-state. This shifting process of self-identification, of solidarity between self and some facet of society, is an order-producing process. When the whole society is perceived as threatened, it can create solidarity at the total societal level. It is a feeling of solidarity resulting from the shifting perspectices that individuals have about the groups with whom they share common attitudes, that is with whom they feel a degree of cultural consensus.

Marx's concept of *class consciousness* may be seen as one variant on the model of ethnocentricism. Marx admitted that solidarity and a feeling of consensus are possible at the national, total system level. But such unity and order strikes him as synthetic, a creation of the ruling class who have used their superior resources to manufacture a form of false consciousness in the society. Marx saw important real divisions in the experience of the material realities of life occurring along class lines. In different social classes, one finds significant variations in values, beliefs, attitudes, and motives resulting from these differences in experience.

Class consciousness is the subjective experience of solidarity with one's class. One acknowledges a degree of identity with that class and the interests one has in common with it. One is also aware of similarity with members of one's class, and of differences with members of other classes. Class consciousness is ethnocentrism, with one's class as the in-group. Class consciousness occurs only in groups which are marked by cultural consensus, but consensus does not, in turn, automatically create such solidarity. Class consciousness results from perceptions of threat, intensified exploitation, conscious intraclass organization and education, and cross-class confrontation. It is most marked at moments of revolutionary confrontation between classes. Thus consensus and solidarity do work for unity and order in the Marxist thesis, but only within social classes. Consensus at the national societal level is always "false," the synthetic creation of a ruling class. Like Sumner, Marx viewed order and tension as two sides of a coin: cross-class hostility leads to within-class solidarity, and this in turn increases the hostility between classes. Marx believed that a supranational sense of solidarity was possible, but again along class lines only. This belief inspired his activity on behalf of an international proletarian movement. Between Marx and Sumner, or for that matter between Marx and Durkheim, one can see the differences in theories of social solidarity created by varying commitments to socialism and nationalism.

Durkheim's fusion of consensus and solidarity is presented in his concept of *mechanical solidarity*. Mechanical solidarity rests on cultural consensus, and operates to the extent that individuals have certain common experiences of society and certain common attitudes which reflect these experiences. Mechanical solidarity is greatest in small homogeneous societies, but it is present to some degree in any society with a long, continuous history, no matter how large and heterogeneous.

But mechanical solidarity means more than similarity in attitudes. It also implies an emotional identification with one's society, a personal conviction that one's society is important and deserves one's support. Consensus and solidarity are not separate aspects of social order: they are closely connected. Consensus creates solidarity, at the societal level. This occurs because the group tends to concretize, to bequeath objective, independent status to its culture. Cultural consensus does not stay at the level of similar outlooks in the minds of many individuals; it becomes a real object to which those individuals, as a group, can relate.

This point is made clearer by illustration. In his first book, *The Division of Labor in Society,* Durkheim treated a society's legal system as one example of the way in which culture becomes an object, and a spur to solidarity. Particularly illustrative of this are those laws which Durkheim called retributive laws. These laws come close to a society's taboos, the issues which relate closely to the society's fundamental moral codes. The violation of these laws creates a sense of outrage in the population. They seek to punish the violator for his temerity, not simply to restore things to normal. Their most negative sanctions are reserved for such violations. Examples would include the lynch "laws" of the past, or our own outrage at murder, kidnapping, treason. The historical starting point of a retributive law was probably a wave of anger and revulsion felt by people at the violation of one of their central beliefs. In ongoing societies, however, both simple and complex, the existence of the law objectifies, reinforces and emphasizes those beliefs. Violation of the law, in itself, creates as much anger and force for punishment as does the particular act. The law represents both some particular cultural belief and the culture or society itself. One defends both in upholding a law, and one offends both by violating a law. In this sense, Durkheim argued, men relate concretely to their culture and feel their oneness with it.

In the last of his books, *The Elementary Forms of Religious Life,* Durkheim looked at the concretization of culture and its effects on solidarity in another institution, religion. One important distinction on which this book is based is that between *sacred* and *profane.* Men operate with two mental categories into which they place everything that they encounter in life. Things classified as profane are judged instrumentally, in terms of their use and functions. Most things are profane things. Sacred things are never assessed in terms of instrumental value. Rather they are seen as intrinsically powerful and deserving of awe and respect. One must relate to them in a special way since their immanent powers can bring both benefits and danger. Religion is that set of attitudes and activities that has to do with sacred things.

In fact the objects dubbed sacred have no intrinsic power. Historical and ethnographic data show that the things which have been sacred to some group or other are almost randomly variable: sticks and stones, streams and mountains, various animals, bits of cloth, and so on. Sacred objects are symbols, multiple codes for a common experience and common expressive need in men. The experience is of the power of culture and social organization. Sacred objects are half-articulated conceptualizations of society or culture, concretized and worshipped.

Durkheim also distinguished, in his study of religion, between *ritual* and *beliefs*.. Given the present concern with solidarity, the concept of ritual is important here. Ritual refers to the overt activities in which the group engages in its relationship to sacred things. What are the functions of ritual? At one level rituals are sacred objects too, symbolic representations of society. But ritual is distinctive because it is both a symbol and a relationship to society. Participation in sacred rituals reasserts and strengthens the sentiments of solidarity with the culture.

In summary, Durkheim felt that social order rests primarily on shared values or cultural consensus. He argued that this culture is objectified in certain institutions, like the legal system or religion. Men can relate to these institutions and to their culture. This relationship creates an emotional awareness of one's place in a group and common culture: the relationship creates solidarity, at the societal level. This not only facilitates social order in its own right, but acts to strengthen value consensus.

Functional Interdependence

A certain paradox can be found in all that has been said so far. The sociologists of this period lived in societies that were rapidly industrializing; that is, they were becoming increasingly complex and internally segmented. Society, as they experienced it, seemed to be characterized by an attenuation of value consensus, and by a decline in the importance of groups which were primarily solidary in character. Yet the societies persisted, with some degree of internal stability and effectiveness. How could answers in terms of shared values and emotional ties explain social persistence in modern industrial orders? The early sociologists tried to deal with this problem in several ways.

Some sociologists were pessimistic in tone. They argued that the perception of a decline of societal bonds in modern society was accurate. This was the tragedy of modern society. It achieved prosperity at a growing cost of societal conflict and disintegration. The long-term results could only be disastrous. Cooley took this position in arguing that modern urban societies destroyed many of the possibilities for primary association, and thus the foundations of its own well-being. Something of the same note can be detected in Durkheim's treatment of egoistic and anomic suicide. To Durkheim, progressive weakening of social controls, marked by a rising rate of deviant, non-social behavior, seemed to be the trend in industrial societies.

Another set of answers were those offered by the "stubbornly insistent" sociologists. They argued that one ought not to be deceived by the spectacular degree of differentiation in modern society. Beneath the surface reality of variation there still existed some degree of shared values and shared emotional ties. This is Mead's view. He felt that the very fact that relationships do occur is evidence of some persisting level of shared meanings. This too is Durkheim's prevailing opinion, despite his occasional pessimism. A level of shared values and solidarity prevails in modern society, though admittedly the integrative ties are weaker than in traditional societies. And Weber subscribed to this opinion: it seemed to him that the diversity of modern society rests on a foundation of shared beliefs in individualism, change, rationality, and so on.

Other sociologists, however, tried to find an integrative mechanism in the very fact of diversity. They gave answers to the social order question phrased in terms of *functional interdependence*. In contemporary sociology this kind of answer has been elaborately formulated. On the whole the earlier sociologists did not equal this elaborate concern with functional interdependence. The theme is there, however, and its early articulation had some influence on later theory. In the earlier period the thesis of functional interdependence, or complementary needs, was pitched to two different levels of social organization. Some stressed it as a variable in the relationships between individuals. Others emphasized it as a process of the social system, a characteristic of the relationships between major processes and institutions in that system. These two models are described below.

Individual Relationships

Several writers in this period see the possibility of social integration in the exchange and contractual relationships which characterize economic life in modern society. Spencer's stress is on exchange. As was described in chapter 5, Spencer viewed society, at one level, as an aggregate of human beings. Moreover he argued that Western societies, in the vanguard of mankind's social evolution, were approaching that optimal condition, the fully industrialized social system. In such a system men would relate freely to each other without the artificial constraints of an autocratic government. Men would be bound together, voluntarily, by a network of rationally motivated exchange relationships, broadly economic in character. To the marketplace some men would bring their strength, others their capital, others their particular skills. Each would get from the relationship what he could not provide for himself yet could not do without. This consciousness of mutual dependence would stabilize society, and create social order. It should be recalled that Spencer assumed an evolutionary improvement in man's nature. The dynamic he called "survival of the fittest," by making man more moral and rational, steadily increased the probability of equitable and rational exchanges between men.

Durkheim held a completely different view of human nature. In his first book, *The Division of Labor in Society,* he questioned the concept of individual rationally-inspired exchanges implied by Spencer's thesis. Yet he too felt that the elaborate task specialization of modern society should be seen not just as a divisive force, but, because of the mutual dependence it created, as an integrative potential in society. He developed this idea with his concept of *organic solidarity.* (This concept he posed as the alternative to mechanical solidarity.) Organic solidarity rests on a system of ethical and normative orientations which are adaptations to a highly specialized occupational structure and economic interdependence. These orientations are such as to facilitate relationships between men differently located in the economy, who act towards each other *as though* they were rationally aware of their mutual dependence. But most men are in fact not so aware. The behavior is "habitual" for most individuals, a result of their conformity with institutionalized expectations about behavior. The orientations and expectations which characterize organic solidarity are socially produced, not individually created. The ethical codes of professions and the legal codes for contracts are not created by individual beings on every occasion that they enter into a relationship. Such things spring from collective responses to the particular circumstances produced by an elaborate division of labor. They facilitate exchanges between men, but not because men consciously will such equilibrium in each of their relationships. Organic solidarity is the consequence of a particular type of cultural arrangement. In the end Durkheim realized that he was talking about a variant of cultural consensus, and he moved away from his initial distinction between mechanical and organic solidarity. But the dichotomy has survived in the discipline, and organic solidarity is often taken to mean what Durkheim had first attempted to outline—a kind of contractual interdependence in individual relations, springing from and morally validated by the normative systems of complex societies.

One of the best known treatments of such interdependence is Tönnies' ideal type of the *gesellschaft.* Directly translated this means simply society, but understood as it was intended, as a contrast to *gemein-schaft*, the term is better understood as urban society. *Gesellschaft* refers to a kind of human relationship and to a form of orientation or "will" which prompts such relationships. Such relationships are rationally motivated by the wish to attain explicit, discrete ends. The individual acts as an autonomous agent in the pursuit of such ends. He is moved by consideration of exchange, costs, rewards. He, and others entering into the relationship, favor a contractual regulation of the rights and obligations of all the agents involved. It is a formalized relationship. The *gesellschaft* contrasts with the diffuseness, absence of egoism, natural rather than rational mentality and the warmth which characterizes *gemeinschaft*. Yet it is a social bond.

> Gesellschaft . . . . superficially resembles *gemeinschaft* insofar as the individuals live and dwell together peacefully. However, in *gemein-schaft* they remain essentially united in spite of all separating factors, whereas in *gesellschaft* they remain essentially separated in spite of all uniting factors. In the *gesellschaft*, as contrasted with the *gemein-schaft* we find no actions which can be derived from an *a priori* and necessarily existing unity; no actions therefore which manifest the will of the unity even if performed by the individual; no actions which insofar as they are performed by the individual, take place on behalf of those united with him. In *gesellschaft* such actions do not exist. On the contrary, here everyone is by himself and isolated.[2]

Gesellschaft as an ideal type is a society of individuals, lacking any identification with a group, acting in pursuit of particular and separate goals. Is this social order? Tönnies felt that it is, though admittedly a fragile order. Indeed it is the only social order possible in a society of the marketplace. Moved by concern for their separate interests, individuals can maintain their relationships over time and actively minimize conflict, to the extent that these things are seen to serve rather than hinder such interests. Society persists because self-interested, functionally specialized individuals see that persistence is instrumental in the achievement of their particular goals. To this end they create organization, legal codes, and so on which stabilize relationships and regularize unproductive tensions. But order of this type is a tentative order: voluntarily instituted, it can be voluntarily destroyed. The enduring natural order of the *gemeinschaft*, which rests on the subordination of individuality, is absent in *gesellschaft*.

Gesellschaft has become an accepted model of human relations in modern society, a description of relationships that are motivated by self-interest, exchange strategies, and calculations of instrumentality. It is the original description in sociology of what we today call secondary relations. As a way of explaining social order, however, neither it, nor the models of Durkheim and Spencer just described, have been as influential on contemporary notions of functional interdependence as has the other theme, focusing on the larger social system.

The Social System

Functional interdependence in the social system is the idea that stabilizing processes based on complementary functions exist in a society between its institutions, structures, processes, or organizations. In a sense this is what Durkheim was reaching for with his belief that exchange and contractual relationships in an organically integrated system do not develop in the ongoing sequence of interpersonal relationships but are, instead, the consequence of large-scale structures affecting these relationships. Comte had a similar belief in the possibility of harmonious relationships between the institutions of the "social organism," a relational congruence which was the mark of a "healthy" society. But both Comte and Durkheim ultimately explained such social stability in terms of cultural variables. Durkheim pointed to institutionalized norms and ethics which smoothed the relationship between men of different economic statuses. Comte argued for a unifying world view—theological, metaphysical or positivistic—which, by influencing the dynamics of each institution, makes possible a common purpose and will in their relationships to each other. Thus interdependence between opposites at one level is explained in terms of cultural consensus at another. More emphatic proponents of system level interdependence, however, sought to keep the explanation strictly at the level of relationships between parts of the social system, relationships which in their own right created social order.

Spencer, when he thought of society as a thing in its own right, rather than as an aggregate of individuals, moved towards this emphasis. The structure of the social system is increasingly differentiating, becoming more complex. This means that there are more and more institutions and organizations, each distinct from the others because of the specialized and essential task it performs for the whole society. A simply structured society is one in which individual units—men, families, communities—can break apart fairly easily; the costs are low, for the units can survive since each unit can perform the variety of tasks necessary for its own subsistence. It is the same with simply structured biological organisms. But one cannot break a complex organism apart without mutilating or perhaps killing it. A highly differentiated society is similar. Its structures are closely bound together because the particular functioning of each draws on the functioning of the rest. The

health of any particular structure or organization is as much determined by its relationship to other structures and organizations as by
its own internal processes. This is an order-producing phenomenon:
institutional interdependence arising from functional differentiation.
Phrased in these terms one does not have to raise questions about individual relationships. It is much more relevant to understand the
phenomenon in terms of the general principle of evolution: the thrust
towards a system equilibrium based on structural heterogeneity. Yet
the two types of interdependence which Spencer described (rational
exchanges between individuals and relational interweavings between
institutions) are complementary processes: a shifting perspective on
the same general order-producing phenomenon in human societies.

Pareto's concept of *equilibrium* is even better known than Spencer's. Pareto developed his idea in terms of a process in a social system
which is mechanically conceptualized, in contrast to Spencer's organic
imagery. The social system is a dynamic cluster of interdependent
processes existing in a constraining environment. One dynamic in this
system is the tendency to equilibrium. This appears to be a tendency
for the system at any one time to achieve a steady state, characterized
by the recurrence of essential processes, the meshing of these processes
with each other, and a certain predictability in the sequences of behavior which are the components of the social system. What produces
this is not any solidification of structures but rather the capacity of
those structures to produce adjustive, compensatory outcomes. As
something changes in one part of the system, all the other parts are
capable, up to a point, of compensating for this change by their reac-
tive counterchanges. The steady state, the meshing of system parts,
and the predictability in the system as a whole continues. This is the
dynamic of equilibrium.

Equilibrium is absolute and stable when the compensations in other
parts of the system serve to maintain the exact qualitative condition of
the system which existed prior to the initial change. For example, a
general standard of living may stay exactly at some point, despite a
sudden increase in certain resource costs, because of a whole series of
compensating adjustments in prices, wages, interest rates, taxes, and
so on. Or an extension of the franchise, such as the grant of the vote
to eighteen year olds, may not alter prior party and political strengths
because of rulings on where the new voters must vote, a series of
minor adjustments in party platforms, parental and community influences on the new voters, and so on.

In other instances equilibrium may be a moving state in which new
qualitative conditions emerge in the system at intervals, but each
change is marked by such adjustments in the other institutions as to

create a new mesh, new predictabilities, a new—if temporary—steady state of the system. In this case the standard of living shifts (if we stick to our examples) or the balance of power alters, but instead of this resulting in stresses and incongruities in society, one finds a fairly rapid alteration in other institutions in response to the initial change.

Pareto seemed to think that a moving equilibrium was far more frequent than a stable one. He also saw equilibrium not as an unalterable fact, but as one dynamic in society which functioned with more or less success to produce harmony rather than conflict in the relationships of the social system. Like Spencer, Pareto saw a complementary relationship between such system-level processes and the traits and relationships of the individuals in society: in this case the needs for relationship and stability in individuals, and the behaviors arising out of such needs. Later sociologists have drawn extensively on the equilibrium notions of both Spencer and Pareto.

Formal Organizations of Regulation and Control

The last group of answers to the questions about social order points, in a variety of ways, to the existence in large societies of organizations which are primarily oriented to the maintenance of the system: organizations whose explicit purpose is to suppress disruptive activities (social control) and to coordinate the various processes of the society (regulation). In this light we shall consider Marx, Pareto, Durkheim, Weber, and Spencer. The first three men lean towards the social control answer, the latter two towards the regulative alternative. But in all instances the organizations of control and/or regulation are seen as dimensions of the political institution, or to put it more generally, as aspects of the state.

Marx saw societal order as the product of formal social control organizations in a stratified society. Ultimate social power rests with the economically dominant class of men. They, however, control exploited and potentially insubordinate social classes not only by the exercise of economic sanctions, but also by extending their influence into the formal organizations of the state, and into those of mass persuasion. The former area of influence means that political power is used in the interests of the economically dominant class and involves all those processes of coercion over which the state exercises exclusive control. The latter avenue of influence means that those who create and spread ideas in society—religious leaders, ideologists, academicians, educationists, intellectuals—on the whole tend to create idea systems which validate the existing power arrangements, and, by spreading these ideas, to produce false consciousness in subordinate classes. This further ensures their docility. Order in society is created by a ruling class, in its own interests, by means of processes of both direct and indirect control. Except for Spencer's views in this general area, all the other perspectives to be described here are addressing themselves to Marx's thesis. Of all the answers to be reviewed here, Pareto's comes closest to that of Marx. His main point of difference from Marx is that he did not see political power as a superstructure to economic power; indeed, he tended to reverse this relationship. The instruments of formal social control, he said, are accessible only to a small circle of men: the political elite. The political elite includes those men who actively seek or have obtained political office, and their hangers-on, frequently their economic hangers-on. This elite exercises power horizontally over other kinds of elites, and hierarchically over the great mass of the non-elite. The channels of mobility into the group of the political elite, either from other elite groups or from the non-elite, are variably open, depending on the society. In some social systems mobility is considerable, in others it is nearly impossible. But whatever the particular situation in this matter, the fact remains that, at any one time, control is the resource only of that small group which is the political elite.

There are two broad strategies for such direct control. The first is the use of force or coercion, the political structure being the one which attempts to monopolize force in society. The second is the use of what Pareto called "ruse." This refers to all forms of manipulation, including bribery, deception, and propaganda. The particular tastes of the rulers will determine their emphasis within this category of social controls. Effective government requires a balance of the two general strategies. In Pareto's terms, order exists in a society not just because of the diffuse conservatism and sociability of the population and the mechanical adjustments of institutions to each other, but also because any society contains a political structure which, in terms of whatever goals seem appropriate to the rulers, consciously works to control the rest of the population.

A very different bias is apparent in Durkheim's work along these lines. Somewhat more than both Marx and Pareto, Durkheim indicated that a complex organizational factor is involved in formal social control. Where both Marx and Pareto had pointed to the central core of politicians in the state, Durkheim pointed to the legal-judicial-law enforcement aspects of the polity. Complex societies, he claimed, create certain concrete agents directly empowered to enforce the norms embodied in the society's laws, to apprehend and punish those who defy those norms, and to rectify the situations which result from such defiance. The agents of the law enforcement institution, though a functionally distinct group, are not a special interest and power group in the sense that Marx and Pareto saw them. Durkheim saw the agents as representatives of their society. They bear the power which that society gave them and which it can recall from them. They defend the norms that are deemed crucial by the collectivity. They have authority, as Weber would understand authority. This legal-judicial-law enforcing institution is a complex of organizations each with its own specialized task. Complexity and specialization increases as the social system grows bigger and more differentiated. In the small simple society, the law enforcement activity is dispersed throughout the group, an activity in which all group members participate. But in complex society, it becomes essential to specify the norms as laws, and to empower certain organizations to oversee the maintenance of those laws. The consequence is the same: social control and social order.

Weber's emphasis is not so much on the control aspects of the state but on the coordinating, regulating structure which it represents. Weber's views on power as authority and authority as a form of consensus have already been described. What is important here is that he related each type of authority to a distinctive administrative organization. Any type of political authority is complemented by an administrative organization which acts to procure resources for the authority center, to implement its decisions, to maintain continuity at moments when authority changes hands, and to siphon information from the wider society to the rulers who make collective decisions. These administrative organizations are subordinate to the ruler, for such authority as they wield is merely a reflection of the authority which he has. Yet the ruler needs his administration, for it is the practical channel from him to the population. This concern with the administrative aspects of power is yet another route for Weber in his debate with Marx. He saw the Marxist power model as too simple because it overlooks the frequent case of a legitimate power arrangement—legitimate, that is, in the eyes of both rulers and ruled. It is also too simple because it overlooks the formal organizational and administrative dimension in national power relations, a dimension which is essential to confront if one is truly to understand political power.

Like Durkheim, Weber felt that the complexity of these organizations varies from society to society. Unlike Durkheim, however, he did not explain this variation in terms of the size and degree of differentiation in the society. Rather it correlates, in his handling of the question, with the type of authority wielded by the ruler and with the amount of rationality, or conscious systematic application of effort to problem solving, which permeates the society's ethos. Charismatic rulers frequently rely on little more than a devoted band of disciples to perform the minimal essentials of coordination. Traditional rulers use a bigger group of relatives, vassals, and favorites, and seek a more sustained regulation of the society, but the administration is still somewhat unsystematic and very much subject to the whims of the rulers. Legal-rational rulers, that is, those whose authority rests on formal, legal, and constitutional arrangements, tend to correlate with bureaucratic administrations. Such administrative structures are much more distinct from the rulers and much more definite in their purposes than the administrative organizations of charismatic or traditional rulers. They are hierarchically organized for maximal control and task performance, manned by professional administrators, and protected to some degree from the arbitrary purposes of the rulers. As an ethos becomes increasingly rationalized, the bureaucracy becomes increasingly complex and increasingly "pure" along the dimensions just described.

Spencer, in common with the last two sociologists, felt that the formal regulatory structures of society became increasingly complex. This is a natural conclusion in view of his evolutionary beliefs. Since he ideologically denied the state any but the most minimal rights to control the lives of its citizens, he could not countenance the idea that this complexity was a growing degree of formal social control. He focused instead on the coordinative, regulatory functions of government. Although his discussion is, as always, made difficult because of his elaborate use of organic imagery, he is more precise than any other sociologist of this period as to the processes involved in effective state regulation of a social system. He pointed to structures which channel information and resources from the peripheries of the system to its regulatory center; to structures which allocate those resources, circulating them and rushing them to vulnerable parts of the system; and to the central decision-making nexus, lying at the heart of this network of distributive and communicative network, and oriented towards threats to the system either from within it, or from its environment. Some of the most contemporary explorations of social integration take exactly this perspective.

Summary and Conclusions

This chapter has described the variety of order-producing variables touched upon by earlier sociologists in their exploration of the vexing questions of what creates social stability and facilitates the persistence

TABLE 6: Explorations of Social Order

THEORIST	Human instincts	Consensus/ shared beliefs	Solidarity/ Emotional ties	Consensus & solidarity	Functional interdependence as individual relationships	Functional interdependence at institutional level	Structures of control and regulation
Comte	Sociability	Consensus universalis					
Spencer	Sociability in evolved man				✓	? ✓	Political coordination and communication
Sumner				Ethnocentrism			
Marx		False consciousness		Class consciousness			Political control
Tönnies			Gemeinschaft		Gesellschaft		
Simmel	Sociability		Sociation				
Weber		Culture, including agreement on authority relationships					Administrative coordination
Durkheim				Mechanical solidarity	Organic solidarity	? ✓	Legal-judicial organization
Pareto	Sociability Conservatism					Equilibrium	Political control
Mead		Consensus					
Cooley	Sociability		Primary groups				

NOTE: A check indicates that the writer discussed the particular order-producing process at length, but developed no distinctive label for it. A check and a question mark signifies implications in the writer's works about the particular order-producing process, but the concept is not explicitly dealt with.

of groups. (The material of this chapter is summarized in table 6.) Answers to these questions were framed in terms of human needs and traits, cultural consensus, emotional solidarity, functional interdependence, and formal control and regulatory organizations. No hard line was drawn, or maybe can be drawn, between value consensus and emotional solidarity as order-creating phenomena. It is also important to distinguish between those who saw functional interdependence as an outcome of individual relationships, often conceived as exchange relationships; and those who saw such interdependence as a macrosocial dynamic of the social system, that is, operating at the level of institutional linkages and dynamics. In the course of this description several of the concepts which were most influential on later sociologists were introduced: Weber's concepts of authority and bureaucracy; Pareto's concepts of equilibrium, elites, and non-elites; and some now famous dichotomies like *gemeinschaft* and *gesellschaft*, mechanical and organic solidarity, sacred and profane, beliefs and ritual.

The substance of this chapter can be linked in a variety of ways to the material already presented in this text. The most important linkage is to the description of sociopolitical events given in chapter 3. As that chapter described it, the nineteenth century was a century of dramatic economic and social change. It also appeared to men of the time to be a period of political instability. Any careful observer of the events of that period found order problematical, and the discussion of stability-producing factors was a major theoretical theme in the early sociologist's writings. The connection of the concerns of these early sociologists to the social changes of the day is direct and obvious.

Intellectual influences of the period also shaped several of the finer points of discussion. Again there was a confrontation between those who saw man as a creature of emotion and those who stressed his cognitive traits. The curious similarities in the metaphysics of Marx and social Darwinism, centering in part on their common assumption of conflict as a social dynamic, surfaced in the similarities between Sumner's concept of ethnocentricism and Marx's of class consciousness: in both cases order in subgroupings of society resulted from intergroup hostility. Again, ideological differences described earlier help us to understand the differing evaluations made by some of these writers of processes which superficially strike us as substantively alike. This is true of the discussion of formal control organizations as mechanisms for social stability, especially in the contrast between Marx's views on political control and false consciousness and the concepts of consensual, authoritative relationships presented by both Weber and Durkheim.

Running through these competing theses of social order are the different images of society described in chapter 5. Views on cultural consensus, small group solidarity, and interpersonal exchanges rest on the varying emphases given by sociologists to cultural and interactional variables as the crucial subject matter of sociology. Explanations of social order in terms of large-scale, institutional interdependencies arise from images of society which are either organismic or mechanical in nature. Finally, from the viewpoint of this particular text, the most interesting thesis may well be that of Durkheim's "mechanical solidarity": the concretization of culture, so that man could relate to it by habit or by emotion. Here we have resolved for us, even if not very satisfactorily, one of the major paradoxes of Durkheim's work: his view of society as omnipotent and ideational, rather than material, and his belief in man as non-cognitive yet subservient and morally compliant with the normative-cultural "thing" which was society.

If one were to compare past views to present views on this question of order, one would have to note first all the enormous influence that past views have had on our present theories of order. There have been some changes in emphasis: a marked decrease in answers which point to human traits as an order-producing cluster of variables; less emphasis on the theme of emotional solidarity; a great elaboration of the system-level interdependence concept, and the motif of communication channels (which figured in Spencer's writings). But the list of possible sources of stabilizing factors has not been added to.

It must be obvious that the various factors are not alternatives in the strict sense. Though no sociologist of the earlier period touched on all the factors, all of them did deal with more than one theme (as indicated in table 5). Their intention seems to be to state, clearly, that there are several order-producing mechanisims simultaneously at work in society. The relative importance of each mechanism is determined by the stage of development, and the degree of complexity and differentiation in the system. Today we are less easy about this developmental model. We lose, thereby, a theoretical device for differentiating between the order-producing mechanisms in terms of their relative contributions to a particular society's stability. Yet it is not enough to be weakly eclectic and say that they are all at work. The task before contemporary sociologists seems to be one of tracing the relationships between those order processes which earlier sociologists brought to our attention.

NOTES

1. For an extended treatment of ethnocentricism on these lines see Robin M. Williams Jr., *Strangers Next Door* (Englewood Cliffs, N.J.: Prentice Hall, 1964), chapter 3.

2. Ferdinand Tönnies, *Community and Society*, trans. Charles P. Loomis (New York: Harper Torchbooks edition, 1963), pp. 64-65.

10

Explorations of
Social Conflict

Like "the problem of social order" the term "the problem of social conflict" is a catch phrase for a number of sociological concerns. Subsumed under it are all the particular interests in various kinds of social instability, confrontation, disorganization, and violence; the efforts to conceptualize, interpret and explain these; and the attempt to determine the extent to which these "problems" for investigation should be treated, by sociologists, as "problems" for society. This chapter is a relatively brief one, but not because early sociologists were unconcerned with social conflict. They lived in societies characterized by many kinds of intense conflict, and they drew on intellectual themes which sensitized them to the importance of such dynamics: the concept of the dialectic, Darwinian evolutionary thought, Malthus' population thesis. The chapter is short because we have already anticipated much of its material in the preceding discussion of social order.

In many ways, interpretations of order and conflict are two sides of one coin. This is particularly clear in the preceding descriptions of ethnocentricism and class consciousness, both of which imply that group ties at one level are produced by conflicts at another, conflicts springing from normative and interest dissimilarity. Similarly explanations of order in terms of consensus, solidarity, the exchange of desired services, or social control can be turned around and used to explain the phenomenon of conflict in societies: conflict is a consequence of the absence of such processes. For a fuller grasp of early sociology's exploration of conflict the reader should look again at chapter 9 with this new question in mind. The discussion in this chapter should be viewed against the backdrop of that material.

To explain social conflict simply by pointing to the absence of order-producing factors is only the beginning, though a useful beginning. One must go on to locate the processes and mechanisms which weaken those order-producing factors, or directly create tension. The main part of this chapter reviews some of the better known attempts by early sociologists to do just that. A later section then looks at their efforts to establish what the sociological position on conflict would be, and the extent to which societal tensions should or should not be viewed as genuine "problems" for societal well-being.

Conflict-Generating Factors

The key to the various answers about conflict developed by early sociologists lies in the assumptions each man made about which relationship in society was the crucial, conflict-generating one. Some saw it in the general relationship of individual to "society." Others located it in the specific relationships of individuals to each other. Still others pointed to the relationship between important groups or sectors of society. This section looks at the various analyses of conflict at each of these relational levels.

The Relationship of Individual to Society

Mead and Durkheim are both well known for their stress on this relationship as the source of social conflict. Chapter 6 described the elaborate linkage which Mead traced between individual and society. The crucial factor was the self: the individual's personality. Socialization and the individual's lifelong experiences of others served to embed "society" in the self as an internalized system of social controls. Conflict thus also originated in the personality, as an "internal" or subjective experience. It might or might not then spill over into behavior and social relationships.

Analytically, Mead viewed the self as having two components. The first was the internalized, social control element; that part of personality which reflects the group's expectations and values. Mead labeled this the "me." The second was self-will, the purely egoistic element of personality which one experienced on a momentary basis as a flickering reaction against the me. This was the "I." In this transitory experience of resistance to society lay the individual's fleeting assertion of autonomy in society. Even the most socialized of beings on occasion asserted this separateness from society. In this recurring tension between "I" and "me" was the source of social conflict.

Conflict of this type might be experienced only within the personality, as the elements of the self made war on each other. Various forms of psychopathology might thus be viewed as instances of social conflict. This tension was particularly acute when an individual was marginal to a group, only slightly involved in its common meaning structures. Under such circumstances the individual was particularly prone to cloak himself in a sense of "I"-based superiority, and, either actively or passively, to be in a state of conflict with society. Since all individuals experienced this uneasy relationship between "I" and "me," the probability of conflict and tension in social interaction was an ever present one. This was particularly so in those aspects of life which called for innovative and impulsive behavior. Mead thus described conflict in terms of an eternal tension in personality, though he also pointed to certain social situations, like marginality and the requirement for innovative behavior, which served to heighten this tension and to increase the probability of conflict in social life.

Durkheim also viewed conflict as a consequence of a confrontation between society and the purely egoistic drives of the individual. There are, however, several differences between his approach and that of Mead. First, Durkheim emphasized the exteriority of social controls rather than the internalization of such controls. The confrontation is, therefore, portrayed as one between the individual and a wider social system, rather than as a tension within the individual. Second, social conflict merits sociological attention only when it manifests itself in behavior. The wholly subjective tension of which Mead spoke is essentially inaccessible to empirical study in Durkheim's eyes. Durkheim saw conflict as an act of overt rebellion by the individual against the normative constraints of society: it is *deviant behavior.* Nor was he particularly interested in isolated instances of deviance. When the analyst can isolate a *recurring* phenomenon of deviance in a population, an actual statistical rate of deviance, one has a social fact which warrants sociological investigation. Third, Durkheim was not prepared, as Mead was, to explain social conflict as an inevitable outcome of personality dynamics. Rather he argued for an explanation in social terms: the confrontation between individual and society is to be seen as an outcome of the organization of the society itself. Thus conceptualized, Durkheim's interest in social conflict as deviant behavior was an enduring one, to which he returned repeatedly in his writings. His most famous statement on deviant behavior is his book *Suicide*.

In *Suicide* Durkheim developed most clearly his thesis that social circumstances, rather than personality dynamics, create deviance. Painstakingly analyzing some of the statistical correlates of the rate of suicide in French society, he isolated three general causes of suicide. Two of these he saw as typical of complex modern society: *egoistic* and *anomic* factors. Both are conditions of society in which the effective link between individual and society is broken.

Egoistic suicide results from the individual's isolation from close, meaningful relationships with others. On the whole, embeddedness in a group is one of the ways in which the individual is linked to society, and absorbed in a system of social controls which are meaningful and important to him. On occasion, though, this link may be broken, as in the case of the divorcé or the widower. The individual is then set adrift from the constraints of the society. He is left to his own devices. Deviant behavior is a frequent outcome. (One can see similarities between this and Mead's notion of marginality.) On other occasions isolation is not an accident, as the case of the widower might be construed. It is instead the result of a cultural system which fosters individualism, urging, as an ethical necessity, that the individual renounce group ties. Such was the case with Protestantism, in contrast to Catholicism. The occurrence of suicide was, consequently, much higher among Protestants. Modern industrial civilization was also markedly individualistic. Durkheim saw all forms of deviant behavior, including suicide, on the increase in modern society.

The concept of *anomie* shifts one's focus away from the individual's location in a web of association to his experience of a cultural system of beliefs and values. Durkheim stressed that one important function of culture was that it specified the desirable goals towards which men should direct their activities. Moreover, he assumed that on the whole there was a fairly good mesh between the realistic possibilities of the situation and what was culturally designated as an acceptable and desirable achievement. Man acquired both the ends towards which he directed his activities and the practical ceilings to those aspirations from his culture. *Anomie* was a cultural *malaise* characterized by a weakening of these controlling mechanisms. There were no clearly specified goals for action. The individual found himself in a highly ambiguous situation, in which an endless array of goals seemed vaguely possible, with no clear criteria for assessing achievement or satisfaction. The intolerable restlessness and anxiety as well as the pervasive suspicion and dread of personal failure which this created led to suicide and to other forms of social deviance. *Anomie* was a blurring of the cultural system.

One condition that might produce *anomie* was an unstable economic situation in which the rapid alternation between expansion and economic depression undermined any explicit system of material expectations. A more basic cause of *anomie* was rapid structural differentiation. As the society became more complex, the common culture was generalized. It became more vague, abstract, empty of content. This was inevitable, given the ramifying network of special interests now subsumed under the broad rubrics of culture. The real problem was caused by the failure of effective "middle level" groups to emerge. Such groups—organized professional or trade groups for example— could develop explicit and realizable sets of goals into which their members would be socialized. Economic instability, accelerating structural differentiation, and an absence of effective organized middle-level groups all characterized Western industrial societies. This was another explanation for the rapid increase in deviant behavior.

Students frequently point out that egoism and *anomie* are very similar. There is, however, a clear analytic difference between the two, a difference which parallels the distinction made in the last chapter between emotional solidarity and value consensus. The immediate referent of egoism is associational, while that of *anomie* is cultural. Durkheim saw *anomie* as an actual condition of the culture. Both the social isolation which is egoism and the cultural *malaise* which is anomie produce in the individual an experience of stress: a sense of loss of "belongingness" in the egoistic situation, a sense of loss of direction in the anomic. However, Durkheim saw a connection between the associational-emotional and the cultural variables in social life. The same connection could probably be made between egoism and *anomie*. Moreover, both clusters of processes were intensifying in mobile, individualistic, complex, economically unstable modern societies. Both factors jointly explained the increase in deviance or conflict.

[It should be noted that Durkheim isolated a third form of suicide, which he called altruistic. This resulted from conditions which were the very opposite of egoism and *anomie*. The individual in the altruistic situation was completely and utterly absorbed in a group which had a very explicit culture. Indeed it could be said that such individuals lost all separate self-identity. Their deaths were voluntary sacrifices for the group, often conforming to very explicit cultural rules. Such were *harakiri* in Japan, *suttee* in India, the suicide of the defeated military leader in ancient Rome. Durkheim felt that this phenomenon was seldom seen in modern societies, except in certain enclaves like the military.]

Relationships between Individuals

Despite their differences, both Mead and Durkheim explain social conflict in terms of what contemporary sociologists call a "boundary relationship." That is, it arises from the relationship between psychological or personality dynamics and the social system proper. The implication of this is that the social system in and of itself tends towards order rather than conflict, although certain social situations may intensify the personality's inherent drive to rebel against social control. These views are explicitly rejected by Simmel, who wrote one of the most extensive statements on social conflict in the history of sociological thought. [1] Weber, who made a briefer statement on conflict, seemed to concur with Simmel. [2] This section concentrates on Simmel's thesis, but refers occasionally to Weber.

Neither man denied the role of personality variables in social conflict. Hostility, egoism, hate, or desire, and the desperate need to escape an intolerable situation may all result in conflict. But social factors are at least as important as personality factors in the genesis of societal tension. Moreover, Simmel applied his famous distinction between contents and forms to this particular question: knowledge of the impulses behind conflict cannot help us to explain the recurring, patterned ways in which it may manifest itself in social life. Conflict often results from social factors, and conflict is a major dynamic in several important social institutions. In summary, conflict situations permeate the ongoing interactions of everyday life, and are frequently social both in terms of the causes of the conflict and in terms of the structures those conflicts attain.

One important social cause of conflict which Simmel identified is differentiation, obviously a social "fact" rather than something immanent in individual personality. Differentiation in relationships creates contrasts and differences among individuals in interests, values, and life styles. In confrontation these differences may lead to conflict. But conflict may also develop out of similarity, particularly similarity in goals and values; and goals and values are social products. (An example is two scientists both intent on the same discovery. Two men in pursuit of the same scarce value are, almost by definition, in conflict.) Power relationships, from the dyad to the large organization, imply yet another locus of tension and struggle in the ongoing dynamics of social interaction. Finally, Weber described a form of conflict which is cultural in its origins, and which spills over into human relationships, producing instability there. This type of conflict is the result of the inherent instability of normative systems which, because of constant shifts in power, the division of labor, the production of ideas, and the challenge of the environment, are constantly challenged by new normative alternatives. As a result individuals frequently confront each other as spokesmen for alternative perspectives. Personality does not create such tensions; the dynamics of the cultural system itself do.

Given the pervasiveness of both social and psychological conflict-producing mechanisms, Simmel felt that social conflicts should properly be viewed not as artificial, pathological, or deviant aspects of society but as inherent features of social life. In a sense, the fact that all social structures are to some extent complex forms of relationship automatically produces conflict, whether overt or covert. Social distance, discretion, caution, suspicion—all forms of "holding back," and all forms of conflict—are the underpinnings of social structure and pattern. Complete harmony is not only unachievable, it also logically implies an absence of complex patterning and a blurring of all entities into an amorphous oneness.

Simmel thought conflict probably has its place in the life history of all intimate relationships. In their initial efforts to establish a relationship, individuals frequently blur their differences, creating an "artificial" homogeneity through their mutual tactfulness. But later, as the relationship grows secure, an airing of differences leads to various tensions in the relationship. Yet this is a natural stage in the life cycle of relationships, a preliminary to the development of more complex bonds resting on dissimilarity as well as similarity. It is a mistake to assume, as Tönnies did, that conflict characterizes only the relationships of strangers. Close communal life is frequently the scene of fierce confrontation. Finally, Simmel pointed out, certain patterns of social life may be viewed as institutionalized conflict situations: games, sports, the legal process, and much of economic and urban life are of this type.

Another image of social life permeated by diffuse conflict was developed by the social Darwinists, Spencer and Sumner. Simmel had arrived at his conclusions by means of a logical exercise with the concepts of conflict and of social relationship, as well as through close scrutiny of the data on such relationships. The Darwinists in contrast drew on themes from biological evolution and from Malthus' population theory, deducing from these the particular hypothesis about the pervasiveness of conflict in society. In developing this thesis they shift from their focus on society as an emergent, organismically structured reality, to society as a species aggregate of human beings (a view which was always been in the background of their theory). Between the individual members of the human species conflict is constant, frequently conflict over the material prerequisites for survival. This process is part of the mechanism of selective survival through which the human species evolves genetically.

Sumner developed this theme most explicitly with his concept of *land hunger*. Essentially this is an argument that conflict between individuals increases as the proportion of land available to each individual decreases. Growth of population is the reason for this changing ratio of men to land. (Malthus' influence is very clear here.) When the emotional and cultural tensions contingent on *ethnocentricism*[3] are superimposed on this fundamental survival struggle, conflict in society becomes a ramifying, many-faceted phenomenon. (For example, the increasing flow of European immigrants to America could be seen as a major conflict-producing mechanism in American society since it intensifies both the conflict-creating variables.)

Intergroup Conflict

Mead and Durkheim had described the tension in the relationship of personality and society. Weber, Simmel, and the social Darwinists saw conflict as a general characteristic of interpersonal relationships, pervasive and diffuse. Marx and Pareto treated conflict as a correlate of major social structures, characterizing the relationship of enduring groups or sectors of the society. Conflict interested them as a social system process.

Conflict is a crucial process in Marx's conception of the social system. His philosophic commitment to dialectical materialism meant that he assumed society to be in tension. His materialism meant that he saw the basic division in society centering on the material, concrete aspects of economic life. Contributing to his emphasis on conflict were his political concerns and his moralistic anger with his own society. The economic conflicts on which he focused were those that centered around the oppressed urban poor. His sociological concept of social class gave him the means of relating philosophical, political, and moral concerns. Marx saw society as a system of permanent conflict. Classes of men are the protagonists in this conflict, and in modern society the war of proletariat against capitalist is the historically significant social conflict.

In speaking of conflict the early sociologists were really talking about a variety of processes: competition, personal ambivalence and stress, discrete acts of nonconformity, a diffuse relationship of opposites, and so on. When Marx spoke of the conflict between classes, however, he seemed to be referring explicitly to violence practiced by one class against another, violence which is not mediated by any commonly held set of rules, violence aiming at the total subjugation or extermination of the opponent. In the relationship of capitalist to proletariat this conflict is disguised, rationalized, and reinforced by the formally acknowledged "institutions" of society. Being the economically dominant class, the capitalist can command the instruments of control and persuasion: the state, the law, the ideas and ideologies of the age are its weapons. Nevertheless, Marx insisted, one should not be deceived by this facade of "legitimacy" and so conclude that the capitalist was not at war with the proletariat. The capitalist systematically exploits the working class by "stealing" from the worker most of the value of his labor or work, leaving him with only that fraction of such value necessary for barest subsistence, and constantly trying to reduce that fraction to an even smaller amount: minimal wages, maximum prices, and monopoly provide the formula of such exploitation. Moreover, the capitalist seeks to reduce the proletariat to utter passivity. The capitalist cannot exterminate his opponent because he needs the proletariat as a productive resource. But his effort is to dehumanize the work force in a very basic way: to deprive it of its rights to self-direction and to induce in it the malleability of the other productive resources, such as land and money.

Undisguised by law and ideology, the proletariat's war on the capitalist is more obvious. It is characterized first by resistance to the pressures of exploitation and control, resistance occurring at the individual and at the group level. It involves mobilization by the exploited against the process of exploitation. Ultimately this resistance leads to an effort not merely to lessen exploitation but to liquidate the processes which create the exploitative situation. Resistance evolves into revolution. Force acts "as the midwife of every old society pregnant with a new one."[4] Although manifesting itself in contemporary society as a war between capitalists and proletariat, Marx felt that every age witnessed a confrontation between the economically powerful and those whom they oppressed. Conflict conceptualized as class war was the crucial dynamic in historical change.

Pareto accepted this model of conflict correlating with some of the most enduring social structures, rather than conflict viewed as a diffuse, elusive dynamic in interpersonal relationships (as Simmel described it). But within this broad acceptance of Marx's perspective he attempted to alter the Marxist thesis in a number of ways. First, he argued that the confrontation was not fundamentally an economic one. It was a battle for power, particularly for political power. Access to the power of the state gave man his most elemental control over society, even over the economic processes of society. All history could be seen as a struggle for this crucial resource. Society was eternally structured along the lines determined by access to power. Every society had an elite, those who controlled the state, and all the other high or low status groups who sought to displace the elite. Even abolition of property, which Marx advocated, would not end such social conflict. A propertyless society would still divide and make war on the issue of political power.

One major battlefront in this conflict over political power occurred between the governmental elite and the non-elite or mass. Although differing from Marx's distinction between propertied and propertyless classes in numerous ways, the mass-elite model parallels Marx's class model in that it focuses on a vertical alignment of strata in which the "upper" stratum monopolizes all the privileges and rewards of the society. Pareto concurred with Marx in arguing that the elite seeks to control the mass with the twofold weaponry of force and ruse, control and persuasion. Like Marx he saw that the non-elite may be roused to revolutionary resistance to its condition. But he did not feel that the gradual intensification of resistance into revolution is inevitable. This process he felt is determined by the degree of social mobility in the particular society. Societies with fairly open channels between the two strata, allowing able and ambitious members of the non-elite to make their way on their own into elite circles, will not move to a state of revolutionary confrontation. Only in rigidly stratified societies, where the natural "leaders" of the mass find their personal ambitions blocked, does the move towards "class" war occur.

Pareto modified Marx's thesis in a third direction by pointing out that the "vertical" conflict between governmental elite and the non-elite is not the only important one in social systems. At least as important is a "horizontal" conflict between the governmental elite and other privileged groups in the society who want to obtain for themselves control of the state. That is, the group who has direct access to political power at any one time is always numerically smaller than the aggregate of privileged people who are potentially equipped to exercise political control in the society. Organized into parties and cliques, the non-governmental elite constantly struggles to oust the existing governmental personnel. Force and ruse are used in this battle as well. Frequently an elite faction will use the mass in its personal struggle for power, rousing the mass to riot and mob violence just so long as the elite's purposes are served. The conflict between factions of the elite may not be as total as the conflict between elite and mass in a revolutionary situation. But it is a constant conflict, while revolutions are occasional events, and observers often mistake a turnover in the personnel of the governing elite for a revolution.

Social Conflict as a Societal Problem

Conflict, tension, instability, violence—the very words are prejudicial. They imply discomfort or pain for individuals, and therefore we tend to judge such situations negatively. But should one unquestioningly extend an evaluation based on individual experience to a world in which relationships are the elementary components? Is conflict bad for systems of social relationships because it may be painful to individuals? What really are the consequences of conflict and tension for societies? Simmel phrased the problem of social conflict in these terms. But, implicitly or explicitly, all the early sociologists who touched on social conflict as a phenomenon arrived at decisions on such questions.

Comte viewed conflict as pathological. He used his organismic metaphor quite systematically. The healthy animal was one in which tension and instability did not occur. It was a being in a condition of orderly, imperceptible development. The same thing held for the societal being, Society. In a condition of health, Society experienced order in its functioning, and steady but gradual development in its capacities. A society torn by crime, revolution, and hostility was unhealthy. Such conditions ought to be studied by a special branch of sociology, the field of social pathology. Social pathology could contribute substantially to the mainstream of sociology by pointing up, indirectly, the prerequisites for a healthy society. For example, Comte himself felt that one cause of conflict in society was a sequence of rapid, uneven cultural change. The implications for governments wishing to maintain stability were clear. Contemporary sociologists constantly accuse themselves of being unsophisticated in their treatment of conflict, of assuming too easily that it is something to be minimized as much as possible in society. They trace this tendency back to Comte, and they are correct in doing this. But if contemporary sociologists generally view conflict as socially damaging, then this consensus is a development which occurred subsequent to the period under review here. Comte's position in that period seems to be an isolated one.

Some sociologists argued that conflict was a normal part of social life, and that Comte was wrong in asserting that it occurred only occasionally. Instead conflict was ubiquitous, evolving naturally out of elementary social processes. Mead pointed to the unstable link between ego and social control. Weber and Pareto, in different ways, saw conflict as an inevitable outcome of the power relationships intrinsic in social life. Weber also underlined the inherent instability of normative structures in the face of environmental challenges, and viewed conflict as an ongoing outcome of this condition. If conflict is pervasive and constant, the organismic analogy to pathology is an inadequate attempt to analyze it. Society differs from the biological entity in this regard. Mead then went on to argue that some manifestations of social conflict may be harmful to society, while others may contribute positively to social progress. Weber and Pareto did not go this far. They were content to say that conflict is normal, a fact of social life. Evaluating it as good or bad is as irrelevant to the sociological task as evaluating cultures or systems of sentiments. Conflict deserves sociological analysis, just as other recurring social processes do.

Many other sociologists, however, were not content to let matters rest at this level. They seemed to feel that it was necessary to combat the cultural prejudice against conflict by pointing out to fellow professionals that conflict was not only normal but also functional. Conflict made positive contributions to the functioning of society. Spencer and Sumner linked conflict to the evolutionary development of the human species, and hence to man's hope for achieving a good society. Marx saw conflict as *the* change-producing mechanism in human history, and since change was progressive in its long-term implications, conflict was a force for progress. Durkheim claimed that conflict, defined as deviance, might be not only a source of social innovation, but also an order-producing factor in the wider social system, for it united the majority in a conscious protective concern for their threatened norms. Sumner, of course, in his treatment of ethnocentricism, arrived at the same general conclusion from a somewhat different perspective.

Simmel, however, most elaborately attempted to isolate the positive consequences, or functions, of social conflict. In small face-to-face groups, he argued, hostility or conflict often correlate directly with the degree of intimacy and warmth in the relationship. When participants are deeply involved in a relationship, feelings of both attraction and hostility, love and hate come into play simultaneously, fusing into a single emotional experience. Conflict manifesting itself overtly in such relationships is fierce indeed, but, so long as it is directed to things which are not central to the relationship, such overt confrontation may be a good outlet for the emotional buildup which lies behind it. In fact the absence of conflict in a relationship is no index of its stability, and *vice versa*. A close, enduring relationship can be full of hostility and confrontation.

Similarly, in the wider society conflict may serve as a safety valve, releasing the accumulated hostilities in the system and avoiding what, for the sociologist, is truly disastrous: the termination of the relationship in withdrawal and indifference, the truly non-social situation. Conflict may also serve to create new and more realistic balances of power, since it provides an arena for testing claims to power, and for that continuing adjustment of relationship which guarantees equilibrium. Conflict also sets the contenders to seek allies, and so produce the ramifying webs of relationship which are societal structures. Finally, in a variety of ways, conflict produces unity and cohesion within the competing camps: it produces a heightened sense of identity, a tightening of organization, a mobilization of energy, a decrease in nonconformity, and a clarification of boundaries. This is in fact so true that groups, especially nations, will often create hypothetical enemies to strengthen their own unity.

Durkheim sounded a note of caution in this quest for the functions of social conflict. He made more emphatic a point which Mead also touched on: it would be as naive to assume that conflict was always functional for society as to conclude the reverse. The question of the functions of a particular kind of conflict is a research question. The researcher would be able to determine whether the conflicts in a particular society were functional and normal, or dysfunctional and abnormal. One indicator which Durkheim himself used was the rate of deviance. A steady rate indicated a normal, and probably functional state of the system. A sudden fluctuation in the rate, especially a rapid increase in the occurrence of the behavior, was an indicator of abnormality and stress in the system.

Summary and Conclusions

The main points of this chapter are summarized in table 7. On the whole it would be legitimate to conclude that earlier sociologists, with the exception of Marx and Simmel, were not as curious about social conflict as they were about social order. As has already been stated, the earlier explorations of order did imply a great deal about conflict, but the fact remains that the primary interest was in order. It would be possible to develop a plausible explanation of this in terms of the sociopolitical situation described in chapter 3, but by itself such an explanation is insufficient since it can so easily be turned around.

To understand the pattern of preference more fully it should be noted that most earlier sociologists attributed the actual social conflicts they observed not to permanent social dynamics but to the historical changes they saw their own societies experiencing. Their interest in change was as great as that in order, and a direct consideration of social conflict became minimized. Second, one has to consider some of the intellectual assumptions on which these men operated, particularly the assumption of "system." This was pronounced for the positivists. It was a constraining overlayer for a Darwinist like Spencer. It is implicit even in the concern for cultural *gestalts,* or complexes of ideas, which intrigued Weber. An interest in society as a system leads to a theoretical concern for the integrative mechanisms in society, although it does not logically exclude some consideration of conflict. Only Marx and Simmel, both of whom operated much more centrally with an assumption of dialectic rather than of system, were led by their most basic philosophic outlooks to think of social conflict in and of itself.

Nevertheless the group did, collectively, identify many of the loci of conflict in social life: the tension between ego and society, the struggle for power, the working through of values, and the dynamics of stratification. In so doing they introduced important concepts to sociology, the most significant probably being Durkheim's *anomie* and Pareto's "circulation of elites." And finally they on the whole agreed that conflict, sociologically speaking, was not to be evaluated as an unqualified disaster; it was an ongoing social process which might have certain positive consequences for the social system. The various approaches to social conflict taken by this group and described in this chapter have been enduring contributions to the sociological belief system. This is particularly true of Marx's elaborate probing into the dynamics of class war, and of Simmel's detailed analysis of the functions of social conflict.

NOTES

1. Georg Simmel, *Conflict and the Web of Group Affiliation,* ed. and trans. Kurt Wolff and Reinhart Bendix, (New York: Free Press, 1955).

2. Max Weber, *The Theory of Social and Economic Organization,* trans. Talcott Parsons (Glencoe, Ill.: Free Press, 1947), pp. 132-36.

3. See chapter 9.

4. Karl Marx in *Capital,* quoted in David Caute, ed., *Essential Writings of Karl Marx* (New York: Collier, 1967), p. 205.

TABLE 7: Explorations of Social Conflict

Theorist	Conflict originates in, exists in relationship of individual to society	Conflict originates in, exists in interpersonal relationships	Conflict originates in, exists in intergroup relationships	Evaluation of social implications of conflict
Comte	✓			Pathological
Spencer		✓		Functional
Sumner		Landhunger	Ethnocentricism	No judgment
Marx			Class war	Functional
Weber		✓		No judgment
Simmel		✓		Functional
Durkheim	Anomie			May be functional or dysfunctional
Pareto			Circulation of elites	No judgment
Mead	"I" vs. "me"			May be functional or dysfunctional

NOTE: A check in a column indicates that the writer discussed the particular order-producing process at some length, but he developed no distinctive label for it.

11

Explorations of
Social Change

Just as the discussion of social order can be used to yield insights into the origins of conflict, so the chapter on conflict in part anticipates this description of early views on social change. Conflict and change, after all, share common ground in that they both represent challenges to the given order of things. The rebellion of personality against social constraints, the confrontation of economic classes and the changing balance of power, all themes in social conflict, can and were used in an effort to understand observed changes in society. Rather than restating these ideas, this chapter will continue the discussion of social change.

Earlier sociologists witnessed the industrialization of the North Atlantic societies and their specific interests were with that type of change. They devoted much energy to conceptualizing and understanding it. Moreover, when they attempted to develop general theories of social change, the industrialization of the West remained their prototype of change and, frequently, their point of departure. They sought to understand massive and fundamental changes in the relationships and beliefs of total societies. Change on a smaller scale, such as the dynamics of small groups, communities, or organizations, concerned them less. While some of the material of this chapter may be viewed as generally applicable to any level of social change, on the whole it explores the efforts early sociologists made to understand the particular changes that they were living through, changes which permeated the whole fabric of society and were, as they rightly assessed it, historically unique. This chapter then looks at the "general" theories of historical and cross-cultural societal change which the earlier sociologists developed from their particular vantage point.

The chapter is organized into two parts: in the first, the early explanations of this type of social change are described; in the second we look at the evaluations and judgements that earlier sociologists made about the thrust or direction of such change. A summary and discussion section ends the chapter.

The Mechanisms of Social Change

This section describes the immediate interpretations that the earlier sociologists made of the changes they observed in their own societies. It then explores the explanations they developed of these changes in particular, and of societal change in general.

The impression of dialogue and argument among the group of earlier sociologists is particularly marked in their statements about social change. They refer to one another. They borrow ideas and elaborate them. They deliberately set out to refute or qualify each other's views. Among the various exchanges the argument with Marx is a strong theme. This section is organized around that theme. It is not a precise, structured debate, but rather a loose interaction of viewpoints.

Marx's Explanation

Marx, predictably, interpreted the changes occurring in Europe as changes primarily in the economic institutions of society. Men had developed new ways of working on nature, of procuring from her the things they deemed necessary for survival. What lay at the basis of all the changes observable in nineteenth-century Europe was a system of new relationships between men for production, and new alignments of men around the crucial means of production. The new arrangements triggered many other changes: in class and power arrangements, in ideas and ideology, and so on. But the core of all the change was in how man produced, and in the social and property arrangements centering on that activity. Europe was experiencing an economic "revolution."

What had produced such a revolution? Marx asserted that prior economic arrangements had generated the new order: previous relationships to property, the groups arising out of earlier modes of production, their special interests, the dynamic conflicts between them. Another cause was the inherent trait in the world of work for maximizing productive capacities, and the technological changes which grew out of this. All these things in combination had, inevitably and mechanically, produced an industrial revolution.

The general theory of social change which emerges from Marx's ideas has several distinctive dimensions. Change of any fundamental and enduring nature must always originate in economic changes, specifically in modes of production and in the ways men relate to the resources essential to production. Economic change is like a stone dropped in a pool; it produces an ever-widening chain of reorganization until finally the whole system of relationships and ideas adjusts to the initial change. But in contrast to the imagery of pool and pebble just used, Marx never assumed a placid or static social system, nor did he argue that change is introduced into the system by some extra-societal force or variable. Rather he asserted that the future of society was immanent in the present; the dynamics of existing economic and social relationships, particularly the points of tension and conflict in those relationships, inexorably created the next stage of society. This evolution of the future from the present was a constant feature of social life, though the pace of such change varied over time from imperceptible to revolutionary. It is a model of change which incorporates conflict and tension as essential ingredients, especially between classes. The critical moments of change are marked by a crescendo of such confrontation: a superstructure of revolutionary confrontation on a foundation of evolutionary, accumulating tensions. Marx's thesis about the nature of recent Western history has been dramatic and pervasive in its impact.

Change as Differentiation

The other sociologists of this period propounded a variety of alternative hypotheses. In terms of its impact on sociological thought, the most influential of these was probably the thesis of increasing structural differentiation. Both Spencer and Durkheim propounded versions of this theme. In contrast to Marx, they did not see change in Western societies as having a primarily economic basis. Instead, they viewed social changes as the result of a process occurring simultaneously in most of the important institutions of society. Specifically, this process involved an even more complex specialization of function and a concomitant acceleration in the complexity of the normative and organizational networks which were society. Where earlier a single social component had performed a fused complex of tasks, several separate organizations now existed, each handling one specific aspect of that earlier complex. The obvious illustration is the contrast between the early craftsman-artisan and the modern factory with its chain of specialized production line workers. But both Durkheim and Spencer insisted that differentiation was occurring more widely and generally than in the economic institution. Political functions once handled by a chief, or a relatively simple king-and-ministers organization, now required a complex maze of specialized governmental agencies. Education, which had originally occurred almost spontaneously in the relationships between children and parents, was now a vast network of interlocking organizations offering an apparently endless set of alternatives for specialized training. Spencer and Durkheim argued that the essential characteristic of the "industrial revolution" was not simply a new set of work and property relations (as Marx had described it); it was an accelerating process of task specialization which could be observed in all the major institutions of society, a process which manifested itself in an apparently irreversible trend towards complexity of social organization. Durkheim termed this "the division of labor in society."

As formulated by Spencer, the concept of differentiation combines the two greatest influences on his social thought: organicism and evolutionary thought. These influences are very clear in his explanation of the phenomenon. He explicitly related the fact of increasing societal complexity to his general law of evolution: it was given in nature that all things either elaborated in structure or disintegrated, and the recent events in Western societies were simply another manifestation of this principle at work.[1] Implicitly, however, Spencer was envisioning society to be like a biological entity, the elaboration of social structure appearing to parallel not only the evolution of a species over time, but the maturation of a single living being from the moment of conception to the period of full adulthood. Differentiation then was one result of a developmental dynamic intrinsic in social life. Spencer seemed to view development as immanent in social organization, explainable in terms of his general law of evolution, and having structural-functional differentiation as one major consequence.

Spencer saw increase in size as another aspect of societal development; it was a correlate of sturctural differentiation. Durkheim, anxious to shake free of any obvious organismic or evolutionary imagery, used the factor of societal growth to *explain* differentiation. By growth Durkheim meant a number of factors in combinations: increase in population and population density; the growing number of cities which paticularly illustrated this demographic density; the multiplication of social relations which this density produced; and, as a crucial dimension of this increase in interaction, an intensification of communication between the parts of the population. Societal growth implied a greater density in society at several levels: demographic, relational, communicative.[2] Societal growth produced structural differentiation.

> The division of labor varies in direct ratio with the volume and density of societies, and, if it progresses in a continuous manner in the course of social development, it is because societies become regularly denser and generally more voluminous . . . . the growth and condensation of societies . . . . necessitate a greater division of labor. It is its determining cause.[3]

Although Durkheim was swift to point out the aspects of social density in his concept of growth, it remains apparent that his ultimate explanatory variable is a demographic one. Population increase and population density seem to be the necessary and sufficient causes of increasing social density. In combination these give rise to differentiation in social organization. There is something unsatisfactory about this explanation of Western industrialization, and of social change generally. Demographic density may indeed always lead to greater social complexity, but this variable cannot, alone, make clear why the West industrialized while other densely populated areas did not. Nor have sociologists been content to leave the ultimate explanations of societal and historical change to such a mechanical and non-social factor as demographic change. Yet Spencer's explanation is not any more satisfactory. In essence he seemed to argue that social differentiation occurs because society, like any other natural thing, develops. It is a quite circular argument. The concept of differentiation has remained an important sociological explanation of societal change. But sociologists still have the problem of explaining this tendency. The old arguments of Spencer and Durkheim are still operative, and are still unsatisfying. Differentiation essentially is treated as a "given" in social dynamics.

Social Change as Cultural Change

A second important alternative to Marx's thesis was the argument that the changes observable in nineteenth-century Europe and America were, fundamentally, cultural changes. An alteration in motives, outlooks, and values had triggered the changes in Western society. Weber, of course, is well known for this thesis, and his views have been described in an earlier chapter,[4] but Comte and Tönnies developed a similar theme. One characteristic common to all three men is that they saw a shift to rationality as the most important of recent cultural changes. Comte phrased this as the emergence of positivism, an empirical, science-oriented *gestalt*. He argued that positivism was penetrating all the institutions of society. Tönnies had given the concept of will a central place in his theory of society, "will" apparently referring to a combination of motive and outlook. The most obvious difference that he perceived in the shift from *gemeinschaft* to *gesellschaft* was a restructuring of will. Modern man was characterized by rational will. He consciously pursued explicit goals with judiciously selected means. He was a cognitive or thinking being. Closely linked to rationality was individualism. Modern man had come to see himself as separate from the groups and relationships around him, as an autonomous agent free to advance his personal interests in an ongoing series of considered social exchanges. Weber ascribed the massive reorganization of social life in his own time to the steady advance in rationality. Rationality was a particular form of consciousness or orientation. As described by Weber, the rational culture contains all the themes already mentioned: scientism, individualism, deliberate problem solving. But overriding all these in his description is an end to "enchantment," a lessening of the impact of magic, religious considerations, ritual, and tradition on the everyday routines of living. Rational man was practical, pragmatic, sceptical, and had a marked sense of mastery or power over his life. These attitudes together with the values of scientism and individualism created a unique and active outlook on the world.

A second theme common to the theories of Weber, Comte, and Tönnies is that the cultural shift towards rationality had produced immediate and far-ranging consequences for the relationships and organizations which make up society. Comte claimed that the major changes of his time consisted of the slow, often stressful, alterations of social structure towards congruence with the world view of positivism. Tönnies linked will to relationship, seeing these two as the primary interlocking variables of sociological concern. Rational will produces the relationships of *gesellschaft*, impersonal, weighed exchanges between autonomous, calculating individuals. Although there has probably always been some *gesellschaft* in human communities, the distinctive feature of modern society is the preponderance of such relationships. The system-wide shift to a rational perspective is the immediate explanation of this growth in *gesellschaft*.

Where Tönnies concentrated on the quality of interpersonal relationships, Weber emphasized the forms of organization which cultural rationality produced. Rationality implied purposive efforts at efficient problem solving. The outcome at the societal level was complex, formal organization; deliberate organizational efforts at collective, sustained problem solving. Such organization Weber called rational-legal bureaucracy, and he gives to sociology its classic formulation of that concept.[5] The consequence of deliberate organizational effort was a very great increase in the efficiency of collective action. Weber saw bureaucratic organization as an increasingly dominant trait in all walks of life—politics, administration, economic activities, education, and so on. Whatever its drawbacks (and Weber was well aware of these), bureaucratic organization increased society's immediate problem-solving potential. Cultural rationality and bureaucracy were closely related, and they were both peculiar characteristics of contemporary society.

A final point common to these interpretations of social change by Comte, Tönnies, and Weber is that they all saw economic activity as one of the first to be affected by cultural changes. Comte linked the emergent industrial order to positivism. Tönnies saw economic relationships as the primary sphere of rational will. Weber, of course, explored the dimensions of Western rationality in his investigation of the economic ethics of a variety of cultures.

What had produced these cultural changes at the time of the industrial revolution? The similarities between the three men break down at this point. Comte, like Spencer, ascribed the changes to some developmental dynamic inherent to society. He claimed to have discovered a law of social development. The shift to positivism marked the culmination of this developmental sequence. It needed no further explanation. In contrast, both Tönnies and Weber traced the emergence of a rational ethos to a specific configuration of historical factors. Tönnies touched on things like the mentality of the trader, the life of the city, a cultural emphasis on "thinking." Factors like these help spread rational will, which then gives rise to more extensive "rational" influences like contract law, and the monetization of economic life. These things advance rationality still further. This combination of factors occurred in the history of certain Western societies, and triggered the changes of the nineteenth century. Weber too pointed to the particular form of urban life and the orientation to trade in Western cities. But he also emphasized the content of certain cultural traditions in the West: the Judaic theme of radical critical thought; the Christian stress on the brotherhood of equals; and finally ascetic Protestantism's focus on work and self-testing. This combination of factors was unique to the West and explains both the development of rationality and the emergence of a bureaucratized industrialized social order.

The general theory of social change behind this interpretation of recent Western history is quite clear. Change originates in the culture system of a society. When orientations, world views, and motivations alter, extensive social change occurs. Culture very often changes because of dynamics internal to it—either through dynamics universal to culture, or through particular historical factors working within it. The former is Comte's position, the latter that of Weber and Tönnies. None of these men seemed to assert the absolute primacy of culture in the sense that Marx asserted the primacy of economic life. This is particularly true of Tönnies and Weber. Instead they described a reciprocal influencing between cultural and relational variables. But culture is given a central status, rather than a peripheral one, in their explanations of societal change.

Social Change from Political Change

Another important hypothesis advanced in this period about the origins of change can be understood as an exchange with Marx. It is a reply, however, to his general theory of societal change rather than to his specific interpretation of recent Western history. Pareto's thesis that the crucial change-producing variable was political rather than economic.

Pareto felt that aspirants to political power were never homogeneous in their sentiments, interests, ideology, and so on. They varied essentially because their basic instinctive configuration, their "profile" of sentiments, varied. Political cliques, parties, and groupings were formed along these lines of difference. Men similar in sentiments and interests grouped together in the struggle for political control, opposing those groups who differed from them in sentiment and ideology. One of the most fundamental political divisions was between those who had a strong sentiment for the persistence of aggregates, that is a strong conservative bent, and those characterized by the sentiment of combination, a facile but innovative group of men. Pareto nicknamed these parties "the lions" and "the foxes." Most societies and most ages contained this basic political division. The two groups alternated in positions of ruling elite and opposition "party."

Pareto insisted that the consequences of a turnover in ruling personnel had far-reaching consequences for social organization. Each group, for example, had its cohort of economic allies. Lions were supported by economic and financial conservatives, men concerned with land ownership, sound investments, steady and cautious economic development, balanced budgets, and so on. Foxes associated with a more speculative group, the financiers and industrial entrepreneurs, risk takers prepared to venture a great deal on the chance of realizing huge profits. The quality of economic life shifted dramatically with a change in political direction.

Lions were men who turned readily to the use of force, and they used it well. They tended to be ideological, to point to higher ideals and values as justifications for their behavior. Their terms of rule were marked by military activity, by an emphasis on "law and order," by an age of faith or ideological rigidity. Foxes never used force comfortably, and they were both more pragmatic and more manipulative in outlook. Their reign was one of "freedoms": of expression, the press, belief. But these freedoms often became empty symbols in the face of military ineffectiveness abroad and a breakdown of order at home. Any blossoming of civilization, however, or growth in the arts occurred in the early period of the regime of foxes, in the first phases of freedom. Thus the cultural dimensions of social life as well the economic altered when there was a political change.

Pareto paralleled the dialectic which Marx saw in the economy with a similar cluster of change-producing tensions in political relationships. No party can hold on to power indefinitely. Its accession to power sets in motion the processes which will remove it eventually from power. First, an accession rallies the opposition to a more intense unity. The longer the opposition stays out of power the stronger and more numerous it becomes, driven by the hunger for political control. Second, effective government demands the use of both force and manipulation. The party in power is strong in only some of these skills, and is forced to use some of those from the other ideological group to keep itself in control of the situation. Its ranks and organization are thus gradually infiltrated and weakened by those who, when the moment of confrontation comes, will go over to the other side. Third and most important, accession to power sets in motion particularistic activities with regards to the allocation of privileges. Men seek to hang on to the privileges they have won, and to pass them on to their offspring, their kinsfolk, their close friends. In the period of the struggle for power the party was a true elite: only those possessing the party's particular virtues achieved positions of leadership and control. Once in power, however, this pool of talent is diluted because of the workings of particularistic concerns. The longer a party remains in power the more this occurs, and the weaker the party becomes in the very skills that once brought it to power. A turnover in elites in inevitable, though the characteristics of the particular case will effect the length of the interval between such changes.

Pareto felt that much of what history recorded as significant change in a society could be understood as political. Such changes occurred against a background of more stable, enduring societal characteristics determined by national character. National character resulted from the pool of sentiments in the population, and changed only at a glacial pace as the distribution of sentiments in the population altered. Other factors like technological developments might also bring about social change (for example, in the conditions of work or the forms of military events). But the pace of innovation and particularly of the acceptance of innovation was itself markedly affected by the political variables already described. Pareto moreover deemphasized technological changes and stressed political and genetic changes.

Social Change and Creative Individuals

The final exchange with Marx's general thesis centers on the role of influential individuals or "leaders" in social change. It seems fair to say that Marx's thesis of social change, as he developed it, could not assign to particular individuals an independent and important role in causing social change. Such change resulted only from the working out of massive social dynamics: the impact of technology on production, system-level relationships to property, the relationships between classes of men. The independent thinker or leader was a myth with which historians had deceived themselves and others. Such men were produced by the social situation and acted out a role demanded by that situation. Marx was modest even about his own influence: he saw himself as the product of an age, his ideas simply as responses to a definite stage in the history of Western society. [6]

Many sociologists concurred with this even when they generally differed from Marx. To Comte or Durkheim or Spencer it seemed unthinkable that any single individual could set himself against the direction of societal forces and change their course. The so-called "great men" in history were produced by their situation: presumably any one of a number of men might have been drawn forth to fill the role.

Others among the early sociologists, however, were prepared to give "great men" an independent role in causing social change. Pareto, Weber, and the symbolic interactionists do this in various ways. On the whole none of them seem to be directly addressing themselves to Marx on this point. Apart from Pareto, this group seemed more generally concerned with any rigidly deterministic social theory, be it Marxism or social Darwinism or doctrinaire "sociologism," such as Durkheim's views on the omnipotence of social forces.

Despite his variance from the others on this point, Pareto is included in this group because his political sociology seems to allow a modest role to the political leader. Political leaders are an effective elite: whatever the talent demanded by the moment, be it wisdom, guile, strength, or ruthlessness, the leader is the one who demonstrates that he has more of this quality than any other. Such leaders exercise mastery over the situation, and they become rallying points for like-minded people in the struggle for power and afterwards in victory (until the various processes for loss of power get under way). Leaders presumably play a role in the articulation of ideology or derivations. This is as much as it is possible to extrapolate from Pareto's political sociology on this pont. It is not much of a role for the leader who is after all still determined by his biological capacities and talents, and who is caught up in the logic of the particular historical moment. His talents are only quantitatively different from those around him: he has more of some skill than they do. His creative role may manifest itself in the formulation of ideology, but ideology has at best a modest status in Pareto's explanatory scheme. Leadership's particular role seems to be to crystallize and bring to a head the processes and tensions already working in the situation. Leadership affects the timing of a power turnover.

The symbolic interactionists, Mead and Cooley, ever anxious about the free will/determinism debate, leave to leadership a role beyond that of simply working within the framework set by a pre-existing situation. They also define a "leader" as possessing more of some ability than others do. In a society conceptualized in terms of communication and empathetic skills, leaders are those unusually strong in these qualities. They possess the skills to communicate with groups very different from those within their immediate experience, and to guess at their needs and responses. In a population where most individuals are only capable of communication with a fraction of the community, leaders communicate universally. The true leader in this sense is qualitatively different from the average member of the society. Mead moreover allowed to the individual a creative or innovative role: the outcome of tension between "I" and "me."[7] Although only embryonic in his social theory, these views in combination certainly seem to allow an effective change role to peculiarly talented individuals.

Weber has the most elaborate formulation of this viewpoint. We have already touched on this in earlier explorations of the concept of charisma.[8] Charismatic leaders have qualities which set them apart from other human beings. They have a personal magnetism, a striking power of personality which cloaks them in immediate legitimacy and makes willing followers out of those who surround them. Such traits are found only in a few individuals: the interchangeability of personnel in the great man role made no sense to Weber. Charismatic individuals appear to their followers as the formulators of new ideas. Very often they do in fact create new belief and value systems. Given the role that ideas play in Weber's change theory, such individuals become potent change factors. They combine two crucial variables for far-reaching change: new ideas and the power or authority necessary for propagating them. Charismatic leaders of this calibre are revolutionary agents of social change, for they enunciate and spread those new world views from which fundamental societal reorganization springs.

In contrast to Pareto, Weber did not seem to feel that such leaders will inevitably arise given certain circumstances, the leader simply being the most able man available in the situation. Weber saw the characteristics of such individuals as rare, and the emergence of a charismatic leader is never wholly determined by sociohistorical dynamics. It is true that some situations seem to demand such leadership. Some cultures, for example, seem to have institutionalized the dynamics of frequent critical societal self-evaluation, and in any society there are times when the legitimacy of the prevailing belief system comes to be widely questioned, and a need arises for new ideas and beliefs. But neither situation guarantees the appearance of charismatic leadership. Only when persons with the qualities necessary for such a role exist does the situation "jell" into a period of revolutionary cultural change. Moreover the image of an absolutely exhausted belief system is a theoretical "type;" it is rarely found in a complex society. The actual historical cases of charismatic leadership and cultural change, such as those of the prophetic founders of major religions, have been cases in which the old belief systems have been fairly well entrenched. The belief systems had their cohorts of priestly and lay support, and had been operating at a level of effectiveness (or ineffectiveness) not much different from that of earlier years. The appearance of a prophetic or charismatic personality explains why the challenge to those beliefs occurred when it did; and the fact that the new beliefs made inroads into the old system depended as much on the power of that personality as on the internal weaknesses of the established system.

The radical restructuring of beliefs and institutions associated with charismatic leadership is, however, only one part of the cycle of change stemming from such leadership. Weber was also fascinated by the processes through which the initially explosive and unstructured revolution evolves into an organized stable situation. This process he called "the routinization of charisma." In this process a vital role is played by the band of disciples or followers who surround the leader—his embryonic "administration." Inspired by his message this group undertakes to spread his views, confronting, and fighting where necessary, supporters of the older system. All this produces organization. More organization is demanded by the need to procure resources to support the faithful, to establish chains of communication from them to the leader, and to deal with the daily problems of this growing community (such as the need for adjudication). The biggest problem of all which this growing organization must face is the problem of sucession. How is the group and its faith to survive the demise of the original leader? Who is then to direct the community, and on what will his authority be based? Various strategies are adopted: the leader's appointment during his lifetime of a successor to whom he passes on some of his special "powers;" the establishment of a hereditary succession, with the "power" presumably transmitted through the bloodline; the formulation by the leader, or in his name, of standard procedures for finding a successor and defining his duties. In this last case the procedures incorporate something of the original leader's mystique. If any of these strategies work, the regime becomes institutionalized and rapidly approximates the system it overthrew, in form if not in content. The originally charismatic authority becomes traditional. The small band of followers becomes an increasingly elaborate and structured administrative organization. The revolutionary message of the prophet crystallizes into a "holy word" or a collection of sacred messages, demanding its priestly group of interpreters, teachers, defenders. The culture becomes static, or evolves gradually in response to a variety of pressures and events on it, or within it. It in turn may be eventually challenged and overthrown by a new charismatic leader.

Judging the Direction of Societal Change

These various conclusions about the nature of societal change—emphases on economic, political, or technological variables, on ideas and leadership, or on a system-wide tendency to organizational complexity—were all seen by their exponents as inductions from the data on actual historical changes. We may note how each man's philosophical and other assumptions shaped his perceptions, and in many cases they themselves felt reassured that their conclusions from the evidence "meshed" logically with their more general theories. This must certainly be the case for Spencer or Marx. But all the men discussed above felt that they were relating rigorously to the evidence about actual changes, in the West or cross-culturally. Did it seem to them that the various kinds of change recorded in history added up to a more general movement of society over time, or were there just unconnected events which cancelled each other? If there was movement, what sort of movement was it? These are the interests generally subsumed under a discussion of the direction of change.

It should be recalled[9] that the period in which these men lived was one which decisively asserted that there was an underlying direction in history, a general thrust of movement towards progressive amelioration. Since it was assumed that all societies were more or less rapidly moving along this path, this thesis about the direction of history is a *unilinear* model of progressive development. A remarkable number of intellectual themes converged on this conclusion. Its roots lay in the optimistic faith in the "progress of civilization" which emerged in the sixteenth and seventeenth centuries in response to the intellectual and scientific breakthroughs of the period. The idea was then incorporated into philosophical idealism, as a bulwark for the assertion of mind's supremacy. It later became a guiding beacon for the radical thought of the late eighteenth century, when it acquired an overlayer of revolutionary rhetoric. In the nineteenth century it seemed to gain support everywhere from the economic, technological, and sheer power advances of the North Atlantic societies, especially when this was related to the new data on other "more primitive" societies. And finally it seemed to receive its ultimate legitimation in the impressively scientific conclusions of Charles Darwin and his disciples. Regardless of variations in background, the earliest sociologists could not escape this chorus: man's lot in society was steadily improving, society and civilization were constantly advancing, all history was a record of this progress. In discussing early sociological views on the direction of change, one very immediate interest is with the extent to which earlier sociologists accepted this interpretation, and with the way they gave precise formulations to it in the context of their sociology.

The group made various attempts to resist the widespread faith in a unilinear progressive development of society. The most marked of these was the denial of development of any type in the long-term historical record. This is Pareto's major conclusion. He did not deny a cumulative record of technological change, but he insisted that most of the changes recorded by chroniclers could not be subsumed under that particular explanatory factor. Most changes related to political events and in that there was no development. Change of this sort was cyclical, or like the swinging of a pendulum at irregular intervals. Events shifted from a pattern of growth and over-extension to a pattern of static retrenchment, and back again. Apart from this were the almost imperceptible alterations in national character, changes which took centuries but which, in any overview of this type of change, seemed to move mankind in no one direction. Pareto's views were elaborated late in the period, against the backdrop of political crisis in Italy and the imminent horror of World War I. It reflects a pessimism which was growing in intellectual circles, but in terms of the interests of this section, it is also the most radical break by a sociologist of the period with developmental thought.

Weber's statement on the routinization of charisma presents us with another cyclical model of societal change. He was, however, far less insistent than Pareto that change is *only* cyclical: indeed he would have rejected that suggestion. It is one pattern of change, a pattern observed frequently enough in the histories of different societies to deserve sociological attention. But he clearly believed that there are other observable patterns of movement in history. The rationalization of culture and organization in the West was a movement which was cumulative and unidirectional rather than cyclical. Moreover his formulation of the cycle surrounding charismatic change is not mechanical enough for one to assert that it will inevitably occur, or even that it will ever occur again. There are too many problematical factors: the appearance of an innovative and charismatic personality; the measure of success obtained by his ideas over established beliefs and organizations (a variable affected by the relative strength of the contending sides); a successful solution to the succession problem; and so on. Further, the new belief system may survive as the doctrine of a sector of the population only, as in the case of Calvinism; or it may become the belief system of a vast region, as did Islam. The only thing that is certain is that, if the leader and his perspective gains a foothold, the process of routinization will occur. The cycle of charismatic revolution and routinization is very far from being an interpretation of the direction of "History." Weber would have recoiled from such a grandiose effort. But to the extent that he demonstrates it to be a pattern in history, sometimes even the pattern in massive, significant culture change, it can be viewed as a criticism of any monolithic theory of universal progressive development.

Cyclical theories reject the progressive development model on all scores. Most of the views on change propounded by sociologists in this period did not go so far. Some accepted the developmental model fully, others sought to modify it in two ways: by claiming that this pattern of change was not universal, but simply the experience of the West; and by arguing that the direction of change, while cumulative and developmental, was not necessarily or wholly progressive in its consequences for men in society. Within the framework of a developmental thesis, therefore, were four competing perspectives: those denying both the universality and the progressiveness of the pattern; those rejecting one or other of those characteristics; and those insisting on both.

The most limited version of developmental social change is represented both by Weber's thesis of increasing rationality and by Tönnies' theory of the appearance of *gesellschaft*. Both are interpretations of the direction of change in recent Western history, and prognoses about the fairly immediate future of the West. Neither argue any continuity between this sequence of events and those in other societies. Other societies do not represent in any sense earlier "stages" in the development of human society. Nor will they necessarily, through some universal social dynamic, approximate in the future the conditions now emerging in Western societies. They have their own unique histories and these, and the history of events yet to come, will determine their future organization. Even the continuities which Tönnies and Weber trace between the present and past of the West do not conform strictly to the developmental model. One has no steady transition through different levels of development, no continuous progress in their accounts. Rather one has the low accumulation of factors followed by a fairly rapid emergence of rational urban society; operating within this new order are processes which indicate the continuation of the present trend into the future. Yet to the extent that the conditions creating the present situation were cumulative over time and the movement of events in recent centuries trendlike in one direction and apparently irreversible, both Weber and Tönnies saw a developmental pattern in modern Western history.

The consequences of this development for man are mixed. On the one hand there is the tremendous increase in effectiveness which Weber saw resulting from the growth of rationality, or the advance in creative and innovative thought and activity found in Tönnies' image of urban society. This implies in the former case a great increase in society's power to handle the problems of survival presented by the environment. In the latter case the consequences were an enrichment and elaboration of civilization. The recent developmental change in the West was to this extent "progressive." Both Weber and Tönnies, however, were so acutely aware of the implications of the new order for human alienation that they viewed the trends of their time with more dread than complacency. Tönnies genuinely mourned modern man's loss of belongingness, the demise of community. Weber feared both the depersonalization and the loss of meaning in the new order, particularly the replacement of real justice with formal justice in a vastly powerful state. Their ambivalence in evaluating the trends in the West means that their models of development do not have any obvious connotations of progress, or of the reverse.

Of those who modified the progressive development theme less drastically, Durkheim represents one perspective, Simmel another. To Durkheim the trend to differentiation was a universal one arising from the general tendency towards increasing population density. The world's population had increased steadily. The population density in most societies had increased, despite the survival of certain very simple societies "fossilized" on this and other dimensions. The population of the Western nations in recent times had grown dramatically and all the indications were for a continuation or acceleration of this trend. Dependent on this variable there were other trends towards increasing density of interaction and greater complexity of social organization. Generally, societies had become more complex. Western societies had recently entered a phase of accelerated differentiation, and societies could be ranked on a single continuum ranging from the primitively simple organization of small tribal groups to the extensive complexity of the Western industrial states. This approximates the classic versions of the developmental thesis. Durkheim, however, was as ambivalent as Weber in judging the consequences of these developments. He saw the enormous variety of tasks that the highly differentiated society can perform effectively, and, like Weber, he viewed this as an enhancement of society's adaptive ability. The highly differentiated society can meet the material needs of its population far more elaborately than the simple social organization. Yet complexity poses a threat to social integration, indicated by soaring rates of deviance and a pervasive *anomie*. Given Durkheim's greater concern for social organization than for individual experience, these malaises of social structure are his equivalents to the individual alienation which Weber regretted.

Simmel, like Weber and Tönnies, limited his generalizations to Western societies, and on the whole to those societies in relatively modern times—since the eighteenth century. In this period, however, he did see development, in the form of irreversible, unidirectional trends towards increasing size, increasing organizational complexity, growing urbanization, and so on. In this analysis he concurred with what Weber, Tönnies and Durkheim had all said. But in evaluating the implications of this development, Simmel differed from all these men. Although he was aware of the stresses associated with urban life,[10] Simmel seemed to conclude that recent developments have been beneficial or progressive in their consequences for men. Simmel's concern was with individual freedom, and he made the point that the individual's freedom in modern society is far greater than it ever was in the small, rural communities of earlier times.[11] The increased size of modern communities, with their expanded networks of association, means that man is no longer tightly bound by the obligations and conformity pressures of the small group. The new complexity of social organization leads to much more elaborate and unique personality development because each man can develop constellations of roles which are uniquely his. There is freedom too in such multiple group membership, since one is no longer wholly dependent on a single group, but instead partially independent on any one of them. Finally the growing organizational effectiveness of modern life gives man the freedom to impose his will over an increasing number of things, rather than to be subjugated by them. In a variety of ways the individual had steadily increased his freedom as a result of the recent developmental trends in the West. An important role in all this had been played by the monetization or commercialization of life. Things had been reduced to value on a single symbolic scale, money. This was an aspect of modernity which Simmel singled out, and which distinguishes his interpretation of contemporary social changes from others already described. And it seemed to him that money had been very influential in producing the fluidity, the mobility, the impersonality, and the sense of control which were all parts of man's new freedom. Recent social changes were, in Simmel's eyes, progressive.

But several sociologists adopt the theme of progressive development without serious modification: the societies of the world are all caught up in a single dynamic pattern of social change. Western societies, in the vanguard of this movement, once resembled the "less developed" societies of today. The movement of society is trendlike, unidirectional, irreversible; the change is cumulative; the direction progressive. Comte saw steady growth toward enlightenment, away from superstition. Spencer felt that the time was fast coming when society would achieve, through structural differentiation, an optimal level of adaptiveness, in which all material and moral challenges could be successfully handled. In his case the movement seemed to be away from primitiveness of organization and of response. Ward and Marx in very different ways read in the data on social change a march towards an era of social justice. In contrast to all the others in this group, though, Marx did not see in the data evidence of a gradual emergence of the good society. Rather he saw the moment when such a society will be formed coming steadily closer, as the misery of oppressed classes and their awareness of what produces their anguish increases. All history shows the drive to that final conflict which will destroy the causes of social injustice. And Mead saw a general movement in history towards "universalism." By this he meant the ability and will of men to communicate within an ever-widening circle. Already the arena of effective communication has shifted from the tiny kinship group to the region and even the nation. Soon, he felt, an age of effective international communication would appear. All these sociologists noted the technological developments of their age. In all cases such developments were seen to accompany and even be essential to the realization of the various good societies for which they hoped.

As they explored the problem of direction in history, many of these sociologists formulated typologies of societies or of social relationships. Those most committed to developmental thought created models of different kinds of societies, and each kind was supposed to represent a stage in the development of society. Comte described the prevailing mentality and the institutions in theological society, metaphysical or philosophical society, and positivistic society. Theological society, in particular, he subjected to elaborate subdivision. Spencer thought society moves through primitive social organization, to complex but militaristic, and finally to complex industrial systems. Marx described the forms of primitive communism, feudalism, capitalism, socialism, and communism. Other men classified aspects of society, but blur the notion of stages. Weber contrasted rational and traditional outlooks; Tönnies, *gemeinschaft* and *gesellschaft* relational systems; Durkheim, mechanically and organically integrated societies; Pareto, the dynamics of conservative and innovative states of the social system. These typologies have survived in the sociological vocabulary, in the first two cases more as an interesting footnote and as the rationale for the Comparative Method,[12] in the other instances as categories which have various uses in present efforts at comparative analysis.

Summary and Conclusions

Early sociologists were keenly interested in the phenomenon of societal change. This chapter has reviewed some of their work in this area. It has looked at some of the explanations they offered for such change, at their long discussion about the possible patterns and directions in actual societal changes, and, briefly, at the typologies to which their discussions gave rise. All this is summarized in table 8.

One interesting aspect of this earlier work was the extent to which it concerned itself with specific, historically recorded changes, and especially with those changes which were described earlier in this book as the Industrial Revolution. There is no doubt that the curiosity of ear-

TABLE 8: Explorations of Social Change

Theorist	The nature of nineteenth Century Western change	General causes of change	General pattern of change	Evaluations of social change	Typologies used in analyzing societal change
Comte	Emergence of positive or rational culture	"Law" of development	Developmental	Universally progressive	Theological→metaphysical→ positivistic→
Spencer	Institutional differentiation	Law of evolution	Developmental	Universally progressive	Primitive→ complex military→ complex industrial
Marx	Economic, class, power changes	Technological/ economic	First develop- mental, then revolutionary	Universally progressive	Primitive communism→ feudal→capitalist→ socialist→communist
Durkheim	Institutional differentiation	Demographic and social density	Developmental	Both progressive and regressive qualities	Mechanical→organic
Weber	Emergence of rational culture and organization	Unique historical factors; and/or charismatic personalities	Sometimes devel- opmental, some- times revolu- tionary	Sometimes cyclical; in the West developmental with both progressive and regressive qualities	Traditional→ rational (for Western societies)
Tönnies	Emergence of rational culture and organization	Unique historical factors	In the West, developmental	In the West, both progressive and regressive	Gemeinschaft→ Gesellschaft (for Western societies)
Simmel	Emancipation of the individual	Urban complexity and the monetization of relationships	Developmental in the West	Progressive in the West	
Mead	Expansion of communication systems	Evolution; leadership	Developmental	Universally progressive	
Pareto		Changes in political leadership, direction	Cyclical	Neither progressive nor regressive	Conservative→ innovative

lier sociologists was primarily with the change that they were witnessing. They sorted out their impressions of it, conceptualized it, and sociologically attempted to explain it. This interested them far more than developing "general theories" of social change. In this they contrast with later sociologists.

As a result of this concentrated interest in a particular series of changes we have been given a cluster of astute analyses of what, for us also, is a very significant historical event: the birth of the complex urban industrial society in which we today live. The earlier sociologists collectively listed most of the characteristics of the new order which we today have come to regard as peculiarly characteristic of it: enormously complex task specialization, the centrality of economic concerns, the commercialization or monetization of so many aspects of life, ramifying bureaucracy, the practical, individualistic world view, and so on. Two trends which later sociologists have also come to regard as characteristic of modern society were, however, not so greatly emphasized by the earlier group, although the issues were not overlooked. One is the role of technology in the social changes, the other is the tendency in the new order towards professionalization, a tendency illustrated by the turn-of-the-century crystallization of sociology itself.

A more negative consequence of this absorption with recent changes in the West is that it introduced a degree of ethnocentricism to most of the general theory of social change that had been developed. Some, like Weber, Simmel, and Tönnies, deliberately limited their analyses to the Western experience,[13] but many others were less prepared to circumscribe their speculations in this way. Although the core of their curiosity was with the recent Western experience, they often implied, and on occasion stated, views on the nature and causes of change which they claimed to be universally applicable. Yet, as for example with Marx's thesis, these interpretations were really most appropriate to the recent histories of their own societies. These ethnocentric blinkers continued to handicap sociological interpretations of non-Western societies.

Another marked feature in earlier work on societal change was its tendency to adopt an evolutionary or developmental perspective on how change occurred. This reflects the consensus among a number of perspectives in the intellectual community of the time. Indeed, given the level of consensus, it is interesting that sociologists expressed the degree of uneasiness with developmental thought that they did. Developmental thinking means that certain types of change are emphasized over others. It underscores the cumulative, incremental types of change, the embryonic shaping of the future in the present, the steady transition from one stage of social organization to another. It seems to pay less attention to processes of dramatic innovation or sudden revolutionary alteration. As Comte put it, only orderly developmental change was normal; other forms of change presumably were pathological. Yet the record of change that the group surveyed showed much innovation and revolution. Several strategies were adopted to come to terms with this, and many of the modifications of developmental thought spring from it: Marx's interpretation in which revolutionary conflict climaxes each stage of development; the cyclical motifs of Pareto and Weber, in which violent conflict have a "normal" part. In Weber's thinking we have an attempt to come in terms with innovation, both as a product of charismatic personality and of rational thought. Rationality, however, though it encourages innovation, itself emerged developmentally. The same theme is present in Tönnies' approach, and Mead too struggles with an explanation of innovative change.

In no other discussion of the period do the values of the different men emerge more clearly than in their views on the direction of recent social changes. Comte saw the dawn of an age of enlightenment and order; Marx predicted equality and social justice; Mead foretold the coming of a free and open discourse between all men; and so on. Even in their fears we see these personal values at play, as Durkheim trembled for the decline in societal integration, Weber for the increase in personal alienation, Tönnies for the demise of community. Only Pareto, in his almost cynical evaluation of both "lions" and "foxes," seemed to dole out praise and blame equally.

In terms of sociology's continuing interest in processes of change, this period passed on to us several concepts and hypotheses about the origins of social change which we continue to use with great frequency. Some of these were described in this chapter, some in the preceding discussion of social conflict: the small-scale but constant adjustments arising out of interaction dynamics, normative fluidity, and personality's tension with societal constraints; the total explanation offered by Marx; and the other important partial explanations in terms of differentiation, power relationships, leadership, and value-motivational changes. Except for those who choose to accept Marx's theory completely (and in modern Western sociology this complete surrender has been rare) the earlier period gives us no comprehensive general theory of societal change. It did, however, selectively highlight strategic aspects of such change in a way which has continued to provide important direction to later sociologists.

NOTES

1. See chapter 4.

2. Emile Durkheim, *The Division of Labor in Society,* trans. ed. (Glencoe, Ill.: Free Press, 1964), pp. 256-63.

3. Ibid., p. 262.

4. See chapter 7.

5. Max Weber, *The Theory of Social and Economic Organization,* trans. Talcott Parsons (Glencoe, Ill.: Free Press, 1947), pp. 329-41.

6. Friedrich Engels, "Socialism: Utopian and Scientific," in Lewis S. Feuer, *Marx and Engels: Basic Writings* (Garden City, N.Y.: Anchor Books, 1959), pp. 68-112.

7. See chapter 10.

8. See chapter 9.

9. See chapter 4.

10. Georg Simmel, "The Metropolis and Mental Life," in Kurt Wolff, *Sociology of Georg Simmel* (New York: Free Press, 1952), pp. 409-24.

11. This argument is presented by Levine, "Simmel's Social Thought", in *Essays on Sociology,* ed. Kurt Wolff (New York: Harper Torchbooks, 1959), pp. 16-19.

12. See chapter 8.

13. The reference here is to Weber on rationality, not his views on charismatic change which seem to be intended as general theory.

Index

271